Sister Moon Lodge

The Power & Mystery of Menstruation

Kisma K. Stepanich

1992
Llewellyn Publications
St. Paul, Minnesota, 55164-0383, U.S.A.

Cover Painting © 1991 Hrana Janto

FIRST EDITION

Library of Congress Cataloging-in-Publication Data
    Sister Moon Lodge : the power and mystery of
menstruation / by Kisma K. Stepanich.
        p.   cm.
    Includes bibliographical references.
    ISBN 0-87542-767-7
    1. Menstruation   I. Title.
QP263.S74   1992   91-36828
612.6'62–dc20   CIP

Llewellyn Publications
A Division of Llewellyn Worldwide, Ltd.
P.O. Box 64383, St. Paul, MN 55164-0383

Woman as Shaman

As women redefine who we are in today's society, an awareness of goddess and female spirituality begins to awaken in our minds and hearts. In our pursuit of self–empowerment, we are discovering a base of shamanic power that has been inherent in all women throughout history. These shamanic powers lie dormant in a very natural part of a woman's physiology: her menstrual cycle.

Each month when a woman bleeds, she fully enacts her power. Yet many women are extremely ignorant of this power and its effects because a patriarchal society has convinced us to regard menstruation as an evil, shameful and inconvenient part of our lives; a part to hide and keep secret.

When in this mind–set, we remain out of touch with our shamanic abilities no matter how much we reclaim and celebrate our goddesshood. It is only after we embrace our cyclic nature that we can fully reclaim our dignity and rightful stance as an important part of society and life.

Sister Moon Lodge shows us how to tap into this most potent core of our being and give birth to the full force of our power. This book provides ancient wisdom that supports us as woman through every transition in our lives. As we rethink and recreate through celebration the honor and dignity of our menstrual cycle, we begin to take part in a greater vision that is balanced and harmonious.

The negative attitudes toward menstruation and birthing are the last chains of the patriarchal hold on women; once broken, the true power of the feminine energy can be unleashed on the Earth's plane, and right relationships will again pass smoothly between the sexes.

About the Author

Kisma K. Stepanich was born July 4, 1958, in Santa Anna, California, and continues to live in the coastal region of southern California. She is of Irish and Romanian gypsy ancestry, from which she proudly draws her spirituality. Grounding into the roots of her heritage, Kisma became an initiated High Priestess of Celtic and Faery Wiccan Traditions. She also holds a ministerial credential with the Covenant of the Goddess, has studied and undergone initiation with several shamans of native traditions from around the world, and founded Women Spirit Rising of Costa Mesa. Presently she directs Moon Circle Lodge Network in collaboration with Brooke Medicine Eagle, and travels throughout the southland providing ceremonial workshops of Goddess spirituality. Kisma is also the author of *The Gaia Tradition*.

To Write to the Author

We cannot guarantee that every letter written to the author can be answered, but all will be forwarded. Llewellyn also publishes a bi-monthly news magazine with news and reviews of practical esoteric studies and articles helpful to the student, and some readers' questions and comments to the author may be answered through this magazine's columns if permission to do so is included in the original letter. The author sometimes participates in seminars and workshops, and dates and places are announced in *The Llewellyn New Times*. Write to:

Kisma K. Stepanich
c/o THE LLEWELLYN NEW TIMES
P.O. Box 64383–767, St. Paul, MN 55164–0383, U.S.A.

Please enclose a self-addressed, stamped envelope for reply,
or $1.00 to cover costs.

This book is dedicated with love and honor to Mary K. Greer,
a sister who midwifed me through the labor pains
that birthed forth this book.

Dear Mary, from the body of my heart, may Goddess bless!

and to

Brooke Medicine Eagle, whose teachings have,
and continue to, inspire me.

Ho. Blessed Be!

Other Books by the Author

An Act of Woman Power, Whitford Press, 1989

The Gaia Tradition: Celebrating the Earth in Her Seasons,
    Llewellyn Publications, 1991

Forthcoming

The Oral Faery Tradition

Celtic Shamanism (Sequel to *The Oral Faery Tradition*)

The Seven Veils of Mahakundalini

ACKNOWLEDGMENTS

In creating a book such as this, many women and a few men have gotten involved—whether they knew it or not! I would like to start off by thanking those people who gave me information I was seeking or who pointed me in the right direction: Kara (from Vicki Nobel's office), the Menstrual Health Foundation, Linda Waite, Jody Sager (Harmony Network), Melanie (Brooke Medicine Eagle's office), and Patrice Wynne (Gaia Bookstore) who was helpful in supplying me with a list of lunar calendars, a list of books on menstruation, as well as menstrual supplies from the woman owned and managed company Many Moons. A special thanks to my editor, Emily Nedell, whose genuine interest made the more mundane handling of the manuscript a smooth endeavor. I would also like to thank Roberta (*Shaman's Drum Magazine);* the research efforts provided by Bob & Jo Thompson (my cousins) who supplied me with my matrilineage, the hundred-plus women who took the survey, and Jack Reidling for his scientific research as well as his love and support and understanding (thank you for rubbing my tummy when needed during my Moon-time).

To the artistic beauty provided by Wahaba Nuit-Cat and Renee Yates, whose illustrations grace the opening of each chapter; Hrana Janto, who illustrated the front cover; the artistic talents of Llewellyn's Terry Buske; and the powerful sculptures created by Amber Dawn Noland; may the Muses continue to grace you all with their blessings. Thank you, dear sisters, for sharing your creations with me and other women through my book.

I would like to thank the wonderful guidance and critiques provided by an expert board of reviewers: Jean Mountaingrove whose comments were never "too picky"; Dr. Susan M. Lark and Dr. Sadja Greenwood whose comments helped provide medical correctness; Susun S. Weed whose guidance made me aware of the political grim reality surrounding the trasmission of herbal knowledge in former times; and Mary K. Greer whose invaluable criticisms and direction helped make this book a reality. To all of you, thank you for the long hours you invested into this project. Your enthusiasm and the inspiration you provided me with was *precious*.

Lastly, I give thanks to being born in a female body this life and being placed into a position of having to experience the menstrual matrix. As a shaman woman, as a Goddess worshiper, as an eco-feminist, I am completely convinced that we (women) really *do* hold the power. It's right here—inside—and each one of us can contact it. We do this through remembering that our wombs—these houses of life—are the core of creation!

Thank you Mother Earth. Thank you Grandmother Moon. Thank you Goddess. Thank you Woman Power. My heart is very full, my womb is very potent. Ho. Blessed be!

CONTENTS

MEDITATIONS, VISUALIZATIONS, EXPERIMENTS

Introduction

I am the daughter of Betty Jewel Pittser (Pitzer), daughter of Myrtle Cora McFarlin (McFarland/McFarlind/McFarlane/McFarlan), daughter of Emma Jane Robinson, daughter of Harriet (Greer). I am also the granddaughter of Alexandria Josephine Kosikovski, who was the mother of Helen, Ana M. and Mary Stefoichie (Stepanich/Stepanick). My mother's lineage has also branched in another direction. My sister, Debra Ann (Stepanich) Aimes—birth name: Debra Evon Case—is from my mother's first marriage. Debbie's daughter, from her first marriage, is Tammie Jeanette Mershon.

How many times throughout history have our lineages branched off? Countless times, but the blood of the Great Mother, the First Mother, flows through our veins, and the generations of woman's acquired wisdom can be peeked at each month during our common denominator—our Moon (menstrual) time.

As we work with the Moon time we connect back-up with the matriarchal Grandmothers who can direct us, adding insight and depth to our lives. But first we must reclaim our bodies by understanding the biology of them. We need to rethink the conditioned mind-set we hold against our monthly physiological function. As we re-examine this area of our lives, we can begin to experience the divinity we contain and recreate ways in which to honor this sacredness.

It was in this vein of thought that I began working with the menstrual matrix: menarche, menstruation, and menopause. I longed to be acknowledged as a creator of life, and felt it was wrong to view such a natural function of life as something shameful, evil, or as a curse. I began rejecting all the thoughts and feelings that, through the current patriarchal religions, I had been taught to have.

My own awakening in this matter was both long and quick, methodical and spontaneous, mundane and magical. As my own self-empowerment began to grow, I found an intense desire to share this new (old) truth with female relatives and friends. Over the last five years I have performed "Women Who Bleed For Life Ceremonies," created a Moon Lodge, shared in menarcheal rites and cronings, and joined forces with other women being pulled toward the enlightenment found through the blood mysteries.

Sister Moon Lodge, though in no way complete, is my gift to the sisters who walk this MaMa Earth. It is my way of reaching the finer web of women whom I will never have the opportunity to meet face-to-face, heart-to-heart, womb-to-womb.

One day, my name will be added to the lineage of the woman's ways; for I too shall be a Mother, Grandmother, Great-Grandmama and so on. Until that day comes, I share with you the wisdom of the Grandmothers' voice: the woman's ways, as received in this Maiden Goddesshood I currently dance.

Ho. Blessed be.

IN THE BEGINNING

In The Beginning

We are re-writing our herstory. I choose to use *herstory* in place of history because I am referring to the story of womankind rather than mankind. Women who are researching and rewriting history have found that women have always played a significant, if not major, role not only in the evolution of life on the planet, but also in the progress of civilizations everywhere. Therefore as women we must speak of our newly revealed past, present and future as *herstory: the story of womankind; the story of Goddess.* We are re-creating the mythologies that explain our worthiness, our position in life. Singing the wisdom words flowing up from the very center of our cores.

> *We are the new women,*
> *we are the old women,*
> *we are the same women,*
> *stronger than before.*

Sisters whose creative talents are bursting forth from this new vein of strength and identity are illustrating, writing, weaving, constructing the images of the divine. We are adding our faces to these images, our bodies, our biology, and showing the community that *woman* is not something to be over-looked, or dressed-up to show-off as a trophy. We are telling our story: expressing the woes against our oppression, subordination, devaluation, desecration, annihilation for the last millennium.

In this resurgence of woman power, we are collectively realizing how vitally important it is to *rethink* several aspects of our biology, the most important aspect being our menstrual cycle.

The following myth is a recreation of my own heart. I do not base it on any factual evidence, but rather the wisdom that dwells within and flows over during my own time of bleeding. The power that lies beneath my own bleeding has *remembered* me to this truth. I give it to you in the attempt to nudge awake your own deep ecology centered around the sacredness of woman's menstrual cycle.

● ◗ ○ ◗

In the beginning of herstory, women honored and held sacred our bleeding. Our cycles were much like Grandmother Moon's cycle. In fact, our bodies truly imitated her cycle so closely that if we kept track of her phase we correctly predicted the time of bleeding. And so the lunar calendar (the first known calendar) was developed by She-Who-Cycles.

Our lunar calendar is a beautiful spiral drawing that shows the different phases of Grandmother Moon. Through practice, we can count off the days in advance and mark them either "red" to indicate the blood time, or "green" to indicate the fertile time. Many of the women use bones to mark their bleeding times. When they have cut thirteen lines into the ivory, we all know that the great wheel of the year has turned one complete cycle and the energy around our planet changes. This energy change will effect us and so we seek to understand the changes anticipated during our bleeding.

The time of bleeding is matrifocal. All women of the tribe bleed during the same phase of the Grandmother Moon's cycle and so we come together to honor this shared mystery of our beingness. Together, we construct small huts away from the main section of the village. Places where we can come together and share the blood; share the pain our bodies sometimes feel just before and during this time; share the deep richness of the wisdom that flows forth during this time, just as the pungent blood flows from the vagina. We call these huts Moon Lodges and have consecrated the surrounding area as sacred; designating the place for only She-Who-Bleeds.

However, the Grandmothers are always allowed to enter our Moon Lodge for they are the wise Crones of our tribe. Since they no longer bleed they hold the blood and the power. The Grandmothers have their own Lodge, which is off-limits to all of us. They gather in their Lodge any time during the lunar calendar. No one quite knows what goes on in the Grandmothers' Lodge, except the wise Crones themselves. They bring forth great wisdom though, and truly guide our tribe. Because their wisdom has blessed the tribe with abundance time and time again, everyone listens to their voice. If they say "yes" we know it is a wise consent. If they say "no" we know that they are caring for the people and the safety of future generations.

Those of us who dwell in the Moon Lodges bring forth another kind of wisdom. We learned that we also contain the ability to connect with the spirit wisdom the way the Grandmothers connect with it. This connection comes through the practice of gathering in the Moon Lodge on a regular basis to share in our bleeding, and we find a great power in this sharing. It is the power that allows us to see future events, or receive wisdoms on healing.

In our experimentation, we have experienced the blood by touching it and rubbing it over our bodies to absorb the magical properties it holds. Eventually we tasted the blood. Through this act we gained full cooperation with our bodies and our relationship with nature and the elements.

We find that the blood is odorless until it is exposed to air. The odor of our blood sometimes attracts animals to the site. These animals come in honor of our bleeding, especially the giant cats that lay outside by our fires and usher forth their deep-throated purring.

At first the men were afraid the animals would harm us. But we knew they had come because of our power; that they were attracted to the power. The men argued with us, and in frightened voices said they must become protectors of the bleeding women by guarding the area with weapons. It was the Grandmothers' "no" that finally calmed their fears.

The Grandmothers teased the men—first honoring the men for their concern over the women—but shared with them that the animals, especially the cats, were familiar with the energy the blood spoke.

"The blood is the elixir of life; the fluid of spirit," the Grandmothers said. "The day the animals no longer come will be the sign that the world is severely changing.

"When this occurs," they spoke, "it will be the ending of the woman's ways; the ending of divinity for woman for a very long time. The ending of peace."

The whole tribe howled their terror at this thought. It was an impossible thought to think that the women would one day not be able to gather to honor our divinity and the blood power. It was harder still to imagine a world without peace!

The tribe has settled back into the practices of cycling. The power and the strength of woman grows. The men continue to revere us. The wisdom and insights brought forth from the Moon Lodge hold importance to the village. And so, the men more than ever (especially after the Grandmothers' voice) encourage the women to step forward and gently guide the welfare of the tribe.

Many of us have begun to bring forth the power of peace—peace, the elusive quality the Grandmothers spoke would one day elude us. I am one of the teachers of this peace. I share it with all the peoples of the tribe—and remind my sisters of the peace power each time we retreat to the Moon Lodge.

It is the chanting of peace that keeps the minds of our men balanced and centered; for men are so quick to forget the love between a mother and a child. They are so quick to pick up arms and protect, whether protecting needs to be or not. In their rashness, they are also too quick to exercise power over anything weaker than themselves. So, some of us use the blood—the power of sight gained in our seclusion to mystify them into positive action.

Slowly, a new order has evolved. As we work with the blood wisdom and focus on nurturance, our men develop their strengths into skills that will benefit the whole tribe. It is within this partnership that a natural hierarchy develops. Women and men are finding the roles which complement the other, roles that, when combined, create a cohesive working unit. There is balance in this partnership.

It is through this partnership that a culture is birthed. A culture that honors and respects woman and man equally. A culture whose roots are planted firmly in the rich fertile soil of woman's menstrual cycle.

Change. Change touches everything. It would be against the natural laws to keep something so constant that it could not change. Change is evolution. Evolution is change. Needless to say, the above imagined culture changed. Whether it was a change enacted by force or another process, it died and was buried so deeply beneath the Earth that it faded from memory, until today.

When looking at recorded history, we can understand that over the last 3,500 or so years, civilizations rose-up out of the steppes and deserts, and annihilated or conquered existing cultures. Through history, we can trace the desecration of woman. Clearly, in many countries women were stripped of any value, any partnershiping in life and reduced to mere possessions owned by man. Soulless, voiceless, worthless, women became the evil temptresses of men.

History goes on to tell us that women were also denied our wisdom and spiritual practices. This was enforced by bringing forth a code of denial known as the *Malleus Maleficarum* (1486) or "Hammer of Witches," which resulted in the Inquisition's rage against women. *Malleus Maleficarum* was the work of Inquisitor General for Germany, Father James Sprenger O.P. It was, and remained for centuries, the classic formulation of the Catholic attack on women— witchcraft.

In the current history of the United States of America, it has been in the last 100 years that women have gained a voice. Up until 1921, menstruation and its by-product, "feminine protection" supplies, were considered immoral and were not allowed to be marketed. So realistically, menstruation has only been acknowledged in today's society for 69 years. This acknowledgement came when Kotex began manufacturing a gauze "sanitary" napkin. However, it has only been in the last 53 years that "feminine protection" has become a huge industry, with an $850 million/year market, and one which is dominated by men. It has been only recently, in the last 20 or so years, that women have begun to *rethink, reclaim*, and *recreate* the heritage and herstory and honor that is rightfully ours.

In my own beauty walk as a feminist/Goddess worshipper, I have come to understand that it is vitally important to give back to women the divine aspect of our biology, the management of our bodies. For it is in this extreme age of post-industrialization, this age of supposed intellectual freedom and cultural diversity, women are still being conditioned to believe that their menses are an inconvenience, something to be ashamed of and something to hide. Many women still view this most natural and sacred aspect of our biology as "the curse" inflicted upon us by God (Eve's sin), in the mythology of the current patriarchal religions. If women can break through this enforced stupidity, collectively we will heal the deep wounds that continue to fester as images of weakness in our ideas about being female. The healing of the female psyche will be the greatest gift to humankind. It is this wholeness that will aid our evolution to the state of balance and peace that is so desperately needed on our Mother Earth.

So, let us teach each other about our birthrights. Then together we can share our new (old) wisdom with the other gender—man— who now seem open to re-establishing a balance and a healing of their own psyches.

The next step of healing will be in teaching our children to respect both women and men as equals; allowing each our own unique biological divinity. The following chapters are filled with the wisdoms of the blood mysteries; *rethinking* the menstrual matrix: menarche, menstruation, and menopause.[1] This wisdom, I give first and foremost to my sisters. It is offered secondly to the men who seek to understand the greater wisdoms, work in cooperation with cycles, and desire true partnerships with women. Lastly, it is for the children who will one day grow into women and men.

As I help write herstory, I strive to bring back the power of their blood to women. For it is this power—this sacred connection to our blood—that births peace in a tribal sense. I believe we can usher forth the peace power that existed at one time—*in the beginning*— and transform our world personally as well as collectively into a world of unity, oneness and partnership.

I share with you the modern chanting of peace. May you speak it and allow your mind and heart to enter back into balance.

May peace prevail on Earth.
May peace prevail in my mind.
May peace prevail in my heart.
May peace prevail in my life.
May I know peace.
May my ancestors know peace.
May my children's children know peace
*   unto seven generations.*
May peace prevail on Earth.[2]

● ◐ ○ ◑

NOTES

1. Coined by Tamara Slayton, The Menstrual Health Foundation.

2. Kisma K. Stepanich, *The Gaia Tradition* (Llewellyn, 1991), p. 276 (As received through the teaching of Ochazanna Klarich).

Chapter One

Menarche

men-ar-che \ *men-är-kē*\ *n[NL, fr. men- + Gk arché
beginning]*: the beginning of the menstrual function;
esp: the first menstrual period of an individual—
men-ar-che-al \ *men-är-kē- əl\adj*
                          —*Webster's New Collegiate Dictionary*

Menarche (New Latin/Greek) literally translates into *men*: "Moon
month"; an ancient and universal measure of time, with the celestial
body that measures it, and *arkhe*: "beginning," i.e., to begin one's
rule, to take command. So, menarche means beginning Moon, or
first menstruation.

   The menstrual blood is the water of life, and should be held sacred. The word "sacred" often means taboo and vice versa. Like
many ancient meanings that are twisted for the benefit of those in
power, the meaning of taboo has been misconstrued, depreciated to
negative connotations. Taboo, a Polynesian word which means: sacred, holy, menstrual, was generalized by anthropologists to mean
"forbidden." It actually refers to what is empowered in a ritual
sense as not to be touched or approached by any who are weaker
than the power itself, lest they suffer negative consequences from
contact. The blood of women, menstrual or postpartum blood, is itself infused with the power that links women to the very heart of the
universe. This power of woman is both heart (womb) and thought
(creativity). Furthermore, the concept of woman power, or any
power, is related to the understanding of the relationships that

11

occur between the waking dream (human life) and the dreamtime (nonhuman worlds).

Women are natural shamans from birth, for we contain the powerful mystery of life within. As young girls we simply have to wait to grow older and blossom, expand, open like a flower (*flow-er*) into the time of our first bleeding. Menstruation has often been called "the flowers," and equated to fruit. Conversely, flowers were seen as wombs, or as the menstruation of a tree or plant.[1] The Bible refers to menstrual blood as the flower which must come before the "fruit of the womb," or the child (Leviticus 15:24).

Just as any flower contains its future fruit, uterine blood is the Moon-flower that contains the soul of future generations.[2] This concept is also clearly defined in India where menstrual blood is known as the Kula flower or Kula nectar. In India, when a girl menstruates for the first time it is said she has "borne the flower."[3] And so, like the blooming of a flower, it is with the first menarcheal experience that the female child passes into a new understanding of openness, sensitivity and creativity.

The shamanistic abilities innate in being female are centered on continuance. Since we contain the divinity within to conceive and form life in our wombs, we experience transformative phases throughout our lives that alter the degree of our power. The degrees of our power, as possessed through the physiological occurrences in the female body, begin at menarche.

In this vein of thought, it is important to view the first bleeding as an extremely significant part of a young woman's experience, because what is experienced at this time will permanently be imprinted on our psyche. It is this imprint that will influence how we feel about our menses, our sexuality, and inevitably the stance we take toward our womanhood.

Unfortunately, many women who are actively recreating and rewriting herstory have undergone extremely negative experiences with menarche, and received no initiation into the honor of womanhood. Because of this many women have feelings of shame, abandonment and confusion. As we begin *rethinking* menstruation, it is valuable for us to try to remember the time of menarche. Women who have had a less than positive experience have a very deep wound that is in need of healing. When menarche is re-explored from an adult perspective, a fresh start on the path to empowerment is initiated. This exploration prepares us to undergo the missed-out first rite of passage that should have taken place, no matter how simple or elaborate. As women, it is this healing that will allow us to share with our own daughter(s) in a positive and supportive manner, this aspect of a female's life that has been silenced and hidden for too long.

I would like to share my menarche remembrance in the attempt to regain my own loss at not having undergone a formal first rite of passage ceremony. I believe that when we share this story with each other we begin the inner healing process and become empowered.

● ◗ ○ ◗

At age 10 the bleeding came upon me. It was Easter vacation and the whole family was at home on this particular day. I was in my bedroom, which I shared with my older sister who was 15 and had been bleeding for a few years. Because of our shared quarters, I was familiar with the bloody underwear and sheets, and knew what sanitary belts and napkins looked like and where the Kotex box was kept in the bathroom in the cabinet under the sink.

The sky was grey the morning I felt the first drop of blood release from my vagina. I sat on the floor at the threshold of our closet and looked at all our shoes, my fingers touching the red, wet spot—the size of a silver dollar—on my underwear. I thought of running out to tell my sister and mother the news, but remembered how embarrassing it had been when my mother and Aunt Jean had come into the bathroom and examined my pelvic area after I told my sister I had a (single) pubic hair. I decided to keep the news to myself. Even though I knew where the Kotex box was, I wasn't quite ready to start wearing one and so I pulled a pair of socks out of the chest of drawers, stuffed one inside the other and put the homemade pad in my underwear.

I felt different, in a way, or at least I knew that something remarkable had just taken place. I knew that because of this phenomenon I could now have babies. In that moment of revelation I wondered if I would receive the heated words from mother that were thrown at my older sister about sex? A new set of rules were now being applied to my young mind. Rules that had to do with how I handled myself on the playground, and with boys.

With socks in place, I stood looking out the window. I glanced at my favorite tree, noticed how the leaves seemed to be a deeper shade of green, the pepper berries more red, and then up at the clouds heavy with moisture. I slipped outside and went to my tree, threw my arms around its trunk and hugged it. I stood there for a little while, smelling the scents of nature that the moisture of rain releases. I sat on the fence next to the tree and looked down the empty street. A light sprinkle of rain released from above. I remember feeling very much a part of nature; safe, secure. That time seemed very magical, special. I believe my mother, or sister, eventually saw me sitting outside in the rain and called me in. There were looks of concern. I guess my face mirrored the powerful emotions my young inner woman was experiencing, because mother seemed to know what was happening. My sister smiled. The two of them had a quiet laugh over the socks. Together they showed me the pads and how to attach them onto the belt hooks. Instructions on how often to change the pads and how to keep track of my cycle on a calendar followed. In fact, for the first time in my life I was given my very own calendar (even if it was one of the give-away calendars Security Pacific Bank gave to its patrons).

The light fades, and the day turns into a half normal, half self-conscious day. A mark in time. The making of a memory. I read once (I don't remember where I read it, or who said it), "How do you know when a memory is happening?"

● ◐ ○ ◑

Nevertheless, this memory happened. Now as I look back I realize that nature had given me my very own private rite of passage. Nature had taken me into her arms and embraced me with the moist, feminine element of water. The mother clouds overhead created a womb-like effect. By hugging the tree I was comforted, calmed enough to enable me to naturally become centered and connected. I opened and felt the heartbeat of MaMa Earth vibrate through the tree trunk. My sight opened and clarity was provided allowing me to glimpse the sensitive aliveness of the elemental kingdom. The mother's mind within was awakened that day as I deeply inhaled the rich scents of nature.

Some cultures believe that a female is at her most powerful time at menarche, and to a degree this is true. I was the most powerful I had ever been. My full power was demonstrated through my own ability to become "awakened" by the mere presence of nature during menarche. This event transpired, I believe, because of my sensitive nature. However, this same sense of "awakening" can be experienced by every female when guided by her own mother and honored with a rite of passage ceremony. And so, my menarche, though non-traditional in our family, had resulted in a ceremony. From that day forward, each time my bleeding came, my mother was always, and has always been, sympathetic and understanding.

As you can see, I am one of the lucky women whose menarcheal experience was very pleasant. But even so, I have had to strive to understand the full meaning behind my biology. It has only been in the last five years that I have really started thinking of this aspect of my femininity as being sacred. Because of a non-traumatic menarche I continued to mature without any real thoughts or views on menstruation. I simply knew that I must keep track of it for fertility reasons. In fact, it has only been since my thirties that I have started to notice more discomfort with my cycle. I've always bled lightly, and it was normal for me not to have many pre-menstrual conditions which incapacitated me either physically or mentally. When the term PMS was so widely broadcast, I truly did not understand what the abbreviation stood for.

In my liberation of reclaiming menarche as a positive and empowering experience, I began to understand just how negative it must have been for those less fortunate then myself. The importance of providing a book dedicated to this aspect of womanhood for my sisters became significant to my own healing process. There was no doubt in my mind that adult women, young girls, and future female children deserved a more positive depiction of menstruation.

Of course, this change of view must begin with the current group of adult women who are spiritually awakening. By changing our own evaluation of menstruation, by remembering our own menarcheal experience for good or bad, by undergoing a private menarche rite of passage, by reclaiming our power, we initiate a mental revolution.

Menarche Journey

Go to a special place where you will not be interrupted for at least an hour. Put the phone off the hook (or turn on the answering machine), a *Do Not Disturb* sign on the door and sit back and relax. Focus on breathing smoothly, fully. With each out breath, release the stresses of the body/mind and the strains of day-to-day living. Release fully with each breath, visualizing that your body is also becoming completely relaxed.

With each inhale, draw in a very pure and healing vibration. Breathe this vibration into every organ in your body; visualize it circulating through each of the seven chakra (energy) centers in your body (e.g. pelvic, womb, solar plexus, heart, throat, third eye, and crown of head). Draw this vibration so fully into your body that every cell is saturated with pureness and healing energy. Now, let your breathing resume its natural flow.

Turn your awareness to your womb center. Place your hands over your belly and concentrate on the feminine energy that is housed in the womb center. Allow your focus to drop deeper and deeper into this center. Begin counting backwards from 10 to 1.

10 . . . be aware of your body

9 . . . falling deeper into your womb

8 . . . connecting to your monthly bleeding

7 . . . surrounded by woman power

6 . . . re-awakening your memory

5 . . . going back in time

4 . . . back to the time of your first bleeding

3 . . . the first drop of blood

2 . . . your Woman-child is now present

1 . . . it is the time of your menarche

Allow the memory of this experience to be re-awakened fully. Perceive the emotional state of your little girl. Remember how you felt—whether it was positive/negative/indifferent. How your body felt—was there any pain? any forewarning of symptoms?

Who were the other people involved in your menarche—mother, father, sisters, brothers, girlfriends, or other relatives? How did they respond to you at this time? Remember everything you can; no matter how vague the memory may seem to be, try to get a sense of what did, or might have, happened.

When the full memory has returned, bring your hands to your heart and slowly open your eyes. Now, very carefully record the memory of your menarcheal experience on the following page.

Menarche — My First Blood

Currently I am age:

At the time of menarche I was:

Today's date is:

Comments:

Now that you have journeyed back to your time of menarche and re-experienced it, the time has come to move deeper into the woman's ways.

The next step is to begin re-learning the wisdoms around our blood that belong to us. The first wisdom is connected to Grandmother Moon and her cycle. The second wisdom is how women's bodies are linked to the Moon's cycle and what is actually happening in our bodies. By fully understanding these two components of the blood mysteries we can gain full cooperation with our bodies and heal the inner wound, thus empowering our psyche. (At first I wanted to use "control over" our bodies, but it has become acutely obvious that control means dominance. We never really dominate our bodies. When we understand physiologically what happens cyclically and what influences them, then we can work in "cooperation with" our bodies, and flow with the energies rather than try to continually direct that flow.) The last wisdom is the ability to really rethink positively all three phases of the menstrual matrix (menarche, menstruation and menopause), and undergo a rite of passage ceremony. This is information that we can grow from, and can pass on to our daughters.

> *Women have a responsibility to reclaim their power as menstruating and menopausal females and communicate this wisdom to their daughters.*
>
> —Tamara Slayton
> *Reclaiming the Menstrual Matrix*

NOTES

1. Judy Grahn, "From Sacred Blood to the Curse and Beyond," *The Politics of Women's Spirituality* (Anchor Press, 1982), p. 272.

2. Barbara G. Walker, *The Women's Encyclopedia of Myths and Secrets* (Harper & Row, 1985), p. 638.

3. Ibid.

Chapter Two

Grandmother Moon

Without peacefulness and harmony, which are the powers of
a woman's heart, the power of the [feminine] light and of the
corn, of generativity and of ritual magic, cannot function.
                                        —Paula Gunn Allen
                                        The Sacred Hoop

Each night I glance up into the sky to check the calendar that has become my guiding light. It was Grandmother Moon who showed me
the inner path to the blood mysteries. She pulled on me, moved
through me until eventually I joined her dance. After dancing with
her, I began to see how closely my life as woman was linked to her
on a cyclic level. The integration of this cycle, this lunar cycle, became the calendar upon which I could predict with almost certain
accuracy the days of several of my physiological functions such as
ovulation and the first day of my bleeding.

   As each cycle passed and my body became more linked to the
lunar calendar, I began to see how the changes in my own personality were also linked to the different phases of Grandmother Moon in
her monthly cycle. The expression "As above, so below," took on a
totally new meaning. I realized that Grandmother Moon's monthly
lunation was the archetype for my cycle, and our relationship was
one that would be life-long. The lunation is a cycle of transformations. Grandmother Moon's rapid movement consists of two
changes throughout her cycle—her position in the sky and changes
in her shape—to the extent that during a part of her cycle she van-
ishes entirely from sight. After continual observance of her lunation

cycle, it became perfectly clear that my physical body not only imitates hers, but also my emotions.

The Lunation Cycle

The lunation cycle is a cycle of phases. One lunation (from New Moon to New Moon) is astrologically referred to as the "synodic period" of the Moon, which lasts an average of 29 days, 12 hours, 44 minutes. There is also a relationship between the Sun and the Moon, called the "sidereal period" of the Moon, which measures a complete zodiacal revolution of the Moon and is a cycle of *positions*. The sidereal period of the Moon lasts 27 days, 7 hours, 43 minutes.[1] What this means is that the phases of the Moon (the lunation cycle) can tell us nothing about the Moon herself, the position she holds in the sky. Rather they refer only to the *state of relationship* between the Sun and the Moon (soli-lunar relationship).

Grandmother Moon moves through the sky constantly presenting an altered appearance, which leads us to believe that it is in the nature of the Moon herself to change her aspect throughout the month. In actuality what changes is the soli-lunar relationship, rather than the Moon alone. Grandmother Moon reflects in her appearance to us the changes in this relationship. As woman, I take this enlightened mystery one step further. For in my lunar-human relationship, I reflect the changes of the Moon. The great relationships on both an astronomical and human planetary level are concretely established (soli-lunar-human).

The lunation cycle is a cycle of periodic changes (changes in the soli-lunar relationship) which can be broken up into four phases. Beginning with the start of the lunation cycle (*conjunction* of the Sun and Moon, at which time the distance in longitude between the two celestial bodies equals 0°), Grandmother Moon is in her "dark" phase. During this dark phase, her body is not visible to our eyes. This phase is considered the time of beginning, and is often referred to as New Moon. Lost in the brilliant light of the Sun, she continues in her cycle until a few days later a crescent of her body shines in the sky. Having entered into the waxing phase, her light and size continue to rapidly increase until the time she is half-full (first quarter), and she is elevated at the zenith while the Sun sets. Her increase in size and light continues until Moonrise in the east coincides with

Sunset in the west; She is of equal stature to the Sun. Grandmother Moon at this time has reached her full phase and releases the fullness of her light upon Earth. During the full phase the Moon is in opposition to the Sun (180°); the maximum distance between them in their relationship.

At this point in her lunation, it seems as if her motion becomes slower. Grandmother Moon creeps into the waning phase as she seems to decrease her light and size. During this waning phase she again reaches a point of being half-full (last quarter), and she is seen at the zenith while the Sun rises. She rises later and later in the night until, approximately three days before the cycle's end, she rises at dawn. This marks the entrance into the starting of another lunation cycle and the phase of Dark Moon. For a more basic study of the lunar cycle, refer to Chapter 1—The Moon, in my earlier book *An Act of Woman Power* (Whitford Press, 1989).

The Phases of the Moon and Menstrual Cycle

If we were to consistently menstruate with the lunation cycle we would be perfectly balanced human beings. Bleeding in synch with Grandmother Moon is, of course, an ideal rather than a reality. Regardless, each of us travels through the lunation cycle, only the "Dark Moon/New Moon" phase of the menstrual cycle can come at any phase of the actual Moon cycle.

Often these two cycles, Moon and menstrual, seem to dance together, and when they do we can connect with our inner power on a deeper level. However, regardless of what phase our menses comes in, each of these experiences can be valued. We have much to learn from them, but for now let us focus on the "ideal" relationship between Grandmother Moon and our menstrual cycles, and use the following as a guide in understanding the special relationship that can and will exist between the two.

Dark Moon/New Moon, which is the starting of the lunation cycle, is the time when Grandmother Moon is not visible in the sky

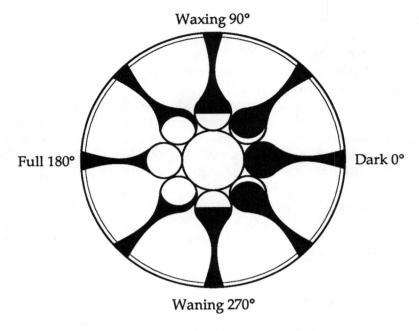

Figure 1. The Phases of Grandmother Moon

primarily because she rises at dawn during this phase, and therefore, is lost in the brilliance of the Sunlight. Her position is between
that of Earth and the Sun (Figure 1). In essence, it can be said that the
New Moon is the starting point of the realm of life.

    During this phase (if in synch with the lunar calendar) we have
finished our time of bleeding, and are starting a new cycle; preparing to ovulate and bleed again. This becomes a time of regeneration
emotionally, mentally as well as physically. This is a time of balance
and strength.

    Crescent/Waxing Moon is the phase when the Moon is from 18 to
36° distance from the Sun. Because the Moon is now visible in the
sky we can view this phase as the definite time of entrance into the
realm of objective manifestation. Like the Moon, our bodies are in a
state of change. We can feel it shifting not only energy-wise, but also
in fluid content. Mentally, we can be more active as new concepts
and possibilities are revealed. This is the phase of spontaneous and
instinctual action.

Full Moon is the phase when the Moon is opposite the Sun (Earth between Moon and Sun) at 180°. The time of creative activity of the spirit becomes clear and consistent, rational and complete. In our bodies, swelling to fullness takes shape. We near ovulation, the time of fertility. Because of the ability to conceive a spirit-child during this phase, the Full Moon also constitutes a beginning. Just as the New Moon can be viewed as the starting point of the realm of "life," the Full Moon opens up the realm of new "spiritual identity"—that of the woman turning from a childless entity into the possible new identity of mother.

Waning Moon is the phase when the crescent shape is inverted (turning eastward). This shape is formed by subtraction of light. Alchemical schools of astrology refer to this phase as the "Balsamic Moon." This phase of the waning Moon symbolizes, in one sense, the final letting go of the seed of the cycle about to end. It also represents the Moon's entrance into the sanctuary of the solar realm; and as she enters, she brings to the Sun the new "seed" of the Earth. During the first part (third quarter) of the waning phase, our bodies may reach a point of crisis known as "pre-menstruation." All energies seem to turn inward. We become introspective, focusing on the physiological changes taking place within.

Toward the middle or end of the waning phase, the blood releases. In essence, we move into conscious growth in meaning and immortal selfhood because we are reaching, and/or have reached that phase of our cycles where we "die and are reborn again." During the course of our lives we cyclically play out the role of immortality by bleeding and not physically dying.

During this waning phase, we consciously form our tomorrows, prepare to birth forth into the light of the New Moon those hidden unconscious seeds that will shape our future.

To take this analysis of the lunar phases one step further, we can divide the lunar cycle into two hemicycles. The waxing hemicycle (Dark Moon to Full) is a period of spirit-emanated or generic-instinctual activity which witnesses the triumph of life. The waning hemicycle (Full Moon to Dark) is a period of individual and consciously controlled release of creative meaning. Therefore, in the lunation cycle we are challenged by two kinds of power: the power of instinct and the power of creative consciousness.

With this in mind, we can begin to consider the lunar path as an indirect way of attaining spirituality. As women begin to reclaim the lunar calendar and link our own menstrual cycle with that of Grandmother Moon's, this calendar, this conscious day-to-day, week-to-week, month-to-month, year-to-year process becomes a natural way of progressive illumination of phase-revelation, of gradual perception—phase after phase—of reality. When the fullest possible revelation is reached, then comes the period of release and of dissemination of what has been learned, until the mind and soul become once more charged—phase by phase—with an increasing awareness of a particular image of reality.

As women, the cyclic character of our life is the most natural thing in the world. To choose to experience this cyclic nature deeply and fully avails us to a spiritual perception of life. Since we are innately spiritual, adapting to the lunar calendar is easy. In fact, the great mystery shrouding women and our changeability becomes elementally defined. With dependence on an inner principle whose chief characteristic is change, it is our *Moonlike* character that reveals the secret to our mysterious nature, and gives insight into the law of change which governs the female psyche, and all phenomenon.

Triggering Your Eyes

As you begin to work with Grandmother Moon, it is important to first familiarize yourself with her monthly cycle. The easiest way to do this is by deciding to "Moon-watch" for one cycle.

Begin Moon-watching at the next Full Moon. Each night check the sky for the Moon and monitor the change in shape and position. Remember there are four definite phases of Grandmother Moon:

1. Full Moon
2. Waning (decreasing) Moon
3. Dark/New (no visible sign) Moon
4. Waxing (first crescent/increasing) Moon

During each of these phases the shape of the Moon will visibly change. Likewise, she will rise at different times and positions. Here is an easy guide to follow:

1. Full Moon rises in the east as the Sun sets in the west.

2. Waning Moon rises later and later in the evening. At last quarter, she is at the zenith in the sky as the Sun rises. Approximately three days before the cycle's end she will rise at dawn.

3. Dark/New Moon is no longer visible because she rises during the day.

4. Waxing/Crescent Moon appears just after Sunset, while the Sun's light still refracts around the Earth's curve. At first quarter when she is half-full, she will be elevated at the zenith in the sky at Sunset.

Therefore, it becomes imperative in your Moon-watching to also check the sky early in the morning, and during the waning phase, throughout the day.

Moon-watching triggers your eyes, which triggers your physiological cycle. Once you get into the habit of using the sky as your calendar, your bleeding time will begin to adjust and eventually you will flow according to Grandmother Moon's cycle.

However, it is important to stress that our cycles will vary from month to month and most notably season to season. (I have found that if you are conscious of the lunar calendar, your cycle variations will never be drastic and often times will only vary for a month or two at a time.)

To add a sense of sacredness to your Moon-watching, create a prayer that you can speak to the female power each night/day as you look up into the sky to trigger your eyes with the luminous light of Grandmother Moon.

Moon-Watch Prayer

At the Full Moon which you choose to begin your Moon-watching with, gaze upon the white light of Grandmother Moon and ask her to send forth the *Moon-Watch Prayer* you will use each night/day for the next month.

> *Grandmother Moon,*
> *I ask that you send forth the special prayer*
> *that you want me to use each night/day in*
> *my Moon-watching of your great body.*
>
> *Send forth this Prayer now.*
> *Allow it to flood-lit my mind, my heart.*
> *Let it flow down with your light.*

Now gaze on her surface and let it come. Record it below. Then stand, raise your arms to Grandmother Moon, and speak your *Moon-Watch Prayer* with power. Continue to perform this same act every night/day for the next month, until once again you face her fullness.

Today's date is:

Moon-Watch Prayer:

Let us remember and let us teach our daughters of this connection we have with the lunar cycle. In conclusion, the lunation cycle is the cycle of the phases of Grandmother Moon. These phases are the different aspects which she periodically presents to us on Earth. They represent, not changes in the Moon herself, but changes in the angular relationship of the Moon to the Sun with reference to the center of the Earth. As women, we reflect these phases through our own menstrual cycle, and on a mental and emotional level as well. By returning to the use of the lunar calendar, we can begin to recenter our spirituality, tuning into the inner dependence we have upon change so that rather than letting our dependency on change control us, we can move in harmony with it.

Moon Journey

After you have completed the month of Moon-watching and you stand once again before Grandmother Moon at the time of her fullness, give thanks for the relationship you have developed with her.

Now it is time to go on a Moon Journey to connect up with the "Moon cycle" within your womb. Find a nice quiet place, preferably under the Full Moon, some place where you will not be disturbed for the next hour. Either sit or lie down. Get comfortable.

Breathe naturally. Be aware of the light shining upon your face. Feel its beauty, its softness, its magicalness. Visualize this beautiful, soft, magical light being absorbed into your skin, and then consciously breathe it in.

With each breath, follow the Moonlight down into your body. Flowing deeper and deeper within until at last the Moonlight has traveled through every particle of your body.

Take another breath, and follow the beautiful, soft, magical light into the place where your woman power lives; your womb. Have a seat.

As you feel comfortable in this place of woman power an apparition begins to materialize before you. It is as if this being is forming out of the very light rays of the Moon. She is, for this Moon Goddess has now come to share with you the wisdoms of the Moon cycle.

Look at your Moon Goddess very closely, and know that you will remember everything about her later.

As you look at her, she moves closer and sits next to you. She takes hold of your hand, smiles and tells you her name. You will remember her name.

She speaks:

Your eyes have been triggered by my light. For the last month you have been dedicated in your Moon-watching, in honoring me nightly with your Prayer. Now let me honor you.

I shall continue to cycle inside you, but you must always be conscious of my light. I will require you to follow me. At times, you will have to search for me, and at other times I will be very present. Sometimes I will ask you to be very carefree with your celebrations of me, and at other times, I will ask that you remain perfectly still and quiet yourself if you want to find me.

Once you develop your inner relationship with me, the power of your Moon time will grow and I will be the guide to the Grandmothers' voice. I will be the channel in which the wisdom will be made accessible. Without my guidance, you will never fully connect with the ancient ones that dwell within.

So, this is what I require: When my body is no longer visible in the sky, and I am known as Dark Moon, I will be housed inside your womb. In order to find me you must become very still and listen. You must dive within and call my name three times. Then I will come and give you guidance.

At the time of first crescent, when just a sliver of my body peeks out from behind the veil, I ask that you consider your attitude and decide that it will be one underlined with positivity for the next cycle. Choose an area of your life that requires attention and dedicate yourself and my waxing energy to it for the next cycle, and then consciously work on making any necessary changes or transformations required.

When my body is full and shines brightly in the night sky, celebrate me by offering your prayers to my light. Honor your woman power. Honor life. Honor creativity.

And last, when my body and light wanes, stop to remember me. As the blood flows, receive my light back into your body, preparing you for my guidance when I am Dark once more.

With those words, the Moon Goddess stands and smiles at you. She tenderly blows you a kiss and turns. As she moves away from you, her image evaporates and becomes the beautiful, soft, magical light of Grandmother Moon.

The Moonlight begins to rise out of your body, and as it does so, you follow it. Rising with each breath you move up from the inner depths of your being. You rise with the Moonlight until it pulls away from your body. As it leaves your body, you become aware of this physical reality.

Allow your mind to focus on your heartbeat, and your surroundings. When you feel safe to do so, gently open your eyes. Look back up to Grandmother Moon and offer thanks for her presence.

Your Moon Goddess name is:

Describe her appearance:

Comments:

● ◑ ○ ◑

NOTES

1. Dane Rudhyar, *The Lunation Cycle* (Aurora Press, 1986), pp. 15-17.

Chapter Three

Woman's Body

Without women's ability to menstruate and keep track of their cycles and of the Moon, we would have no mathematics, music, accounting, science or medicine. In other words, menstruation is the base of modern civilization.
—Judy Grahn

In herstory, women know and cooperate with our bodies. We chart the changes we experience monthly on lunar calendars, know our time of ovulation and fertility, understand how to apply self-help methods to relieve the physical symptoms felt before and during menstruation, practice safe and natural forms of conscious conception, use absorbers to catch our blood rather than "protection" and or "sanitary" supplies. (The word "protection" implies a need for covering, or concealment, and the word "sanitary" implies something unclean; but in herstory, we refer to our feminine supplies as "absorbers" which aid in catching our blood to be used or disposed of as we choose.)

For each of the above subjects there are many valuable books available today for a woman to gain deeper insight. I strongly urge every woman who is undergoing her own transformational awakening and becoming more spiritually attuned, to take time to research and understand the physiological functions of her body more fully. This is our magic. Sadly enough, today many women have no idea as to what is happening each month in our bodies. Throughout this book I will make reference to those books on menstruation that I feel are the best in their field. I urge you to invest a few dollars in books to gain the knowledge women have lost due to the enforced stupidity of the patriarchy—it's well worth it!

Our Cycle

The *vulva* are the lips of our *cunt*. (At one time I was offended by the word "cunt," but the more I worked with it and used it interchangeably with "vagina" I found that it was a very descriptive word for this part of my body. It was a term that I should in no way be embarrassed and/or offended by. Jeannine Parvati has written: " . . . discharge the fear of patriarchal punishments. We can only be embarrassed by our anatomy and the English descriptive words by keeping them hidden, unused except in situations of anger, hysteria, and pain. 'You cunt' can only hurt our little girls if we mystify the word by responding shamefully. Let us not prejudice our daughters to their own bodies by being embarrassed by the word 'cunt' ever again."[1] Passing through the vulva, we enter the chamber of the *vagina*. At the end of the vagina is the threshold of the *uterus* known as the *cervix*. Crossing the cervical threshold into the uterus is entering into the "womb of life." Herstory teaches us about our bodies (Figure 2).

Woman's ability to create life is dependent on two *ovaries*, one on either side of the womb. Within each ovary rest the *ova*, the egg cells of life. Each month, an ovum will mature. The mature ovum is released from the ovary and propelled to one of the tunnels. Before the ovum can enter the tunnel, flower-like appendages known as *fimbria* must open, revealing the entrance to the tunnel. After the ovum has entered through the fimbria it can move through the tunnel (known to medicine as the *fallopian tube*). It is this tube (which opens into the top of the uterus) that allows the egg to either meet with a male sperm or continue to move into the uterus where it dissolves and passes from the body.

Ovulation Awareness

If one is synchronized with the lunar calendar, ovulation will normally occur around the Full Moon. At the time of ovulation, the egg, or mature ovum, is released from the ovary. It is then picked up by the fallopian tube and stays there for 12 to 36 hours. It is

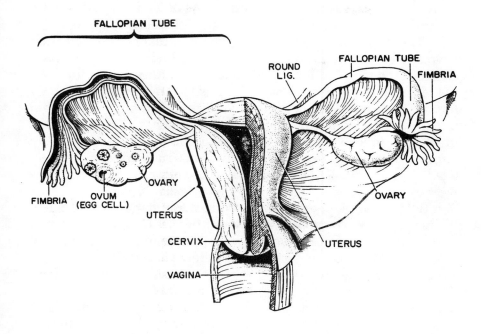

Figure 2. Herstory teaches us about our bodies.

during this time that the egg can be fertilized. If sexual intercourse takes place at this time, the sperm will travel from the cervix to the vagina and on to fertilize the egg in the fallopian tube. When the egg was released, the egg sac left behind in the ovary began producing a hormone called progesterone as well as continuing to produce estrogen. Progesterone triggers production of a food source in the lining of the uterus where the egg, if fertilized, will be nourished and grow.

If fertilization does not occur, the uterus food lining (the endometrium) is no longer needed. The production of both progesterone and estrogen decreases, and the endometrium begins to break down. This is the beginning stage of menstruation, known as premenstruation. Thus ovulation occurs approximately 12 to 14 days before menstruation. It is very rare that ovulation will occur more than once a month, but if it does the second egg will release within 24 hours after the first one.

The importance of understanding the ovulation process is that a woman can work in cooperation with her body and focus on her choices to conceive or not. Fertility awareness directs our attention to the natural knowing of the body. It is true that women are only fertile for a 36 hour period, although sperm can live up to 72 hours in mucus, which extends the time we can get pregnant. Think of all the unwanted pregnancies that would be avoided if women were taught this wisdom as young girls and we really consciously practiced applying this knowledge! We might not have the ridiculous political struggle over Pro-Choice/Pro-Life that is plaguing our nation today. The plain and simple truth of the matter is, that when women take back responsibility for our own bodies, when women understand the process of our own physiology and are *aware* of those aspects, we can truly choose when to conceive a spirit child. Accidents can, and always will happen, but basic awareness and understanding of our cycles will greatly diminish accidents.

Though to some this may seem too simplistic due to the failure rate of certain natural birth-control methods such as the rhythm method—which I hope is never taught to our children as a form of protection—I believe we must begin applying the wisdom (as discussed above) in the attempt to find alternatives to the methods used today. The methods readily practiced today seem to disconnect women from our bodies and natural cycles. There are better alternatives, and we will never know which they are until we start somewhere. I believe the starting place is in relearning about our cyclic relationships and our bodies.

Because the sacredness of menstruation has been taken away from women, we have been stripped of the power over ourselves that we innately contain. Again, the stupidity enforced by the patriarchy has succeeded in demoralizing women to the point where we are now fighting amongst ourselves. It is a shame that women do not yet bond together and put an end to the segregation that is infecting our half of society.

Just as we can tell the approach of our menstrual period a few days beforehand, ovulation also tends to be preceded and accompanied by recognizable symptoms. All fertile women have these symptoms and can learn to recognize them. Most women have already noticed them without realizing that they are of regular occurrence and bear a constant time of relationship to the succeeding menstrual period.

Some of the possible symptoms experienced around ovulation can be:[2]

1. A twinge of pain or strong ache on one side or the other in the pelvic area. This is called *Mittelschmerz* (German meaning "pain in the middle of the cycle.")

2. Mid-cycle bleeding or spotting. Consider three days after this bleeding as a fertile time. With careful observation, however, it will be noticed that this bleeding will be combined with ovulatory fertile-type mucus. (See explanation and Figure 3).

3. Increased breast tenderness, or fullness.

4. Increase in sexual desire.

5. Lower back discomfort.

6. Constipation.

7. Mood changes.

8. Increased desire for certain foods.

9. Swelling.

10. Senses becoming more acute.

11. Increased oiliness of hair and skin.

Many of these symptoms can be confused with pre-menstrual symptoms, and are often the beginning of the PMS symptoms. The two clear signs of ovulation, however, are an increase in vaginal mucus and body temperature.

The Temperature Method depends upon the usual rise of the basal body temperature at about the time of ovulation. (Basal body temperature is the temperature of the body at rest, taken at a relatively constant time immediately after awakening.) A temperature record can hope only to define days of infertility following ovulation and lacks specificity, because the body temperature may be subject to disturbances by influences that have no connection with ovulation. Furthermore, the time relationship between ovulation and the shift of the temperature to a higher level is imprecise; sometimes the rise of temperature occurs before ovulation, or it may be delayed until some day after ovulation.[3]

Mucus secretion is the discharge of mucus from the vagina, usually on three to seven consecutive days before ovulation. It is different from the occasional secretion at other times (e.g. immediately before the onset of menstruation). If we take the time to observe the phases of mucus we will note that beginning mucus is sticky. It changes to a more creamy consistency and then becomes stretchy (Figure 3) before ovulation. The mucus can be light or heavy, transparent or cloudy, white or yellow. Sometimes we may only notice an unusual "wetness" as an indication of the secretion and not actually see the discharge.

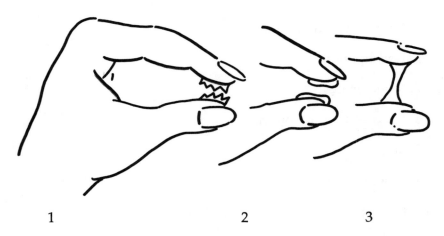

1   2   3

Figure 3. Checking the mucus: 1. Beginning mucus is sticky; 2. Fertile mucus is creamy; 3. Most fertile mucus is stretchy.

It is important to remember that sperm requires mucus to live, and will live up to 72 hours (3 days) in vaginal secretion. Therefore, if we are aware of ovulation, we would want to discontinue intercourse at the onset of increased mucus discharge and not resume sexual intimacy until three days after the last day of any stretchy, clear mucus, which is referred to as "peak" mucus.

You may be asking yourself what does all this have to do with spirituality and *rethinking the menstrual matrix*. The best way to answer this is to simply say that to know, to understand, to cooperate with our bodies balances our internal energies, heals our wounded psyche, and opens the channels that will allow our inner woman power to flow forth into our lives. And, as a very wise Crone, Jean Mountaingrove, once wrote to me, "Consciously choosing whether to bring forth a child is a very empowering act and requires careful ethical evaluation of our ability to nurture a child at this time."

Premenstruation

This is the phase when the lining of the uterus (the endometrium) begins to break down and slough off the walls of the uterus due to hormonal changes activated by the hypothalamus and pituitary gland. These glands produce FSH-RF, follicle-stimulating hormone-releasing factor and LH-RF, luteinizing hormone-releasing factor. Because of all the activity both hormonally and physically, many symptoms occur that have become labeled "PMS"— PreMenstrual Syndrome. Before I delve into the symptoms of PMS there are some very important things I want women to understand.

PMS has become an umbrella term to cover many negative issues in a woman's life. But in herstory, women who bleed do not suffer from the delusion of the patriarchal definition (spoken or unspoken) of the term PMS. Rather we acknowledge it ultimately to mean *Proudly Menstruating Sister*! In that state of mind we prepare our attitudes in advance so that we will be able to better take care of ourselves by finding some time to slow down and rest when we bleed. When we take the time to rest we can really acknowledge what is happening to us and celebrate our divinity. By keeping this attitude, we begin taking care of ourselves to handle safely and comfortably the changes we are experiencing premenstrually. It means that we come first, and we will take *any* necessary steps to place our comfort first. As a "PMS," we no longer need to "take it like a man" and pretend we are not experiencing physical discomfort.

PMS is a very real part of many women's lives. Health authorities claim that 40 to 90 percent of all menstruating women have premenstrual symptoms to some degree, and 5 to 10 percent of employed women are affected severely enough to miss several days of work every month. The symptoms are numerous and affect every

organ system of the body. Over 150 symptoms have been documented (PreMenstrual Syndrome is *not* the same as premenstrual
symptoms—it is a more severe and limited constellation of symptoms). Some of the most common ones are:[4]

irritability	acne
anxiety	boils
mood swings	allergies
depression	hives
hostility	cystitis
migraine	urethritis
headache	less frequent urination
dizziness	asthma
fainting	breast tenderness and swelling
tremulousness	rhinitis
abdominal bloating	sore throat
weight gain	hoarseness
constipation	joint pain and swelling
sugar craving	backache
cramps	

It is common for many of these symptoms to occur at the same
time. The biggest factors that increase the risk of having symptoms
are:[5]

over thirty
emotional stress
diet
birth control pill side effect sufferers
difficulty with weight control
no exercise
pregnancy complicated by toxemia
you have had children

Very serious study in the last decade has been given to this element of a woman's life. As a result of these studies, four basic sub-
groups or types of PMS have been created.[6]

Type A (for "anxiety"): anxiety, irritability, mood swings
Type C (for "carbohydrates" or "cravings"): sugar craving,
    fatigue, headaches

Type H (for "hyperhydration"): bloating, weight gain, breast
   tenderness
Type D (for "depression"): depression, confusion, memory
   loss.

Eighty percent of women suffer from Type A. These symptoms
may be due to imbalance in the body's estrogen and progesterone
levels. A non-fat diet and vitamin B can greatly reduce this type.
Sixty percent of women are Type C, which is due to low blood sugar.
Again diet plays a significant role. Type C's diet should consist of
"fuel" foods. Vitamin B and magnesium are also important. Type H
is experienced by 40 percent of women. These symptoms are caused
by an excess secretion of the pituitary hormone ACTH (adrenocor-
ticotropic hormone). The Type D is seen in only 5 percent of women,
and is often in conjunction with Type A, which is seen in 20 percent
of women. Estrogen levels have been found to be low in women
with Type D.

The more usual menstruation symptoms such as cramps, low
back pain, nausea and vomiting (*dysmenorrhea*), are thought to be
due to spasm of the uterine muscles. However, recent research has
found that primary dysmenorrhea is due to an imbalance in local
chemicals produced by the uterus. These chemicals are called pros-
taglandins.

In applying self-care to our times of premenstruation, it is important to be aware of our symptoms and take the necessary steps to
help lessen their discomforting effects. One of the most valuable
books I have come across on this subject was written by Dr. Susan M.
Lark entitled *PMS, Premenstrual Syndrome Self Help Book* (Celestial
Arts, 1984). This book is a woman's guide to feeling good all month.
It provides a completely practical all-natural plan for relieving over
150 symptoms of PMS. Dr. Lark provides charts in which one can
evaluate her symptoms, and then provides dietary eating habits, exercises, yoga positions, acupressure, massage methods, and vitamins and minerals for PMS relief.

Premenstrual discomfort is a very real part of many of our
lives. If we can begin to find comfort for our physical symptoms, we
can turn our minds and energy toward the more creative inspirations that naturally flow up from our own depths at this time. It is
during the premenstrual time that women can get in touch with our
inner strength. In conjunction with the lunar calendar, this is the

time of the Waning Moon. All focus is turned inward, and we can begin looking at the hidden secrets stored within and empower ourselves with woman essence, rather than be distracted by physical debilitating discomfort.

Menstruation

At the onset of our bleeding, many of the above symptoms magically disappear. Bleeding marks the end of one cycle and the beginning of the next. As soon as the flow begins, the body prepares for a new cycle by releasing a hormone (FSH) from the pituitary gland. While the uterus sheds its old lining, the FSH hormone causes an egg to begin to mature within the ovary.

With our bleeding we also seem to find release from the exhaustion of premenstrual pain. The struggles of both body and mind, to find balance between the many outward demands of a female's life and our inner resources seems to reach its peak. Just like Grandmother Moon who is retreating from our sight, women seem to naturally want to retreat and embrace this aspect of the cycle alone. The loss of connectedness to our bodies during our times of bleeding is unhealthy, for menstruation is a time of healing. What is happening in the core of our being is a phase of regeneration. We are ebbing and flowing with the creative expression of life, and for a woman to maintain biological, psychological, sociological and spiritual well-being it is vitally important that we reclaim our blood, our flow, and use this time to insure the future continuance of our strength and endurance by nurturing and caretaking ourselves first.

As women, we must recall our healing wisdom with each cycle and find the inner and outer balance of well-being. By once again embracing the menstrual cycle we can become educated in the art of being female.

Observing Your Cycle

It is now important to observe your cycle for the next month to familiarize yourself with the messages your body gives you. Most likely, these messages will be similar each month, and once understood, you can anticipate the symptoms connected to them. Continue to Moon-watch, but focus on your body. Begin after your next bleeding has ended.

Ending date of Moon Time:

First week following

Check your vaginal mucus every other day. Record the date and a brief description (sticky, creamy, stretchy, white, yellow, clear, minimal, heavy, etc.):

1.   3.

2.   4.

Note your body water content (e.g. swollen, slender, etc.):

What is your mental attitude?

Describe your emotional attitude:

Second week

Check your vaginal mucus every other day. Record the date and a brief description (sticky, creamy, stretchy, white, yellow, clear, minimal, heavy, etc.):

1.   3.

2.   4.

Date of ovulation/noting any physical symptoms/ messages:

Note your body water content:

What is your mental attitude?

Describe your emotional attitude:

Third week

Check your vaginal mucus every other day. Record the date and a brief description (sticky, creamy, stretchy, white, yellow, clear, minimal, heavy, etc.):

1.   3.

2.   4.

Record any premenstrual symptoms you are experiencing:

Note your body water content:

What is your mental attitude?

Describe your emotional attitude:

Fourth week

Check your vaginal mucus every other day. Record the date and a brief description (sticky, creamy, stretchy, white, yellow, clear, minimal, heavy, etc.):

1.   3.

2.   4.

First day of bleeding:

Record your physical symptoms of menstruation:

Note your body water content:

What is your mental attitude?

Describe your emotional attitude:

Last day of bleeding:

Comments:

Blood Absorbers

Women wear tampons because it is a form of *convenient protection* that does not slow them down. By relying on "the plug" they can hide the blood, pretending that today is just any ordinary day.

For women who are getting back in touch with this aspect of their being, and who are in the process of reclaiming their blood as sacred, the choice of feminine absorbers becomes important.

When we bleed we are instinctively more gentle, quiet, slowed down and moving about our daily lives with an inner focus shaping our views. We are open and flowing. By using an internal absorber, such as a tampon, we are blocking the flow, cutting off our power.

There is an art to bleeding. Flowing is a creative act, and when it is stopped up, I believe the psychology of woman is negatively affected. We depend on this part of our cycle as our release, and inhibiting this function in any way is liable to cause irritability. So, to find the perfect solution for absorbing our blood, we must take time to review this aspect of bleeding. The methods of catching menstrual blood throughout the ages have depended upon what materials were readily available. For example, American Indian women used bird down, cattail down, moss, buckskin, rolled buffalo hair, soft buffalo skin, shredded bark, and sheep pelts.[7] Egyptian women used soft papyrus tampons, while women who lived close to the sea used sea sponges.[8] In early American history, women used soft cloth. It was not until 1886 that "disposable towels" were developed even though they were not marketed because advertising such a product was still considered immoral. Kotex manufactured the first gauze pad in 1921 but did not begin advertising until 1924 in *The Ladies Home Journal*. In 1936 tampons were first put on the market, and of course, today there are many diverse products for our selection. As already noted, feminine protection is a huge industry with an $850 million/year market. The problem with today's product is that the FDA does not require manufacturers to list ingredients used or to perform safety tests. Since 1977, women have been subjected to harm directly caused by the use of these products. Toxic Shock Syndrome (TSS) and vaginal ulcerations have been linked to the absorbent ingredients used in tampons, and the plastic inserters housing the material respectively.

In 1981, the FDA recognized the link between higher absorbency and TSS. After numerous studies, in 1987 an article appeared in the *Journal of the American Medical Association* stating again that it is the absorbency of the tampons, not the chemical composition, which is the main cause of TSS. Proposed regulations in 1988 mandated that all tampons be subjected to a uniform test for absorbency. A numerical range gauging the number of grams of fluid absorbed by the tampon, similar to the ranking system for sunscreens, would assure that all tampons can be compared.

For women who are set on wearing tampons for convenience, it has been noted that the least absorbent tampons are Tampax Junior and Regular. The most absorbent are Kotex Super and OB Super. It has also been noted that there are "regulars" that are more absorbent than some "supers," e.g., Playtex Regulars are more absorbent than Tampax and Kotex Supers. The use of *manufactured* tampons leads to increased risk of TSS. Symptoms include: fever of 102 degrees or higher, vomiting, diarrhea, dizziness, fainting, a sunburn-like rash, and a sudden drop in blood pressure. If these symptoms ever appear and you are wearing a tampon, immediately remove it and call a doctor or go to an emergency facility. Women who receive immediate and proper treatment usually recover in two to three weeks. A last word on manufactured tampons: change them frequently (2-6 hours), don't wear them unless you are menstruating, avoid all deodorized products, and if the brand you use is housed in a plastic case, then be more careful when applying it as it can scratch the vagina.

I believe that when you buy manufactured products you are supporting a patriarchal industry whose leaders have denied women our dignity. Menstrual products originally sprang from women's ingenuity and belong in the hands of women. Nancy Friedman, author of *Everything You Must Know About Tampons*, suggests that women should challenge this industry and take it over. "Menstrual products are women's concern," she states. "It's time to make them women's business as well."[9]

Unfortunately, sanitary napkins, like tampons, are another manufactured product that must be seriously considered before using. The recycled cotton fibers that are found in commercial products are first used in the agriculture industry on seeds and soil to increase water retention, then later put to use by both tampon and sanitary pad manufacturers. Pads are permeated with the super absorbent chemical, sodium polyacrylate, a salt-based chemical that turns to gel when in contact with liquid. Also, the majority of pads are made by a chlorine-bleaching process which produces deadly dioxins. Dioxin is produced when chlorinated compounds, such as polyvinyl chloride and other chlorinated plastics, are burned; dioxin is formed by the paper industry's use of chlorine to bleach wood pulp from brown to white and increase absorbency. The bleached pulp is then converted into a variety of paper products, including commercial menstrual pads.[10] Dioxin is considered one of the most toxic substances ever produced, and is being investigated as the cancer causing agent in Agent Orange.[11] Minute quantities have been shown to cause cancer, liver disease, miscarriage, immune system depression, birth defects, and genetic damage in laboratory research animals.[12] Even though there is no direct evidence for dioxin's effects in humans, cell culture work shows that it may be linked to breast cancer, liver cancer and various carcinomas.[13] Women *should* not be exposed to such dangerous and life threatening circumstances simply to absorb menstrual blood! Regardless of whether or not the FDA feels that the quantities of dioxin found in commercial feminine menstrual absorbers are a potential health risk, it is time we took matters into our own hands and put an end to such insanity. By taking matters into our own hands we can create our own feminine supplies guaranteeing that we are wearing menstrual lingerie rather than unhealthy "protection."

We must remember that the time of our bleeding is a slowdown of energy. A time where we are indirectly, internally, unpretentiously guided toward healing ourselves. If we experience this time as an inconvenience we will never slow down enough to allow the healing to take place, to regenerate us to face the next cycle. Feminine absorbers are designed simply to catch the blood, not to pretend it is not there.

If you choose to make your own absorbers, take the time to examine the materials available. Cottons, flannels, and velvets (natural fibers) are the best materials for constructing napkins. The core can be cotton balls, more cloth or sea sponges. Napkins must be changed more often, but are ecologically safe because they are not thrown away. We simply wash them out. There are two easy patterns that can be used. One is much more elaborate and imitates the pads available in the market place. The other is a flat cloth that is folded-over twice and can be used alone or layered with different stuffings depending on how heavy or light your flow is (Figures 4 and 5). There are also several woman owned companies now manufacturing safe feminine products (Appendix A).

Figure 4: The Pad

1. Take a piece of cloth approximately 10″ x 15″ and fold the long edges in 2″ on both sides.

2. Then fold again into the middle.

3. Turn the edges under to form tabs.

4. Sew edges down and attach velcro to the inside of the edges.

5. Stuff the inside with cotton batting or sponge, and herbs if you'd like. To make the belt, measure your hips, double the length. Cut a 4″ piece of cloth the length of the doubled measurement and sew into a casing or tube by folding the material in half and sewing along side one edge and turning inside out. Insert elastic and sew ends together forming a circle. Attach velcro to the outside of the belt where both sides of the pad will match up.

Figure 5: The Napkin

1. Take a piece of cloth approximately 8-1/2" x 10" and finish off edges with a zigzag stitch.

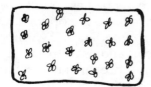 

2. Take a second piece of cloth approximately 5" x 10" and place over middle of the bigger cloth. Sew the smaller piece onto the bigger piece along edges with a zigzag stitch.

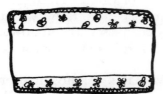 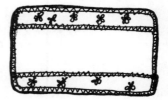

3. Fold the cloth into thirds forming a napkin.

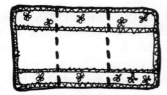 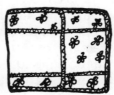

4. For stronger bleeding days, the cloth can be made longer and folded four times. Also, the inside of the napkin can be stuffed with sponges and/or cotton batting. This napkin works well if made out of flannel and used with cotton panties.

Sea sponges can be used in place of tampons, although they may contain bits of sand, and are prone to get moldy. A string can easily be attached to one end, or not depending on how easy they are to get out (your vaginal muscle tone). Using sponges is a good way to get in touch with our blood. Handling both the sponge and blood can help to overcome the self-disgust the media has conditioned us with. When washing out the sponges we have the opportunity to smell our blood which is a very powerful experience. If we are truly an experimental woman, tasting our blood allows us to gain a more intimate connection with our psyches and prepares us for the life-blood that covers our spirit-children at the time of birth.

Fertility and Conscious Conception

Because this book is dedicated to the menstrual matrix (menarche, menstruation, menopause), I choose to leave the above topic for another time when I have undergone my own conscious conception and given birth to a spirit-child. At this point in my life I still stand as Maiden facing the threshold of Mother. I recognize that women need to re-discover the wisdoms behind fertility and conscious conception. We have been out of contact with our powers for so very long we tend to think of birth control as a way of controlling unwanted pregnancies.

It has been said that fertility is woman's unique initiation into Spirit, and that Spirit sees the subtle forms before the creation of matter. Fertility awareness is a woman's birthright. Through understanding the preceding information regarding the menstrual cycle, we can be aware of our fertile time. This understanding of our physiology allows us to work cooperatively with our ovulation cycle and choose whether to conceive or not.

For women who are infertile, the body still undergoes a natural cycle. The above information can be worked with to maintain connection with the female power ushering forth a sense of balance. Perhaps infertility can be worked with during what would be the "ovulation" phase to gain insight into the steps required in helping the body become fertile again. Our spirits will guide and heal us if we listen to them.

The conscious mind tends to look in favorite directions however. Closing our eyes and turning our ears inward turns the mind in a fresh, new direction. We are awakened to the possibilities available. By reclaiming the fertile body and the rich messages that come forth with each turn of the cycle, we can align ourselves with the larger family within. We can begin to hear the whisperings of a spirit-child approach and can delve into our own being to understand more fully the approach of the incarnate soul. This awareness is the beginning of conscious conception.

As Jeannine Parvati Baker says, "Conscious conception is the attempt to put the soul back into fertility."[14]

● ◐ ○ ◐

NOTES

1. Jeanine Parvati Baker, *Hygieia: A Woman's Herbal* (A Freetone Collective Book, *1978*), p. 5.

2. John J. Billings, M.D., *The Ovulation Method* (The Liturgical Press, 1964), p. 16.

3. Ibid., pp. 19–20.

4. Susan M. Lark, M.D., *PMS, PreMenstrual Syndrome Self-Help Book* (Celestial Arts, 1984), pp. 19–20.

5. Ibid., p. 21

6. Ibid., pp. 24–26.

7. Carolyn Berry, "Celebrating the Blood: Indian Women and Menstruaion," *Bread and Roses*, Vol. 3, No. 2, 1984.

8. Nancy Friedman, *Everything You Must Know About Tampons* (Berkeley Books, 1981), p. 34.

9. *Mademoiselle*, September 1986, p. 166.

10. Tamara Slayton, *The Ecology of Being Female* (Menstrual Health Foundation, 1990).

11. *Agent Orange and its Associated Dioxin: Assessment of a Controversy*, A.L. Young and G.M. Reggioni (Eds), Elsevier Science Publishers B.V. (Biomedical Division)1988; *Women and Health*, 1990, Vol. 16(1), pp. 79-93; Michael A. Kamrin and Paul W. Rodgers, *Dioxins in the Environment*, (Hemisphere Publishing Corp., 1985)

12. Archives of Biochemistry and Biophysics, 1990 Mar, Vol. 277(2), pp. 382-388; Biochemical Pharmacology, 1990, Vol. 39, No. 3, pp. 485-488.

13. Toxicology Letters, 1990, Vol. 50, pp. 275-282.

14. Jeannine Parvati Baker and Frederick Baker, *Conscious Conception: Elemental Journey Through the Labyrinth of Sexuality* (Freestone Publishing, Co., 1986), p. 20.

Woman · Woman · Woman · Woman · Woman · Woman · Woman ·

Kisma '90

Chapter Four

First Rite of Passage

One day she is a child; the next she is a new reality, part of an ongoing process of life that inevitably conditions her self-understanding . . .

—Penelope Washbourn,
"Becoming Woman:
Menstruation as Spiritual Challenge."

Menstruation symbolizes the advent of a new power that is *mana*. Mana, like taboo, is a Polynesian word used to describe a sacred power which may be transmitted through sacred objects of substances. The sacred power of menstrual blood contains life-giving and life-destroying possibilities. As in any case with sacred power, mana should never be taken lightly. Menarche is a female's passage into the realm of mana. Standing at the threshold of this experience, the girl who now has a woman's body but is still a child in spirit and social standing, needs a celebration to help ease her into a new understanding of self-identity. The ritual, or First Rite of Passage, helps this woman-child redefine the self in the context of the purposes of nature, helps to understand her physicality in relation to the procreativity of nature, and helps her to begin deciding about her goal and purpose in life in the human community.

In a survey I did on menstruation (see Appendix B), almost every woman indicated that menarche had been connected to *fear*. Many were not sufficiently prepared psychologically, yet almost all felt that they were considered to be grown-up; their young lives

55

having changed literally overnight. Not one woman surveyed had ever undergone a rite of passage ceremony. The overall feeling was one of sorrow. Even though these women understood that menstruation was a "way of life" which they had "better get use to," they were confused, unsure of what it really meant and why it was suppose to be such an insignificant part of their lives when it felt so important. One woman was so coldly indifferent to menstruation that she questioned me as to the validity or importance of such a survey. In response to the one question regarding the celebration of menstruation she wrote *"why bother?"*

Menarche is a very serious time in a female's life: a one time experience because it is the first, though we continue to undergo the same process every month for perhaps another 30 plus years. Herstory reaches out to touch the woman-child during this experience, making it one of graceful acceptance; a symbol if you will, of the potential of one's body for the enrichment of self and others. As the mothers of daughters, we must help them experience this change in the most positive and supportive way we can. Let us teach them to value, rather than shrug off, this monthly cycle and to attend to their life power. Let us help to transform the anxiety and premenstrual tensions into the thought that as women our creative potential depends at all levels on giving up something, on letting go of aspects of ourselves for future gifts.

Menarche is letting go of the childhood freedom, the innocence and the simplicity of our bodies for ever more, but only to emerge like the butterfly from the cocoon into an enriched understanding of our potentialities as life-giver. Ultimately we gain the ability to understand our body in relation to our personal maturation; our value to self as well as to the community. Experiencing menarche gracefully can mean being able to integrate the negative and positive aspects of menstruation into the personality, helping us to embrace this continuing event rather than ignoring it or formally viewing it as a negative—as is so prevalent today. Perhaps then, we can become a whole expression of aliveness rather than a partial one.

Traditionally menarcheal rites have marked the beginning of fertility, honoring the female child's ability to have children, rather than honoring the girl herself. Herstory goes beyond the already existing cultural rites found in history; those rites that have been explained by anthropologists in many different ways: economic, sociological, psychological and spiritual, all of which reduce the female child to an object rather than a person.

Herstory changes the experience of menarche, taking it out of the hands of the Health Education teachers who present Health Education classes that present it as something mechanical, and place it back into the hands of the women to be taught as something sacred. Let us prepare our female children from birth onward for the time of menarche. We can share our own bleeding time with them, helping to demystify the fear of blood and the projected cultural mind-set of uncleanliness. By using the first three chapters of this book as a guideline, we can teach the biological/scientific/medical aspects of our bleeding time to give our daughters an intelligent background on their menses. Depending upon our personal practice of celebration, we can allow our daughters to attend our monthly celebrations (see *Full Flower* section for menstrual celebrations). As they grow toward menarche they will do so as blossoms unfolding, unfolding, unfolding until at last they arrive to the menarcheal experience, undergo a first rite of passage into the status of womanhood thus becoming a full flow-er.

The way of welcoming the woman-child into her creative potentialities and the manner of celebration used should depend on the personality of the child. It is important not to create an environment that will produce anxiety in her young mind, nor cause her embarrassment. Consult your daughter continually through her development toward menarche as to how she might want her womanhood recognized.

The following are suggested variations on theme for you and your daughter to consider when planning to celebrate her menarchical experience.

She Who Gives Away:
For the Daughter who is Quiet, Shy or Reserved

She who has the demeanor of the Goddess Quan Yin—soft, gentle, oftentimes very quietly absorbed in her own world—will benefit from this rite of passage. (For a more in-depth study of Quan Yin refer to Merline Stone's book, *Ancient Mirrors of Womanhood*.) Mother and daughter celebrate this divine revelation. After the first blood has appeared, mother and daughter spend the following 24 hours alone. They take a walk in the woods or along the beach. Perhaps they journey together in an inner meditation to receive a blood-name for the new sister. The mother allows time for *She Who Gives Away* to explore her blood, be with her bleeding, write her thoughts down, illustrate her emotions, create a poem, or perhaps her first Moon Bag. (Refer to Chapter Nine for further instructions.)

The day quietly draws to an end with a special meal and mother giving a very special Blood Gift to *She Who Gives Away*. The Blood Gift is a gift that is associated to menstruation. It can be as simple as a poem welcoming the young woman into her new position, or as elaborate as a very special power tool. Other gifts can be: a book (such as this one), illustrations, vulva (cowrie shell) necklace, menstrual Goddess figurine, feminine supplies, red dress, red flowers, lunation journal, lunar calendar, etc.

It is important to understand the needs of your daughter. *She Who Gives Away* is the female who must unfold even further into the time when she will want to partake of a full-blown rite of passage ceremony in which other women attend in her honor. Sometimes, *She Who Gives Away* will choose not to be involved with groups until she has come into her own sense of power as an adult. *She Who Gives Away* cannot be pushed, therefore, simple encouragement and guidance toward the evolution of her spiritual identity will awaken her to her own power and desire to celebrate with other women.

She Who Gives Away will gain the confidence that this aspect of womanhood is not something to be ashamed of or looked upon as unclean.

She Who Cycles:
For the Daughter who is very Open with the Family

She who perhaps leans toward the energy of Artemis will benefit from this rite of passage celebration. The Artemis child is an extrovert. She plays more with male children than other females, but when she does play with females is often domineering. She is very drawn to animals and extremely protective of them. (For a more in depth study of Artemis, refer to Jean Shinoda Bolen's book, *The Goddess in Every Woman*).

Mother and daughter spend the first 24 hours together after the first blood appears, exploring this new aspect of her young life in very much the same manner as given in the above section. That evening the family prepares a special dinner in honor of *She Who Cycles,* at which time they share their words of support with her. Each family member presents her with a special Blood Gift.

She Who Cycles needs to share this aspect of her womanhood with men and experience their support. For a woman who has a sympathetic husband, or the couple who have raised sons to honor and respect women, this family party is extremely rewarding. *She Who Cycles* will feel comfortable with her bleeding and not look upon it as an inconvenience.

She Who Bleeds For Life:
For the Daughter who, at her Young Age, already seems to be a Goddess Worshipper, and who seems to Innately Understand the Mysteries of Life

This is the daughter of the Goddess Diana, Aradia. (For more information on Aradia refer to *Aradia* or the *Gospel of Witches*, Charles Godfry Leland, 1899.) She has walked with you in your cycling, asked questions and shared her own feelings. If you are a woman who celebrates regularly with a group of sisters, honor *She Who Bleeds For Life* with a First Rite of Passage Ceremony.

As given in the first two woman-child categories, after the first blood appears, mother and daughter spend 24 hours alone. The ending of the second day is celebrated with a family party. On the third day schedule the First Rite of Passage Ceremony celebrated by mother and her group of sisters.

On the day of the ceremony before it begins, *She Who Bleeds For Life* is placed in a warm bath and left to focus on the cleansing that is taking place each time she bleeds. Instructions are given for her to relax and focus on the energy of creation that has been awakened inside. She is encouraged to simply rest and "let flow."

The women prepare the sacred space, adorning the circle by hanging red/white/black cloth on the walls, cover the floor with special rugs, and adorn the altar. The three colors (white/red/black) represent: the rich blackness of our inner mysteries, the rich redness of our blood, and the rich white mucus of fertility.

Flowers, in all stages of opening, can be placed on the altar symbolizing the blossoming, or phases, of womanhood. Each woman places the gift she brings for *She Who Bleeds For Life* on the altar. A white and a red candle (white to represent Grandmother Moon/red to represent the menstrual cycle) is placed in the center of the altar. A chalice of collected menstrual blood, or pomegranate juice, is placed in the center of the altar between the two candles.

When sacred space is sufficiently prepared, the circle is cast. The mother returns to her daughter in the bath. After dressing in a red gown, *She Who Bleeds For Life* is taken to the circle. In her right hand she carries a white cloth stained with her menstruum as a sign that she is indeed a flow-er.

At the entrance to the circle, mother and daughter are halted. The Crone (or eldest of the group) requests the proof of the blood. The proof is handed to the Crone, who in turn passes it to the circle of women. After all have witnessed the first blood and nod approval, Crone will then admit mother and daughter into circle.

Mother guides daughter into the center of the circle and presents her to the women by speaking her new blood-name received during the meditation journey taken during the first day of bleeding. All who have gathered greet *She Who Bleeds For Life* by speaking the blood-name.

A sister steps forward and explains the significance of the red-white-black materials decorating the room. A second sister steps forward and explains the varying stages of the flowers and the symbology they hold. The mother takes her daughter to the altar and shows her the white and red candle. The daughter is instructed to pick up the white candle and light it off a work candle, or altar candle. She is instructed to gaze at the flame while the mother tells her:

This white candle symbolizes Grandmother Moon. It is the energy of this circling orb which pulls on the body, which influences the body. We re-connect our energy to Grandmother Moon's energy when we experience menarche. Visualize yourself opening and allowing the essence of the Moon's cycle to re-align with your own. Together you will wax and wane. Together you will celebrate your fullness, honor your emptiness. You are one.

The women gathered chant:

Grandmother Moon and I are one,
waxing and waning,
empty and full.

Grandmother Moon and I are one,
living and dying
through each cycle.

Grandmother Moon and I are one,
she is my guide,
I bleed her light.

Replace the white candle on the altar. The mother then stands behind her daughter and takes both of *She Who Bleeds For Life's* hands and places them over the belly of the bleeding womb. Mother speaks:

Feel your belly, which may or may not be swollen. Feel the womb, the place of beginning. The place of transformation. The womb is the place where all creation births. It is here that your woman energy rests. Within this divinity, within this mystery lives the power of the universe. Repeat after me:

I am sister with my womb.
We share peace from this day forward;
for the rest of my breathing days.

The red candle is then picked up and lit off the Grandmother Moon candle. Again the daughter is instructed to look upon the flame. The mother informs her:

The red candle symbolizes the blood of the womb, the blood of life. Creative, strong, powerful. It is the ancient mystery of woman that is being celebrated this day. You are now this essence. From you, the blood now flows. You are honored with the great function of creative energy. Rejoice in the pungent smell of the blood. Rejoice in its redness. Honor life.

The women then chant:

Sister to the Moon
Sister to the Sun
Daughter of the Earth herself

She gives away this day,
gives away this day,
she gives away to the power of Life.

The red candle is placed back on the altar. The Crone now steps forward and picks up the chalice containing the menstrual blood (or juice). She faces *She Who Bleeds For Life* and explains:

This is the blood of the Mother. Ever are we mindful there can be no birth without the spilling of the life blood. Since we are women who bleed, let us merge our life blood with each other and restore the power and mystery of womanhood.

The Crone places the cloth that *She Who Bleeds For Life* gave as the proof of her bleeding inside the chalice to allow her blood to mix with the woman-power blood.

Next the Crone asks, "Do you accept your power?" If *She Who Bleeds For Life* says "yes," then the Crone closes her eyes and opens to receive a message from Goddess to bestow upon the girl. When blessing is received, Crone shall dip her fingers in the chalice and mark the third eye, or Shaman's eye, of *She Who Bleeds For Life* with blood (or juice) at the same time she verbally bestows the blessing.

Once marked, the Crone shall then announce to all gathered:

Behold, (the blood-name), no longer a woman-child
but a young-woman who has received her woman-blood.

The time has now come for each sister to move forward and present their Blood Gift, offering at the same time words of encouragement, blessings, and power.

● ◗ ○ ◗

To those dear sisters who have been bleeding for years but have never undergone a menarcheal rite of passage, it is never too late to perform such a ceremony. In fact, I believe it is one of the necessary ceremonies a woman needs in order to heal the wounds of the psyche. In my book *An Act of Woman Power*, I devote an entire chapter to this type of ceremony and provide a complete outline of the *Women Who Bleed For Life Ceremony* that I perform for groups of women all over the country. This ceremony is so fundamentally life-changing (and I use the word "fundamentally" to make the point that it is the "base" of woman power that is most affected by undergoing this ceremony) that the women who undergo it truly walk away transformed.

The reasons I feel it is so very important for women to perform a rite of passage ceremony, though they have been bleeding for years, is because the woman-child is still waiting for this recognition, the honor attributed to this divine aspect of our womanhood. The woman-child has never been celebrated into the status of womanhood, but was expected to assume it overnight. Many of us have actually lived in a state of trauma ever since menarche.

Herstory heals women. Herstory honors the menses. Herstory celebrates the blood mysteries. Herstory gives back to women self-identity. Herstory promotes dignity.

First Rite of Passage

Let me honor you. Today you shall undergo your First Rite of Passage. Look at your face in a mirror. You are looking at the Woman-child inside your body. The beautiful, sweet little girl that requires (deserves) acknowledgement into the status of womanhood.

Dear Woman-child, your bleeding has come, taking you into a new phase of female consciousness. In this phase you are now a channel for creativity. Be aware of your cycle and your connection to Grandmother Moon. Honor your bleeding each month and spend a few hours, or as long as desired, alone. Experience the releasing of your blood-flow as a healing tool; balancing your mental, emotional, and physical bodies. Draw from the rich well of intuition and listen to the voice of the Grandmothers speak the woman's ways to you.

I acknowledge you as She Who Cycles. Acknowledge your own divinity now by lighting a white or red candle. In doing so you are shining your light into the world vibration. Hold your candle before you, look at your face in the mirror and affirm:

> *I am Woman, I am, I flow.*
> *I am Whole, I am, I know.*
> *I am Power, I am, I grow.*[1]

Take a very special essential oil (a personal fragrance) mixed with a little red ochre (or your menstruum) and anoint your third eye, your heart, and your womb. Dear She Who Cycles, this is the blood that promises your healing and self-empowerment. From this day forward acknowledge your divinity each month during your bleeding. Take back this sacredness and power. Blessed be.

Close your eyes and focus on the affirmation just spoken. Allow your mind to quiet and listen to your inner voice; the voice of the Grandmothers. Listen and receive a new Blood Name to use when you seek audience with the Grandmothers during your Moon time. Then listen a little longer to see if a power chant will emerge from the depths of your womb.

Dance now, and sing your heart out. Draw a picture, write a poem, do something creative. Or, if you want, sit very quietly and honor your special biology.

I give to you this gift of reclaiming your divine right. May your woman power grow.

This is my Blood Name:

This is my Power Chant:

In the space below, draw a picture or write a poem to celebrate your passage into womanhood.

● ◗ ○ ◗

NOTES

1. Stepanich. *An Act of Woman Power* (Whitford Press, 1989), p. 51.

*FULL
FLOWER*

Moon blood   Kisma '90

Full Flower

We are living our herstory. Re-claiming the divinity of our being, our existence as women with the biological function of conceiving and giving birth to life, with the physiological function of bleeding monthly. We are affirming our woman power; our voices ushering forth the belief in self:

> *I am Woman, I am, I flow.*
> *I am Whole, I am, I know.*
> *I am Power, I am, I grow.[1]*

We are dancing with our sisters under the Full Moon's light, sharing our private passions with our lovers, creating babies with conscious understanding that we are opening a place for a returning spirit to incarnate, striving to complete a fragmented picture of womanhood and listening quietly to the inner Goddess as she whispers her love to us.

Some of us are just awakening; this perhaps being the first book ever bought in connection with woman power and Goddess. Collectively, we are coming full flower. Opening forth our blossoming faces, exposing them to the spirit of life, we are ready to speak our own thoughts, demonstrate our own likes and dislikes, express our needs, stand firmly in our own beliefs.

Above and beyond the dictates of history and its struggle between the sexes in the war of matriarchy versus patriarchy, we instinctively know that there is a new way of living. Neither female or male dominate. Neither Goddess or God dictate. Rather, it is the way of letting go and burying the past; living fully in the day of female and male partnership, Goddess and God co-existing. A place where there is no "one way," no "right way." A place where ego, political corruption, man-made religious dogma, hierarchy of social standing, sexual supremacy, anthropocentrism (i.e., humans believe themselves to be superior to all creation), starvation, child-abuse, rape, and inadequate housing will be banished.

Before this new way of living can blossom, each of us must begin preparing the fertile soil for the sowing of seeds. The fertile soil of our minds are in need of re-conditioning, eliminating the negative mind-set that menstruation is an evil, a curse awarded womankind by an angry God who became outraged at woman's natural instinct to delve into the mysteries of life and obtain the knowledge to help facilitate her understanding of nature, cycles, and relationships. This societal blighting on woman has injured our spirits; resulting in a withering of power. The disease that has been caused by this mind conditioning has almost caused our spiritual death.

For some women, survival meant remaining wild; becoming the outcast, the notoriously concocted evil witch, who unfortunately was battered even more severely than can ever be imagined. But today, as we recondition our minds and sow seeds of new theology and meditation, we begin to cultivate the wild woman into the very fragrance of our blossoming spirits. Whenever there is social change a degree of wildness is contained therein. And so it is the same for women as we begin rethinking menstruation.

The greatest healing women can experience is reclaiming our divinity. The ability to bleed monthly and not die is divine. The ability to conceive, nurture and give birth to life is divine. This ability is not a curse, is not evil, is not inconvenient, is not dirty, is not harmful in any way, but is divine in every aspect.

It is through the reclaiming of our divinity that wholeness grows and spreads throughout our hearts and minds and bodies and souls and spirits. (Soul and spirit to me are two separate yet interlinked elements of existence. I believe that the soul is the conscious carnation we are in the living, and the spirit is the life force energy that exists within or without a physical body. The soul animates. The spirit enlivens.) As this healing takes place we come to understand that we can begin the shifting towards balance in our relationships and living.

As women begin *rethinking* the menstrual matrix, the shame and curse we have been burdened with begins to mentally dissipate. It becomes a nuisance, a pest, a gnawing of immature behavior. Breaking through the bonds of enforced stupidity, the mind begins to breathe again. The mind opens to receive the energy of the heart as it travels up the energy channels, uncoiling through each of the seven chakra centers in the body (pelvic, womb, solar plexus, heart, throat, third eye, and crown of head).

As women *reclaim* the menstrual matrix, the element of self-esteem/self-love flows forward. The heart fully opens and allows the energy to rise and enter the re-conditioned and fertile soils of our minds. The seeds are sown into thoughts of balance and wellness and wholeness and cycles. Let us move into this new phase of re-thinking, restructuring, recreating the blood mysteries and menstrual health.

As women who bleed, we are full flow-ers.

● ◐ ○ ◑

NOTES

1. Stepanich, *An Act of Woman Power* (Whitford Press, 1989), p. 51.

BLOOD SHAMAN

Chapter Five

Menstruation

men-stru-a-tion \ *men(t)-strə -wā-shən, men-strā-* *n:* a
discharging of blood, secretions, and tissue debris
from the uterus that recurs in nonpregnant breeding-
age primate females at approximately monthly
intervals and that is considered to represent a
readjustment of the uterus to the nonpregnant state
following proliferative changes accompanying the
preceding ovulation; also: PERIOD.
—*Webster's New Collegiate Dictionary*

The word *menstruation*, as in menarche, comes from the Latin mens,
meaning "month," which in turn comes from "Moon," which is the
root of the following words also: mensuration (measuring), dimension, immensity, metric, diameter, as well as many others. So menstruation is a measurement of time, or measurement of the Moon
within a month period of time. Once again we are shown how
women and Grandmother Moon are so very closely linked.

Since all peoples are born through woman, the bodies of male
and female alike are formed from the substance of the womb; the
solid matter of our bodies is produced as a "crust" from the thick-
ened, curdled and clotted blood of woman. The blood that runs
through the veins of the unborn baby is the blood of the mother.
Within this blood is contained the wisdom of life as perpetuated
through the continual birthing of life. Therefore the wisdom of humankind originates from Great Mother (i.e., the very first Mother of
our species) and is centered in the blood, the soul-stuff given by the

73

birthing mother and being a direct link back through the generations to Great Mother. The Great Mother is the original shaman.

Shaman Woman

The term "shaman" has come to be associated only with the
male gender of our species. The shamans are the medicine men of
indigenous peoples around the world. In history, women were
forced away from medicine ways and finally excluded from the
spirit realm. Few people realize that the word originally applied to
both men and women.

Vicki Noble ("Shakti Woman," *Snake Power Magazine*, 1989)
gives a modern definition of the the shaman woman (or female
shamanism) as "a gradual mastery of oneself, and a healing or 're-
covery' from the chronic dis-ease of our time." She goes on to clarify
this by saying that:

> What is of special interest to women in shamanic process is
> our biological inclination to respond to organic cycles. Be-
> cause of what has been felt as our "bondage" to the hormonal
> cycle we experience every month, combined with our condi-
> tioning to surrender to our "lot in life," a woman comes more
> easily to the act of being a vessel for the healing power.

Shaman woman represents the ability to transcend levels of
awareness through the ability to bleed. When a shaman woman undergoes apprenticeship she does so first through the tool of her
body. Through this understanding comes the mystery of the blood
(self-empowerment through reclaiming it as sacred) and the demystification of the evil the menses has been connected to (at the onset of current patriarchal religions).

The five senses become acute skills as we work with the blood
and its cycle, and through the knowledge of the blood and the cycle
we are able to begin working in cooperation with our bodily functions. As we become empowered from this cooperation, a sense of
bonding with nature takes place. See my book, *The Gaia Tradition*
(Llewellyn, 1991), for an in depth study of bonding with nature,
Mother Earth, through the Goddess energy of each season.

It is the shaman woman whose very essence is linked to the elements of nature; an insight is gained as to how the elements of our
nature work separately as well as together in relationship with other
natural cycles such as that of Grandmother Moon, and then that of

Grandmother Moon and the Sun, and ultimately that of Moon-Sun-Earth (as discussed in Chapter Two).

Finally, a sense of balance is achieved for the shaman woman as she begins working in cooperation with body, nature, and universe. This achievement is the healing of the broken spirit of woman on Earth. Once the healing of spirit begins to take place, the doorways for the greater mysteries open; the doorways attached to the mind and fear. By overcoming fear it becomes possible to journey deep into the mind, into other dimensions of possible existence wherein the spirit world resides. Fear of the unseen is diminished and with it the conquering over fear of death. As fears dissolve, the shaman woman can begin to nurture all elements of life.

When fear is diminished shaman woman begins to trust in herself and listens to her inner voice and allows it to act as a guide. She begins making the changes required to manifest the visions birthed inside of her during the bleeding time. Shaman woman speaks out and upholds the ethical laws of nature, of life. She looks at the past and present to gain insight into the future.

"So, the work for contemporary shaman women," Vicki Noble tells us "is to learn to move, to act, to do what our inner voices tell us we need to do, even if it seems socially inappropriate!"[1]

As shaman women our power comes from the menstruum.

The Power of Blood

Power is conceived of as being supernatural and paranormal; a matter of spirit involvement and destiny. However, woman's power comes automatically by virtue of our femaleness, our natural and personal acquaintance with blood-menstrual blood. There is no need for women to fear blood. We understand its worth. Blood is life. This life blood is also the menstrual blood; holy and feminine and real. When the life blood releases monthly from the vagina, we transcend linear time and pass into a heightened state of awareness; a deep connection with cycles, and the relationship we have to them.

This heightened state of awareness brings with it a variety of experiences and feelings, "from the fertility of ovulation and its nurturing or emotional outreaching, to the infertility of the menstrual period and the dark, passionate sexual power that exists there for its own sake."[2] This sexual power is likened unto the Tantric Kundalini. The Tantric Kundalini image of the female is a serpent coiled in the lowest chakra (pelvic) of the human body. An aim of Tantric yoga which is performed to release, or contact this serpent, is to "realize Kundalini" by certain exercises and meditations, such as yoni-mudra, contraction of the perineal muscles. This includes training men to suppress ejaculation. If Kundalini could be induced to uncoil and mount through the seven chakras to the brain, crown of head, the adept would experience the bliss of her emergence as the "thousand-petaled lotus" from the top of the head, which means the union of the self with the infinite.[3]

Shaman woman uses this power of the blood each month during her bleeding; for she realizes that it is her responsibility to find the necessary channel in which to birth her creativity. The awakened Kundalini is the greatest channel of the blood power.

Kundalini Awakening Journey

Find a very quiet place where you can take the following journey. Make sure it is a place where you are assured of no interruptions.

Sit with your legs Indian style and with spine very erect. Close your eyes and breathe deeply. Begin to focus on your breath, allowing your mind to quiet. Counting from 10 to 1, allow each breath to take your awareness deeper and deeper inside.

> 10 . . . relax
>
> 9 . . . you are following your breath in
>
> 8 . . . deeper and deeper in
>
> 7 . . . very safe
>
> 6 . . . very relaxed
>
> 5 . . . deeper and deeper in
>
> 4 . . . still very alert
>
> 3 . . . very safe
>
> 2 . . . very relaxed
>
> 1 . . . very deep within

Now drop your focus to the base chakra, the pelvis or the vagina, and visualize this area of your body becoming very relaxed and very open. You are going to begin breathing through this opening. With each in breath, draw up the pure, rich, nurturing energy of MaMa Earth. Pull it up into your vagina and hold it there. Continue to breath and pull up this energy until you have a sense of fullness in your pelvis.

Focus on the energy you are holding and visualize it starting to spin. It is beginning its cycle inside of you. Note the direction that it is spinning in. Allow this energy to spin and grow so that its motion fills up this chakra.

Within the center of this spinning motion visualize a color growing. This color is your personal base chakra color. This color is your Kundalini power color. Let this color grow in intensity until it lights up this chakra.

Focus on both the motion of the energy and the Kundalini power color and be aware of any physical sensations that may be taking place.

Drop your focus once more to the very center of this chakra. An image presents itself to you. It is peeking out at you. Look very closely at this image for it is your Kundalini.

Allow this image to begin to grow in size until it fills up this chakra. Be aware of any physical sensations, such as heat.

Listen now and see if your Kundalini has any information to pass on to you.

Focus back on the image of your kundalini and allow it to shrink in size until it disappears.

Focus on the color and allow it to diminish in brightness until it disappears.

Focus on the spinning motion of the energy and allow it to slow down. When the movement is very, very slow, take a deep breath and release the energy of MaMa Earth back out through the vagina and allow it to return to its place of origin.

Take a very deep breath and note any physical sensations that may be lingering in this chakra.

Counting from 1 to 10, begin to rise with each exhale of your breath until you are back in the here and now.

1 . . . rising up

2 . . . feeling very relaxed

3 . . . exhaling up

4 . . . aware of your physical body

5 . . . feeling the floor under you

6 . . . exhaling up

7 . . . aware of your surroundings

8 . . . exhaling up

9 . . . fully back

10 . . . exhaling and releasing your journey

When you feel comfortable, open your eyes. Before you forget, note the images that you experienced on the following pages.

Motion of energy in your base chakra:

Sensations attached to this motion:

Color of base chakra/Kundalini power:

Sensations attached to this color:

Kundalini image:

Sensations attached to this image:

Message received:

We are able to access the Kundalini naturally each month during our bleeding time, for as the blood begins to flow, the great Kundali shifts her position and moves up into the second chakra (energy center), the womb. With this understanding we must start focusing on the serpent power of our blood and experience new levels of empowerment. When we bleed, we are connected to the very thin veil between living and dying. In essence, when we menstruate a part of our physical beingness has died and is leaving us. This refers to the tearing away of the endometrium; the shedding of the uterine lining each month. This organic death process natural to the female opens new avenues of understanding for both women and men. However, for women, in our role as original shamans, our collective wisdom knows that both life and death are connected to the spilling of blood. This is demonstrated in its entirety when a woman gives birth.

The birthing mother is quintessentially shamanic for she stands at the gateway between death and life. She peers into the death realm, not knowing for certain if she will come out alive. She reaches over to bring through another new soul. In this altered state of consciousness—a state of natural ecstasy—the birthing mother, in her role as the original prototype of shaman, willingly faces death to give life to a new soul. Most forms of what we call shamanism are analogous to a mother giving birth, as the apprentice had to master facing death without fear to save and/or heal a soul before he could call himself a shaman.

However, women who choose not to ever give birth still contain shamanic abilities and can access them through the monthly bleeding. It is during the blood time that traveling into other realms of existence and communing with the life spirits is easily accomplished. This is made possible when fear of the unknown is diminished as discussed in the previous section. Therefore, the real shaman power of menstruation—in a more fundamental view—is in its regularity.

It is this female shamanic ability that has from time immemorial created fear and envy in the other gender. Man can only gain access into the life spirit if he has mastered an apprenticeship into shamanhood or he himself lies at the door of death; the shedding of his own life blood pouring out from a wound, or a malfunctioning organ. In fact, it has been man that made taboo the menstruum while at the same time incorporating the use of the color red for magical significance in his role as shaman.

The Color Red

The color representative of life and death is the color red. It is the magical essence of the body; the pulsing of the heart; the reservoir behind the tears. Red is a psychic quality, not a material one, though it has a material dimension. To Native American Indians, when ultimately perceived in a sacred manner, the color red is a quality of a being.[4]

In history the female blood color alone was often considered a potent magic charm. Many primitive cultures rendered anything sacred by coloring it red and calling the red color menstrual blood. Often it was thought that blood-red paint was a powerful medicine, and was painted over the body of sick people in an effort to cure them. The "Blood Goddess," whose body was stained red, was considered divine because she never dropped or wasted menstrual blood. I believe that the sacrifice of animals and / or humans for the life blood developed only when man decided to denigrate the blood mysteries and the worship of the Goddess, and that the notion of a blood-thirsty Goddess came about by male interpretation. The original worship of the Blood Goddess most likely involved a blood altar where containers of the Priestess's manstrual blood were set forth out of reverence.

In Europe it was once traditional to cover a cadaver with red ochre to assist the ancestor in being "born again,"[5] but during the 16th century the menstrual blood became so taboo that it was converted to an uncleanly act of life. The red cross then became the sign for the menstruating woman.[6]

Today it is important for us to view the menstrual blood and its color in a new light. We must find the healing powers of its cycle.

The Red Power As Healing

The red power is the shaman woman ability to initiate, to catalyze, to transform, and through these to heal. The menstrual cycle represents the healing power. Since life for women is cyclic, bleeding is a regular exchange of the inner and outer powers, in balance; a time for going within, a time for relating to others, a time for bringing forth the visions seen through the eyes of the shaman. It is the oracular ability that is sharpened at this time which brings with it the power to hear, and the voice of spirit.

Like the Kundalini, our blood power represents the shamanic healing force that rises up through the body and regenerates every cell; replenishing and recharging our bodies, insuring that strength and endurance that is so characteristically female.

The regenerative healing power of the menstrual cycle is central to female shamanism. For as is routine in shamanic apprenticeship we, too, learn to traverse the three worlds: the Upper World, the Middle World and the Under Word.

During our monthly cycle we journey out of the body to the Upper World during the Waxing Moon gathering creative inspiration. We live in the Middle World during ovulation and express our divinity with the Full Moon light, and dive deep into the Under World, like Inanna's descent, during the New Moon when we menstruate and gather the wisdoms of healing and living from the darkness of the soul; where in essence we die and are reborn. In addition, we face death at the time of childbirth when we travel out of body into the invisible realms to bring back a spirit to incarnate in our babies. Women are, in essence, conduits for the mysteries of life and death.

The red healing power is obtained through the temple of our own bodies. When we listen to our bodies through each phase of our cycle we bring back to perfect balance our feminine lives through the ability to self-heal each and every month. When we use the healing power we gain deeper insight into *who* we are. This inner understanding is derived from the quiet moments we initiate during our bleeding. When we get into the habit of publicly acknowledging that we require quiet time, alone time, during our periods we get more in touch with the *who* of self. We draw from our inner power (blood power) the inspiration and visions of the next step we must take. We assume the posture of shaman woman, and as we come out of the quiet time we have the confidence to *initiate* the necessary action required to actually take the next step in fulfilling our vision. This knowledge coupled with the renewed sense of confidence propels us forward.

As with all change there comes a period where movement comes to a temporary halt. However, with the blood power actively initiated, we *catalyze* the standstill by honoring self and gaining new inspiration which enables us to shift direction and continue the *transformation* required to bring about the completion of what was originally envisioned. Celebrating the Full Moon is a tool shaman woman uses to accomplish this means. In the innate ability to understand the intrinsic nature of cycles, through her we learn to view the Full Moon as the time of temporary standstill. It is a time to be reflected on, to view the changes that have taken place, to honor self and life, to take a deep breath, to look into the full light shining in the darkness and see the next step required. From this light we gain renewed inspiration.

As transformation completely takes place, we obtain the added power from the Kundalini power of knowing we are capable of conducting our lives in a manner in which fulfillment of personal needs are met. The inner Kundalini power of the blood is married to the outer power of physical change; we become empowered—Shaman Woman!

Full Moon As A Tool

At the next Full Moon plan to have a private ceremony. Prepare a few days ahead, by evaluating a project you are working on.

The night of the Full Moon go to a place where you can sit safely and where no one will interrupt you. Face Grandmother Moon as she shines brightly in the sky. Raise your arms up to her and sing your Power Chant received during your First Rite of Passage. Sing this chant as many times as you want. Dance if you want. Be free in your celebration.

When the time is right (you will sense this), sit down and get comfortable. Continue to gaze upon the Moon's face. Speak out your project, the progress you have made to date and give thanks for the progress. Then speak out the problem area(s) that seem to have slowed your progress down. Ask for clarity on what steps need to be taken next. Listen. Receive this clarity as it washes down upon you through the luminescent rays of Grandmother Moon.

When you have received information, give thanks for it. Stand and sing your Power Chant again. Dance some more if you feel inclined to do so.

Before you go to sleep that night make sure you write down all the information you received.

It is through this sense of empowerment that *healing* takes place. Change, whether it be on a physical, mental or emotional level generates healing when the change stems from our own initiative.

The above knowledge can also be applied to times of forced change. The blood power gives us the added edge of being able to recognize change at its onset and immediately assess it. By applying the same routine we psychically undergo during our bleeding (which implies some quiet time), we are able to examine the options available, see the most beneficial outcome, focus on the required action needed, and then face the forced change from a rational stance and take control by initiating the direction we choose to catalyze, thus transforming our lives and, in the end, experiencing healing rather than desecration.

Let us approach our lives with this formula in mind. It is this formula: to initiate, to catalyze, to transform, and through these to heal that is the wisdom of the blood power. Women contain the innate ability to access this formula intimately. The shaman woman bases all healing on this formula. The ancient healing, the healing of today, the healing of tomorrow is based on the natural tendency of women to turn inward and access the subconscious for information to balance our lives.

In this ultimate sense of understanding the menses and our monthly cycle, how can it be considered by society and especially by women as such a negative natural phenomena?

The Rhythm of Wellness

At first crescent we emerge from our body temple; reborn, moving into the light of creative action. As the Waxing Moon grows in size and brings with it light, we see more clearly the path that we envisioned in the darkness of our body temple. We walk down the path developing awareness that there is no end-point, that health and happiness are possible in each moment. We share and learn with others during this process; explore and create. The design of our personal lifestyles are initiated.

Full Moon shines boldly; a beacon light. Listening to our body temple we have heard the sounds of fertility and rejoice with the world and all forms of life in our ability to create life should we choose to do so. We channel the energy received from the environment which is being transformed within. We share and celebrate and send out our life energy to affect the world around us. If we choose to conceive we share the sexual fire with a mate and move on toward the consciousness of becoming a nurturer. If we choose not to conceive we take precautions, and lovingly accept ourselves for this decision.

Sometimes it is important to be selfish and focus primarily on self; nurturing and supporting self. As discussed in the previous section, this attention on self is required as part of the formula that is the wisdom of the blood power. Likewise, it is also important to honor the professional side of our life and congratulate personal achievements and celebrate them. If we always wait for someone else to give us the acknowledgement we deserve, some of us will be waiting forever.

Full Moon hypostatizes the goals achieved, our visions, our creativity, freezing it for an instant in time so we can look at it and honor the changes that have taken place, renew inspiration and proceed with the next transformation. We have seen above how the energy of the Full Moon can be used as a tool to help us accomplish our means.

The light begins to wane. Naturally and consciously we seek the confines of our own solitude. The signals of our body temple tell us that the womb is preparing to weep; to release the house that was created to nurture and feed new life. Respect toward the body temple changes are acknowledged by focusing on the physical messages and administering proper balancing practices: paying attention to the foods eaten, drinking herbal teas, massaging the body, assuming yoga postures that relieve tension, relaxing the body, and which facilitates insight.

As the Moon visibly retreats, seclusion is honored; a choice to integrate the body, mind, spirit and soul during the time of bleeding is undertaken. The quiet time, the slowed-down time has arrived. The body temple is cleansing itself, regenerating and healing every cell. The soul is allowed to glimpse the wisdoms tied to the life blood. We learn to love our whole self. We learn to assume charge of our lives by living in process and channelling life energy. We learn to work in cooperation with the body temple, and make the choices that ensure our optimal health, our optimal well-being. As we release our energy with the blood, our bodies relax as if having just died. We advance into a state of completeness, ready to face the world again. Shaman woman is brough forward at this time and the Kundalini power awakened.

However, quiet, alone time is not always easy to achieve for everyone. But I am a firm believer that every one of us contains the ability to initiate the necessary changes in our environment to allow all the quiet, alone time required. We must be willing to speak up and out for what we need. Taking one step at a time facilitates change in a harmonious way. Even if the first step is a 15 minute break during the day at work away from every one, or in the evening at home. Sometimes a strong voice must be used: "I do not want to be interrupted for the next 15 minutes."

For mothers with infants, or young children, remember that children require naps. The first half-hour of nap-time can be utilized as quiet, alone time.

If each one of us examines our lives, we will see where that first step lies. We must be the one to initiate the change. No one else will do it for us. Each and every one deserves what we require to become a whole and balanced shaman woman.

Finding Alone Time

Take a few minutes to sit down and go over your regular schedule during the week and then on weekends. See where you can begin to take some alone time. Write down the possible days and times:

What steps must you initiate in order to be able to have this time to yourself?

Affirm that you will take this alone time. Write out your affirmation.

How do you feel after taking your time?

Do you want to try increasing the amount of time you take for your alone time? If so, again note the possible days and times.

What steps must be initiated in order to receive this time?

How do you feel after taking this alone time?

Continue the above process until you find the time that is perfect for you. Once you have gotten into the habit of taking alone time, you will fall into a natural pattern with it and it will not have to be such a conscious part of your planning. You will simply take it. Good luck.

NOTES

1. Vicki Noble, "The Shakti Woman," *Snake Power Magazine*, Vol. 1, Is. 1 (October 31, 1989).

2. Ibid.

3. Barbara G. Walker, *The Woman's Encyclopedia of Myths and Secrets* (Harper & Row, 1983), p. 517.

4. Paula Gunn Allen, *The Sacred Hoop* (Beacon Press, 1986), p. 69.

5. Walker, Ibid. , p. 639.

6. Walker, Ibid., p. 644.

DANCING THE BLOOD DANCE

Chapter Six

Celebrating Femininity

Yin is like a mother-of-pearl image hidden in the deepest re-cesses of the house.

—Carl G. Jung

We need to reaffirm our bodies as temples of our holy spirits. We need to let our religions stay open-ended, non-ossified and continuously evolving. We need to study matriarchal records and current feminist knowledge, and to integrate our knowledge with our practice. We must develop collective systems of spiritual exploration, based on the natural ecology of our physiological body functions and those of MaMa Earth. We need to develop our psychic powers and our respect for non-verbal sensory as well as speaking our truths. Our theory must come out of our own practical experience, inclusive of all peoples.

As we express the mythology of Goddess and herstory created through current day experience, we realize that woman spirituality is political because it transforms our relationship to society; the arts are its means of communication. The spiritual is once again being recognized as the core of art-making and art-experiencing. The image is the key to our transformation of culture. The change cannot come about without the reinforcement of new icons and symbols of female power.

Herstory is creating a new language of myths and symbols and images. The images of Goddess with our faces and our bodies. Images that proudly broadcast to the world that Goddess is the guardian of the indwelling source of authentic conscience and spiritual guidance, the divinity within, the transpersonal center, the "Self," and that we women are the channel through which the Goddess will reemerge into our existence once again. These images of woman, as Goddess, are bringing her back home. Our task has been to find the way to access this powerful tool of communication; visualizing the sacred female. In the attempt to do so, we find that our art is coming from the power of shaman woman; the soul.

In our attempt to find Goddess within, we allow her to come back as the Muse of the arts. It is she who is the inspiration behind the explosion of our creativity. As the Muse within is found, we express the releasing of this creative energy.

Through art, we are recovering the key to wholeness, of unity. We come to understand that we must create new symbols which in turn are creating a new way of seeing and being in the world. Whether our art be tangible such as in paintings, sculpting, jewelry, clothing, masks, etc., or dramatic through the expression of dance or theatrics, we are empowering and enriching our lives and the lives of men as well; for all of us need the Goddess. As the new symbol of female identity and sacredness is firmly established in our culture, a new symbol for male identity will be birthed; one that is not connected to dominance and violence.

In Honor of the Bleeding

Ritual is the avenue of self-empowerment. Women are innately religious. We understand the depths and heights of spirituality. Through our monthly death and rebirth, through shaman woman eyes, we elucidate the cycles of nature, the basic alchemical complexion of the elements, the ebbing and flowing evolutionary course of life.

Through ritual, we travel a conscious path of evolution. In celebrating our femininity and Goddesshood, we enter into the spiritual arena of life. We undergo a transformation emotionally, mentally and spiritually that births us into the place of initiation. As we undergo our initiations into herstory we are placed on the Path of Holiness, becoming a representative of the feminine nature or energy of life.

Ritual, and especially those connected to the Moon and our bleeding time, is related to our understanding of healing, because healing is the outcome of integration of spirituality. Rituals of transformation are meant to mark the "something-lost/something-gained" inherent in all change. Ritual is also a way for us to integrate the past, present, and future.

Blood rituals remind us of our power as women; our divinity; the sacredness of our body temple. Moon rituals remind us that in order to change we must move according to the natural cycles of birth, release, death, and rebirth. Through all ritual, we learn to live these cycles with grace.

As grand-daughters of Grandmother Moon, as daughters of MaMa Earth, as priestesses of Goddess, as sisters and lovers and mothers we need to begin creating our own ceremonies[1]; pulling from the archaic resources that are an accumulation of the collective, and allow our ceremonies to flow spontaneously and effortlessly from the well of our souls. Rather than getting caught up in the way other women have performed ceremony, let us birth our own wisdom and add our voices to the choir that is already uttering forth. That is what herstory is: an ever changing, ever-widening collective of woman spirit.[1]

Blood Ritual

Sit back. Take a deep breath. Think about how you might celebrate your menses. What kind of ritual you would plan. Now actually create an outline of your ritual.

Day and time of scheduled ritual:

Intent/focus of ritual:

Items you will need:

Chants to use:

Ritual Outline:

Comments after ritual:

● ◑ ○ ◑

Part of the process to create powerful rituals involves examining the most basic tools that are available at our finger-tips. Tools such as the monthly blood, our bodies and how we adorn them, movement for evoking power, and our voices. I would like to share some of my experiences in each of the above areas that were birthed through my own attempt to celebrate the feminine.

The Blood Jar

As I awakened to the power of the menstrual blood I began to see how important it was to collect my monthly release. I stopped using tampons and/or store bought sanitary napkins and started using feminine lingerie. These absorbers are constructed out of flannel. The first time I used a flannel absorber I knew I wanted to create a Blood Jar in which to soak the absorbers in water after each use. At first I simply found a container with a lid, filled it half full of water and hid it under an orangish-red towel in the corner of my bathroom. After each absorber had a good soaking, I squeezed the excess water (now a beautiful red) off the flannel, handwashed it and hung it up to dry. (I find that I can keep the blood water until my next bleeding. During that time I use it in ritual as much as possible. The blood water left over is used to nourish the plants inside my house as well as in the garden.)

In ritual, I place a chalice full of the blood water on my altar and use it to call in a power; such as the Goddess personification I wish to work with during the ceremony. I also use this water to anoint sacred tools and the women attending in a manner of consecration. Consecration is the act of making an item or person ready to receive and channel the energy being worked with. In sacred circle, first I purify the space, items used, and participants usually with a solution of salt and water. Purification is an act of releasing the vibrations of the mundane world; releasing negative thoughts, mental stress and physical tension. The act of consecration is acknowledging that all within the sacred circle are ready to move forward into ceremony, fully focused, grounded and centered, in the here and now.

In some rituals, I simply hold the chalice up and invoke the blood power of the feminine. I do this when I desire to travel deep into the woman's ways and receive guidance. Whenever ritual comes, whether planned or spontaneous, I always have the most exalted offering available at my finger-tips.

On the first day of my next bleeding, I choose which plants to nourish with the remaining blood water. After grounding and centering myself; moving into an altered state of consciousness, I approach the plants in reverence and acknowledge the Devas (spirits) of the plant. I usually chant a prayer blessing over it.

> *Sacred Plant that releases life breath into my world,*
> *thank you for your beauty*
> *thank you for your oxygen*
> *thank you for your spirit.*
> *In honor I give back to you the life-blood.*
> *Receive it with thanksgiving.*
> *May you continue to bless my life with your presence.*

After I speak the prayer blessing, I pour some of the water around the trunk of the plant. I like to touch the leaves (brush off the dust on my indoor plants), and finish by blowing my breath over the plant and then inhaling its breath. This exchange has proven to be very successful. All my indoor plants thrive, and the garden is abundant!

Through time, my Blood Jar has become more ornate. Although I still use an old fashion one pint canning jar and metal lid lined with a rubber sealer, I house the jar in a beautiful red satin drawstring purse that a girlfriend gave me one year at Yule. I often wonder if Ali would have given me the expensive Liz Claiborne

Figure 6: The Blood Jar

purse had she known it was going to be used in this manner? I'm glad she did because my Blood Jar is displayed in my bathroom with dignity, rather than hidden under a towel (Figure 6).

The Blood Jar has become a continual reminder of my ability to reclaim my period as sacred. The richness of the purse and the boldness of the red satin is a symbol of my divinity. I believe that by reclaiming my blood to dispose of as I see fit, has developed a power within my mind that will never be diminished. Through this practice of collecting my blood, I have been able to shock other women by handing them a chalice filled with life blood during ceremony. During those shocking times I am able to help women demystify their fear of blood. The shock opens closed doors. By encouraging them to gaze into the black redness, I guide them through channels and down the corridors of their minds bringing them in touch with their shaman woman. They see, reflected in the light of the blood, their own ability to reclaim their power. It is generally through this type of shocking experience that women begin to want to start rethinking menstruation.

To say the least, the Blood Jar becomes a mystery to anyone who sees it; a compelling, feminine mystery. Women will peek into the red, satin purse and boldly ask questions. Men want to peek, fantasizing that something wonderful is connected to the use of the purse—how right they are!

Adorning the Body Temple

Many of us have become aware of color vibration, whether through chakra enlightenment or personal seasonal colors. I have come across a significant power enhancer using color and style of dress. Several years ago I got into the habit of wearing red clothing during my menstruation as an outwardly sign of my divinity and femaleness. I found that this small personal statement really enhanced my self worth. I walked around saying (no matter how anonymously):

> *Red is beautiful,*
> *red is powerful,*
> *I am bleeding,*
> *I am in my woman way.*

Often, it seemed as if I drew strength from this quiet statement. I didn't care if anyone else realized *why* I was wearing red, it simply seemed as if the people who I did come in contact with during my statement time received, on a subliminal level, the full impact of the message and power of my spirit, because I often found a sense of respect and generosity come back my way.

I began experimenting with this concept of dressing according to the phase of my cycle. At first, I split the monthly cycle into two halves: Waxing and Waning. I began wearing more body contoured clothing, and especially pants during the Waxing phase. I felt that since this phase was one of *action*, I needed to tailor my dressing needs toward one of activity; especially of a spontaneous nature, and loose clothing seemed to get in the way, slow me down, prevent me from moving quickly. Yet, during the waning half of my cycle I dress in flowing, loose fitting dresses and skirts. My body is then swollen and uncomfortable, and, of course, during this phase I usually bleed, and so chose a style of clothing that went with my moving slower, more comfortably. I found that such simple changes actually helped me "flow" with my physical and emotional shifts through each cycle. This conscious effort to work with my body externally, also helped to bring my internal energies into balance.

As a result of the above, I took this concept further by breaking the cycle up into the four phases (Dark, Waxing, Full, Waning), and adding color specificity to each phase. Wow! What a change in my mental and emotional state. Immediately I noticed a stronger spiritual attunement. Of course, body comfort was greatly enhanced. The following data is how I work with adorning the *body temple* during every cycle. I discuss each phase, suggesting not only color and clothing styles, but jewelry, accessories, perfumes, hair styles, make-up, and body painting (See Figure 7 and the color plates in the center of this book). Have fun experimenting and finding what works best for you. I guarantee that by using a system personalized to your cycle, you will create a very solid foundation for expressing your shaman woman.

Again let me stress that bleeding with the lunation cycle is an ideal projection and not everyone does.We all movethrough the cycle. However, I work at keeping my relationship with Grandmother Moon as close as possible, so more often than not I do bleed according to her cycle. Therefore, the following is based on my cycle, which is in accordance with the lunar calendar, and is offered only as a guideline. Naturally, if you bleed during the Waxing or Full Moon phase of the lunar calendar then experimentation will be required to personalize this formula just for you.

The Dark or New Moon Phase. Grandmother Moon is hidden from our sight, withdrawn into her own reality; fully realized, cleansed, rejuvenated, ready to begin a new cycle. Until she peeks her face out from behind the black curtain of her self-chosen seclusion, she rests a little longer making sure the totality of her strength is there.

In this phase of my cycle, I have already finished bleeding and use this time of darkness and quiet to access my inner Goddess. I rest in a passive state of mind. My emotions are recharging. My body is

Figure 7: Adorning the Body Temple

The Dark or New Moon Phase

Colors: black, brown, burgundy, deep purple, forest green, rust, navy.

Clothing style: longer dresses and skirts (more fitting but with a slight flare), shawls, vests, jumpsuits, wide-leg pants, African/harem-style pants, longer length blouses that layer over skirts.

Accessories: belts, scarfs, leggings or layers of socks, enclosed shoes, power tools that are nonthreatening such as medicine bags, woman power shields, crystal/gemstone energy pouches, etc. Hats are wonderful to wear at this time, as are capes with hoods.

Jewelry: sacred, power items that might normally be worn for special ceremonies, symbolic pieces that represent your standing in your Spirit Lodge.*

Hair style: unbound hair, wild hair, unadorned hair.

Perfumes: rich, Earthy scents—musk, patchouli, cedar, honeysuckle, jasmine, sage.

Make-up: eye shadow colors—burgundy, browns, rust, deep purple, forest green; *eye liner*—black, brown, navy; *blush and lipshades*—darker shades.

Body painting: a personal power symbol such as the pentacle or spiral pointed on your body over the solar plexus areas in a dark color will enhance your inner journeys during this phase.

The Waxing Moon Phase

Colors: light orange, yellow, pink, olive greens, turquoise, peach, white.

Clothing style: short skirts and dresses (formfitting), shorts, African/harem pants, jeans, t-shirts, tank tops, blouses that snug my body.

Accessories: belts and shoulder-sling purses, or waist-wrap purses, daypacks, tennis shoes or slip-ons.

Jewelry: earrings.

Hair style: swept back from face and worn in ponytails or braids, headbands, barrettes.

Perfumes: light and airy—lavender, lemon, sandalwood, peppermint.

Make-up: bare minimum; *eye shadow colors*—pinks, golds; *eye liner* —purple, green; *blush and lipshapes*—pinks.

Body painting: none.

---

*The *Spirit Lodge* refers to your state of balance; how you are viewing life at that time; what you are spiritually working on for your own evolution; or what you are magically working on.

Figure 7 (continued)

The Full Moon Phase

Colors: white, blue-greens, bright pinks, brilliant blues, silver, golds, violet, green.

Clothing style: anything goes; expression of sexuality and femininity, seductive, soft, mostly skirts and blouses.

Accessories: scarfs, sandals, shawls, love charms.

Jewelry: earrings, bracelets and anklets, toe rings.

Hair style: curls, ribbons, soft layers (half pulled up, the other half flowing down).

Perfumes: lusty scents—favorite perfume, carnation, cinnamon, clove, rosemary, vanilla, the Kama Sutra scents.

Make-up: eye shadow colors—blues, greens, golds, rose; *eye liner*—blue; *blush and lipshades*—rose, gold, shimmery colors.

Body painting: in my unpredictable nature during the Full Moon, I got my first tattoo; a symbol of how deeply and passionately I loved Jack (my partner). However, for those of you who are not interested in *permanent* body painting, hearts, vulvas, and the sign for Venus (commonly used to represent woman) can be painted over your heart (left breast) or above the pubic hair line. The inner thigh, close to your cunt lips is also another great place, especially if you are planning a love session.

The Waning Moon Phase

Colors: plum, red, deep pink (especially during my bleeding time); deep blues, minty greens, purple.

Clothing style: long, flowing skirts, layers of blouses and vests; clothing for body comfort.

Accessories: slips and camisoles, Moon bags (during bleeding time), big purses, feminine supplies.

Jewelry: necklaces, rings, bracelets, earrings, pendants, symbolic pieces thatshow your worship of Goddess.

Hair style: soft braid pulled to one side, part of hair pulled up and pinned with a beautiful barrette, softly bound ponytails worn to one side and flowing over the shoulder in front.

Perfumes: gardenia, heather, myrrh, orange, orris, rose, violet.

Make-up: eye shadow colors—plum, purple; *eye liner*—purple; *blush and lipshades*—plum, red.

Body painting: a red spiral over the womb area is very powerful especially during your bleeding time.

Note: Please refer to the color plates in the center of the book to see how I look during these phases.

empty and lithe. During this phase I am my most serious, and approach my spirituality from a very powerful base. Because I still stand so deeply within (even deeper than when my blood flows), I adorn my body with rich, ark colors. I wear dresses that are not quite flowing but that tend to hug my body and are long. I am the medieval witch; the Great Goddess whose power knows no bounds. I wear my most sacred and occultish jewelry; the items that I consider to hold power. My hair is wild and free, falling down my back. The shades I cover my eye-lids with, and/or circle round the rims, are dark, ruddy shades. Scents connected to the deepest part of the forest rise from my skin. Occasionally, I will carry magical pouches filled with a variety of protective herbs and stones, amulets, or non-threatening power tools. A Tarot deck gets stuffed in my purse at this time. Belts and scarfs and leggings cover me. I am hidden from the world; a reflection of my inner self.

When I dress this severely for the two to four days of the Dark or New Moon, people truly leave me alone! I look too ominous to approach; scary, way too serious for others to handle.

The Waxing Moon Phase. Grandmother Moon creeps out into the open. Her anxiousness to bring light to the world becomes apparent as the size of her body and volume of light continually increase. The light brings with it action energy; the desire to be with others and share. Suddenly all kinds of opportunities become magically revealed. New ideas are set into motion, projects started, and personal environments enhanced. During the Waxing Phase I suddenly find myself wearing clothing that is more formfitting. African pants, shorts, short skirts or dresses, blouses that move with my body. I seem to choose colors that are pastels: yellows, pinks, olive green, light orange, turquoise blue, peach, white. My hair is swept back in ponytails, braids, pulled back with barrettes. With the increased light and energy, I am on the go and don't want to be bothered with anything. I wear minimal make-up; a dash of rose blush, pink eye-shadow, if any.

Earrings are the primary jewelry worn as I don't like to feel over-burdened. All power tools are left at home. Belts are occasionally worn. To allow my hands maximum freedom I use over-the-shoulder sling purses. I find I forget to use perfume at this time because I am on the go, but when I do put on a fragrance it is a light perfume, often times sandalwood or lavender oil. I am the Virgin Goddess; one-in-herself.

Although I am more assertive at this time (my yang energy raging), I feel sexual and more prone towards aggressive behavior.

The Full Moon Phase. In full glory, Grandmother Moon shines boldly down upon all life on Earth. She is exalted and celebrating in her light. Everything is revealed; nothing is hidden.

As I celebrate this phase of my cycle, and usually because I am ovulating, I tend to reveal my body a little more. I wear blouses or dresses that are lower cut, revealing my cleavage, or are snug fitting. My skirts will be flowing or fitted, long or short, but always extremely feminine. I wear more lace and ribbons. The colors I wear are usually white, but can often be bright and colorful, especially floral prints.

My make-up is playful, seductive, as is my hair. I like to use my hair during this phase to add a touch of sensuality and softness to my face. I am Ishtar, Oshun, Aphrodite; lover of life. I speak more through gestures than words at this time. Laughter explodes easily from me. My ankles and wrists are adorned with lots of bracelets. Fringed scarfs caress my hips or are wrapped around my head. I can be pretty unpredictable during this phase and so I usually allow my emotional state to dictate how I will dress and present myself for these three days.

Because of my overt sexual nature at Full Moon, I wear heavier perfumes, lusty scents like jasmine, patchouli, gardenia or carnation (musk would be another scent compatible with Full Moon); scents that are aphrodisiac in nature.

The Waning Moon Phase. The size and light of Grandmother Moon declines quickly. All energy seems to turn inward. The darkness begins to swallow the mind and one can either ride the ebbing of the light into the dark, gaining access to an inner world, or fight it and struggle against the course of the cycle.

My body moves into a state of discomfort and swollenness. The residue of sexual femininity stays with me, however, and I find that I continue to dress more feminine but my style is more flowing and loose. Longer skirts and layers of blouses and vests allow my body the comfort it requires. In my "slowed-down" state (once bleeding has begun), I tend to wear more jewelry, e.g., necklaces, bracelets, rings, earrings, pendants. More often then not the jewelry reveals my Goddess worship. I wear scarlet colors: plums, reds, deep pinks, and ocean colors: deep blues, minty greens, purples. The scent of heather and rose are usually worn at this time.

I am Venus on the half-shell rising from the depths of the ocean; rising from the depths of woman power. I am in touch with my body. Yemaya, powerful and ferocious.

● ◗ ○ ◗

As revealed above, my own unique personality and Goddess connections take on new power when worked with in such a physical manner. In time, I sectioned my wardrobe off into four parts (for each phase). When I purchase new articles of clothing, automatically, I buy according to the phase I'm in. Rather than be confined to one color scheme for the better part of the year (such as prescribed through the personal seasonal color analysis), I flow a whole spectrum of color as I travel through each cycle.

Perhaps I am a stickler, or an extremist, but I have certain clothes that are strictly worn during each phase and no other, such as my bleeding time. By doing this, I have found that the articles absorb the base energy of each phase and that of my own inner rhythm and not only enhance the power, but aid me in making each transition with relative ease. It took about three months of working with this concept before it began to flow. I found it changed when the season shifted and I brought out a new wardrobe. However, each season was easier than the next to establish, and within the course of one Moon cycle I found my new seasonal color/style vibration for the current season established.

Adorning Your Body Temple

Experiment with your statement of dress according to the Moon cycle and your menstrual cycle. Begin by observing your natural tendencies for dress throughout the next month. Then introduce minor changes at first, such as wearing shades of red during your Moon time. Or light colors during Full Moon. Observe how these changes may or may not consciously effect you. If you find they do, then go one step further and split the month in half: Waxing/Waning and experiment. Should you decide to devote an entire cycle to this concept, then work with all four phases: Dark/Waxing/Full/Waning.

As explained above, it took about three months of continuous study to personalize my wardrobe according to my Moon cycle. Have fun!

STEP ONE: Observe the way you naturally dress for one month, taking in to consideration the weekly phase of the Moon and your own cycle.

Week One

Moon Phase:

Your Cycle:

Describe your dress:

Week Two

Moon Phase:

Your Cycle:

Describe your dress:

Week Three

Moon Phase:

Your Cycle:

Describe your dress:

Week Four

Moon Phase:

Your Cycle:

Describe your dress:

STEP TWO: Begin experimenting with just the Waxing and Waning Phase of the Moon, adding your own cycle. Dress accordingly.

Waxing Phase (Crescent Moon to Full Moon)

Your Cycle:

Describe how you changed your dress to coincide:

What effects did you notice?

Physically:

Mentally:

Emotionally:

Spiritually:

Waning Phase (Day after Full Moon to Dark/New Moon)

Your Cycle:

Describe how you changed your dress to coincide:

What effects did you notice?

Physically:

Mentally:

Emotionally:

Spiritually:

STEP THREE: Now take it one step further by consciously dressing according to your cycle in each of the four phases of the Moon.

Waxing Phase

Your Cycle:

Describe how you changed your dress to coincide:

What effects did you notice?

Physically:

Mentally:

Emotionally:

Spiritually:

Full Phase

Your Cycle:

Describe how you changed your dress to coincide:

What effects did you notice?

Physically:

Mentally:

Emotionally:

Spiritually:

Waning Phase

Your Cycle:

Describe how you changed your dress to coincide:

What effects did you notice?

Physically:

Mentally:

Emotionally:

Spiritually:

Dark/New Phase

Your Cycle:

Describe how you changed your dress to coincide:

What effects did you notice?

Physically:

Mentally:

Emotionally:

Spiritually:

Comments:

● ◐ ○ ◐

Dancing The Blood Power

When the blood flows, performing certain movements greatly enhances our power. Movement raises energy; magical dancing has been connected to ritual since the earliest recollection in herstory. Whether we dance in private or with our circle of sisters, Dancing the Blood Power is extremely intimate. In its intimacy, we may find ourselves becoming sexually inspired. Likewise, Dancing the Blood Power also raises energy and becomes (what I consider to be) ecstatic dance. I always attain altered states of consciousness when Blood Dancing. I find that certain movements bring on trance-like states, and as I attain an ecstatic state, or a hypnotic state, I often feel as if orgasm is a breath away.

Dancing the Blood Power can help heighten our psychic awareness and receptivity by bringing us into closer contact with the subconscious mind; and also by being so receptive, to be able to raise power by channeling the primitive emotions and forces drawn out of the depths of the unconscious mind. The power of blood can be accessed on a transcendental state. Freeing the body at the same time that our blood flows, helps to loosen physical bonds; our spirit can soar when this occurs. On a much higher level, the ecstatic trance can bring forth the archetypal personalities to speak through us, and even carry us through the astral realms and bring us into personal contact and realization of Goddesshood.

Walking Damballah

Through our natural shamanic abilities, women can access a trance state almost immediately once the groundwork (or training) has been accomplished. To learn to attain a trance-like state requires minimal practice. The Voudoun have a powerful work called Walking Damballah, which induces an altered state of consciousness.[2] It is a movement that imitates the pattern of a side-winder snake and can be performed standing or lying down. Damballah is extremely useful for women because it is the movement of Shakti (Kundalini) power; the female Goddess energy housed at the base of the pelvic area. The movements of Damballah activates the Kundalini and causes it to rise. As the Kundalini rises during the bleeding time, a combined feeling of releasing and receiving is experienced. The blood energy pushes out; the Shakti energy rushes in. To experience Damballah, you:

1. Stand with your feet hip distance apart. Stand tall, shoulders back, opening the chest, belly held firm.

2. Release your chest forward, bending over toward your thighs. Allow your knees to bend at the same time. Take a full count of four to perform this movement. When you come to the final position, keep your back flat.

3. Contract your hips, tucking them in and forward. Uncurl your spine one vertebra at a time. Your head is the last thing to return to the original upright position you started in.

4. Repeat steps 1–3 while stepping forward with your right leg about 12 inches in front of the left. Keep your weight on the ball of the right foot; don't touch the heel down. Now repeat with the left foot stepping forward.

5. Once the steps have been performed successfully, add breath. Exhale as your chest goes forward; inhale as your hips contract.

6. Once your breath matches the movements, add the chanting of the letter "O."

Allow the energy to rise within. Open to it, and experience the power. You may need to practice this a few times before you experience anything, but once you do, Damballah will become one of your favorite Blood Dances.

The Womb Dance

Womb Dancing can be performed laying down, sitting, kneeling, or standing. The hands are always held over the womb; left hand over the belly, right hand over the left.

When laying down, keep the knees bent so you can make tiny pelvic movements by contracting and releasing. The movements are so tiny that if someone were watching they might think you were lying still.

When sitting, the belly is pulled in and pushed out very slowly then circled to the right, then back to the left. This movement is performed over and over and over again.

When kneeling, place your right foot over the left. Allow your knees to open slightly. With a breath in, lift up onto your knees. Hold for a count of 8. Breathing out, lower back to your heels.

In a standing position, keep your knees slightly bent and rock your pelvic front—back, front—back, and then from side to side twice. The second cycle the pelvic moves in a "box"—front, right, back, left. Then pelvic front, left, back, right, ending front. Go back to the beginning and perform the sequence again, continuing on to the second cycle, etc.

Use the tone of "Ma" continually. Remember your breathing should always match your movements. When you breathe in, the movement moves back in. When you breathe out, the movement moves out. In the case where the pelvic moves in a box, begin breathing out.

Frog Dance

This position is called "The Frog" because your body looks like a frog when you are leaning forward. Also the frog was an early symbol of fertility in Goddess worship. The Frog Dance is more a position than a dance but helps bring on an altered state. Assume a kneeling position and then sit back on your heels allowing your knees to adjust a slight distance apart for comfort. Keep your hands at your sides and lean forward until your forehead touches the ground. Release, and as you do so, turn your head to one side and rest your cheek against the floor. Hold this position for as long as you can. Don't forget to breathe. If you have a recording of shamanic drumming, use it in conjunction with this position. As you assume this posture be conscious of your connection with Mother Earth and lend her a listening ear. This posture is excellent for relieving cramps.

Bear Shaman (Figure 8)

The Bear Shaman posture is powerful when used during your bleeding time because it activates the very intense Healing Spirit of the Bear. The Bear Spirit is considered a mighty healer in many regions by the indigenous people. The woman who really needs to heal her inner psyche in connection to her menstruation may want to begin with this Blood Dance. It is a stationary posture, like the Frog, that will bring on a trance-like state. When assuming the Bear Shaman posture come into a kneeling position with knees slightly apart. Make fists with your hands and touch the knuckles of each hand together and rest them against your solar plexus (belly button) area. Keep your elbows out and your shoulders relaxed. Tilt your head slightly back. Breathe slow and evenly. Imagine the Great BearMother behind you, your head leaning into her belly, her paws holding your head. A shamanic rattling tape is best when used with this position.

The more you use this position the more information you will receive on healing. Healing rituals of this nature are used extensively around the world. The understanding that trance can heal must be extremely old, for modern hunter-gathers, such as the Bushmen, guardians of the most ancient human traditions, use the strategy simply to keep everyone in their band well and also to heal.

Since we undergo a healing process each time we bleed, allowing the healing wisdom to come through is especially easy to do in conjunction with our innate shamanic abilities.

Moon Dance

Moon Dancing was created through my own efforts to reconnect with Grandmother Moon and the bleeding time. I found that imitating the three phases of Waxing, Full, and Waning bridged the gap between my own energy and those of a more esoteric nature. The dance is performed standing while facing the Moon. Begin by

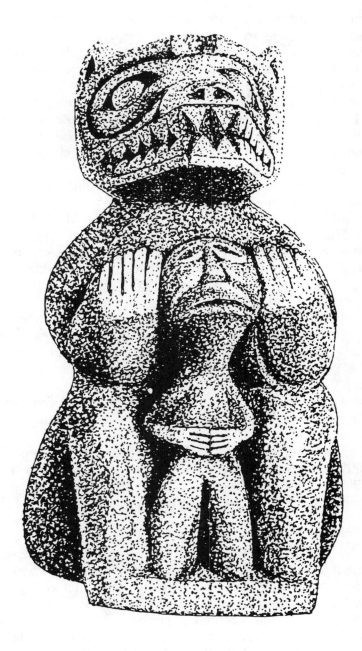

Figure 8: The Healing Spirit of the Bear Shaman Posture

breathing in and raising your arms to shoulder height, and then releasing breath while bringing the arms over your head in a curved position (palms in) creating the Full Moon. Again take another breath, this time reaching up to the Moon to connect with her energy, and then lowering your hands as you breath out, bringing them to rest on your womb to connect with your energy.

The dance now begins. Breathe in. Raise your right arm over your head in a curved position. Breathe out, and bend slightly to your left bringing the curved arm, or Crescent (Waxing) Moon into exalted position. Hold.

In the bent position, breathe in and curve your left arm above your head so that you now hold both arms in a curved position over your head. As you exhale, raise back up to a centered position bringing the Full Moon into exalted position. Hold.

Breathe in and lower your right arm to your side, keeping your left arm raised. As you exhale, bend to the right bringing your curved left arm which symbolizes the Waning Crescent into its exalted position. Hold. Inhale, hold the position.

Releasing your breath, allow your body to completely relax, bend your knees, curve your arms, head and upper torso over and just hang. Hold this position for a few minutes and continue to breathe. You are now the invisible Moon; the Dark Moon or the New Moon.

Breathing in, roll up one vertebra at a time until you come to a standing position. Begin the dance all over again starting with the right arm.

I have found that you can take the movement to a kneeling and then sitting position with little effort or thought; it is nice to have the flexibility to allow a dance to naturally end by slowly moving closer to the ground until you are sitting on MaMa Earth.

Grandmother Step

The Grandmother Step is taught by Brooke Medicine Eagle (an Intertribal metis) and is a very simple dance that can be performed to achieve a centering/grounding effect. Either to hand clapping or a drum beat that imitates MaMa Earth's heartbeat—dum-dum (the stressed "dum" is the accented or strong beat)—begin moving to your left. On the strong beat you step to the left with your left foot. Your right foot follows, but you step lightly onto the right foot while emphasizing picking up your knee. This dance moves in a circle. If other women are present it can be danced with arms around each other forming a very tight circle. With each step down you are speaking a prayer to MaMa Earth; thanking her for your life, her support, abundant food.

Grandmother Dance

The Grandmother Step is the foundation for this dance. After successfully dancing the step in a round circle you are ready to dance the Grandmother Dance, which is also taught by Brooke. If you perform the Grandmother Dance with a group of women it might be best to have one woman act as leader and verbally give the following directions throughout the dance so it flows.

Again, dance to hands clapping or a drumbeat imitating MaMa Earth's heartbeat. After the circle is moving smoothly to the beat, look around the room and acknowledge yourself as the beautiful women you are in this day and time, in the present. Take time to really see each other.

Let the eyes begin to soften, lowering the lids until all that you see are the feet and legs of the women in the circle. Forget about the personality of the women; let go. Acknowledge each woman as all women who, down through time, have danced in circle and connected.

Dance your own mother who may never have had the chance to acknowledge her own divinity. Dance for her. Dance your connection with her. Then dance for your Grandmother, your mother's mother. Keep dancing on back with each Grandmother even if you did not know them, or cannot picture what their faces looked like. Dance for the women of all time.

Move further back in time, to the Grandmothers of all two-leggeds, then the four-legged Grandmothers, the swimmers, wingeds, trees, waters, the one-celled Grandmothers. Go back through time and pull one Grandmother to you, whatever her personification. If she is a dolphin, pull her to you and dance her power, feel her. Talk to her now. Hold out your left hand and let her give you something: a thought, a feeling, a word, a song, whatever it is, receive it.

Now hold out your right hand to see what there is for this Grandmother and give it to her. When you have given her your gift, begin to dance back up through time to the present. Finish by acknowledging each woman who is present again. When completed, sit in a circle and share the wisdom received from the Grandmothers. Often times the information will pertain to the women's ways as were followed in the beginning of herstory.

Dancing the Blood Power

This dance is about moving your body temple in any way that feels good. Let your body take you into an ecstatic state: you may clutch your womb (connecting with your power), cup your breasts (connecting with Goddess power), or raise cupped hands on either side of your head (Figure 9) to connect with Moon power.

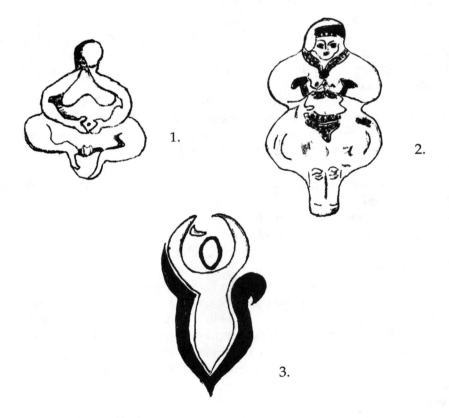

Figure 9: Dancing the Blood Power Hand Movements:

1. Connecting with your power; 2. Connecting with Goddess power;
3. Connecting with Moon power

As you Dance the Blood Power let the emphasis be on drawing energy in through your vagina. Always use this in combination with the psychic energy created by deep and full breathing. Visualize red-gold energy flowing through each chakra of your body to help consciously expand your aura.

Temple dancing of this nature has a fortuitous side effect in that it not only builds up sexual magnetism but creates a more positive frame of mind which is thus engendered with accompanying good feelings which helps to perpetuate a state of continuing good fortune.

Trance is induced with slow repetitious or fast movements (that may bring on a state of hyperventilation) that are performed with focused intent to connect with your own power and either Goddess or Moon power. Remember, practice makes perfect, and in this case, practice makes power through an ecstatic trance-like state. So, dance and experience what you contain within!

Experiments With Dance

Choose the Blood Dance that you are most drawn to. Re-read its section above, committing the instructions to memory so you will not have to stop and read them during your experiment. To be sure you have all the necessary steps of the dance memorized, take a minute to write them out. When the two sets of instructions are identical prepare for the experiment by obtaining the necessary music suggested and/or desired.

Dress in comfortable clothing. Take a few minutes to ground and center yourself. It is important you prepare yourself for trance dancing because, in essence you are going into sacred time through an alternative form of ceremony. I suggest that you use the format presented in the Moon Lodge Journey (Chapter Eight) to create your sacred space. Offering prayers to deity is also very important. When you feel ready. Perform the dance. When you have finished, take the time to reflect on the effects it had on you. I believe it is important to experiment with a dance three times before deciding whether or not you benefit from it.

Chosen Dance:

Memory instructions:

Moon Phase:

Your Cycle:

Comments:

Session Two:

  Moon Phase:

  Your Cycle:

Comments:

Session Three:

  Moon Phase:

  Your Cycle:

Comments:

Final decision to continue to use dance:

Our Voices

As we attain deeper insights to what our woman power is all about, how closely linked to Grandmother Moon and MaMa Earth we are and, most importantly, as we begin to channel Goddess energy in our daily living we need to birth forth the rich power of intellectual communication through our words. We need not fear our words any longer, but rejoicingly and actively seek to speak our truths.

Words are powerful, they are the vibration sent forth for good or ill. Through our words we can persuade others to see the way we see. Through our words we can hurt others. Through our words we can soothe and calm a child's fear. As we celebrate femininity we raise our voices to perpetuate the transformation in our environment that we are undergoing consciously.

It is so very important to speak, chant, sing, our personal truths; those compelling ideas that resonate with what is most sacred, with what seems right. When such ideas are collective, we can call them mythology: how it was *in the beginning*. The collective mythology of woman has become the herstory of Goddess. This story belongs to the realm of all living myth. The truth of the Goddess is the mystery of our being. She is the dynamic life force within. She is the dance of life, and her song is Eros, the energy of creation.

> *Va-La-Ra-Ya-Ma.*
> *Thou art water,*
> *Thou art Earth,*
> *Thou art fire,*
> *Thou art air,*
> *Thou art the void and*
> *Thou art the Supreme Divinity*[3]

As we give voice to her energy of creation we send forth our magick into the world; allowing the Goddess to come back to us as the beacon for the emergence of self that is not separate from the world in which our lives are embedded but a part of a greater being. In the language of the world religions, "this is merging with the One."

Let us use Our Voices to change communication standards, to tell our story, to beckon the Goddess home, to transform our consciousness. The following passages of Our Voices are but a miniscule sampling of the diverse ways in which we can begin actively uttering our truth to the world.

Invoking the Elements/Quarters/Gateways

As we prepare for sacred space in which we will perform our power, let us always remember to speak to the invisible realm of spirit-keepers who so graciously and willingly come to our aide and protection. Remember that what we have called matter is not separated from spirit; matter is impregnated with spirit. Therefore when we call upon the forces of spirit, our physical world is activated and all matter becomes magically and ecstatically animated.

In sacred circle we use Our Voices to establish the quarter gateways. We do this by invoking the element, or guardian, of the gateway.

Each quarter (and there are four: east, west, south, and north) have correspondences that create a picture. The most standard correspondences of the Wiccan tradition for each quarter are:

> *East:* element Air, mind/intellect, time of day—dawn, beginnings, season of spring, Crescent Moon, sacred tool—wand/censor, high-flying birds, the color yellow, and the elemental sylph.

> *South:* element Fire, spirit/body, time of day—noon, middle, season of summer, Full Moon, sacred tool—sword/censor, fire-breathing dragons/cats, the color red, and the elemental salamander.

> *West:* element Water, heart/emotion, time of day—twilight/evening, endings, season of autumn, Waning Moon, sacred tool—chalice, mermaids/dolphins, the color blue/black, and the elemental undine.

> *North*: element Earth, bones/body, time of day—midnight, repose, season of winter, Dark Moon/New Moon, sacred tool—pentacle, stag/bear, the color white/black, and the elemental gnome.

As women, we must begin looking at the quarters from a new perspective and see how each corresponds to the cycles of our bleeding and the phases of our lives. The following is offered as a guideline in writing your own quarter invocations.

Woman power of the east
send forth your clarity
shed your light upon the path
inspire me with purity
from the beginning of my first blood
until the last
I call forth your simplicity
to aide me with my life.

Woman power of the south
strong and mighty passion
flame the power inside of me
awaken my creativeness
flame it life through my blood power
I call forth your spirit
to aide me with my life.

Woman power of the west
flowing power of the womb
sacred blood, mystery blood
blood of life
blood of death
blood of transformation
I call forth your sacredness
to aide me with my life.

Woman power of the north
the deepness of my inner soul
strengthen my wisdom Crone
that dwells eternally within
send forth the Grandmothers' voice
to guide me through each Moon
I call forth your wisdom
to aide me with me life.

Calling Home Goddess

Whether we are in sacred ceremony or we simply feel the need to speak out to our Goddess, let us do so with meaning and intent. Religious prayers have become utterances filled with useless self-pity, begging, and bargaining. When we call out to the Goddess, let Our Voices ring with inner power and the energy of creation.

The following prayers are my own and demonstrate the personal nature in which they hold meaning for me.

Holy Mother, Wise Mother

> Holy Mother, Wise Mother
> I call to you this day
> asking for your guidance
> along my woman's way.
> Through each Moon
> I come to know
> the sacredness of my soul,
> Oh Holy Mother, Wise Mother
> come inspire me.

> Holy Mother, Wise Mother
> I am your daughter
> searching for the answers
> that will quiet my raging soul.
> Through the blood
> I see my questions
> flowing out of me
> and when I look upon this blood
> you quietly answer me,
> Oh Holy Mother, Wise Mother
> you always inspire me.

Acknowledging Blood Power

> Mother Hera, Virgin Hebe,
> the miraculous power of your menstrual blood
> is life's supernatural red wine.

Tasting the Blood

Great Mother, Kali-Maya,
I come to bathe in the bloody
flow of your womb
and drink of it In holy communion,
as Goddess,
I drink of the fountain of life;
hic est sanguis meus.
Through your blessing I will rise forth
to the threshold of your mighty throne.

Offering Your Blood at the Blood Altar

I honor the Soma, sea of milk
secreted by the Moon-cow,
carried in the white pot,
belly of Mohini the Enchantress,
I take part in the active part
of the soul of the world.
Soma, sacred name, secret name
of thee Mother Goddess.

Lakshmi's mystic drink, blood of wisdom,
Sa ambrosia—the blood of Isis,
Amrita, the milk of the Mother Goddess,
Mead of Medhbh, the Fairy Queen Mab,
I, too, am the carrier of mogya

Lilith of the Red Sea,
Chang-O of the Full Moon festival
of the autumnal equinox,
Eostre of the red spring equinox egg,
Kurukulla of the east red caverns
Tara of the Tantric fairy ring,
Eve of the womb-temple of Delphi
Artemis of Ephesus of a thousand breasts,
your mysteries shall be celebrated this night.

Prayers and Blessings

There are times when we wish to utter a prayer or a blessing onto the spirit of another. Let us give pragmatic thought before using Our Voices in this way. Remember this simple rule: whatever words you utter towards or about another, the energy and intent behind those words will return to you threefold. Choose always to make all your words an act of power aimed toward the betterment of this physical life and all relations, rather than just at the time of prayer and blessings.

Taos Pueblo Prayer [4]

My brother the star, my mother the Earth,
My father the Sun, my sister the Moon,
To my life give beauty, to my body give strength,
To my corn give goodness, to my house give peace,
To my spirit give truth, to my elders give wisdom.

A Gabon Pygmy Song [5]

Moon, O Mother Moon, O Mother Moon,
Mother of living things,
Hear our voice, O Mother Moon!
O Mother Moon, O Mother Moon,
Keep away the spirits of the dead,
Hear our voice, O Mother Moon,
O Mother Moon, O Mother Moon!

Menarche (First Rite of Passage) Blessing [6]

Blessed be my womb, where Life comes from,
the sacred source of my Creativity and Power.
Blessed by the white, the ocean of light
Sacred Moon Elixir, Conduit to Life.
Blessed am I by my Desire and Pleasure.
Blessed am I by the blood of my womb.

Sacred Ambrosia of Immortality
Blessed by my cyclic transformation of Self.
I bind myself to my Self.
I am Sacred Woman.
I bind myself to all who bleed
who have bled
and who will bleed to Life.
Sacred Women.
I bind myself with Life.
Blessed Be.

Cycle Regulator Prayer

Mensa, Goddess of the Moon,
measurer of time,
unveil the calendar of your light,
guide me through the night,
make my cycle right.

River Song [7]

Oh, I Take delight in the peace of a river
flowing so gently to the strength of the sea.
And I take delight in the love that is growing
just like a river between you and me.

Blood of Life [8]

I give away this blood of Life
To all my relations,
And I open my womb to the Light.

Give away, give away,
Give away, give away,
I open my womb to the Light.

Power Songs

The songs we sing in private at the time of our bleeding, or during personal ceremony, can be used as tools to ground and center our minds, open our hearts to allow inner power, Goddess power, and Moon power to connect. The Power Songs are much more effective when they are your own. When a Power Song comes to you, it should be memorized immediately. The words can be shared with others, but the tune (melody) is the vibration of the power and should be Sung only in private and not given away to another. The reason for doing this is to maximize a vibration as completely yours.

My teacher, Black Wolf, shared this wisdom with me. She told me that I should have one song, one Power Song that was mine alone. Each time I required access to the dreamtimes I should sing this Power Song three times; once outloud for my own spirit to hear, the second time whispered for my power totem to hear, and the third time silently for the spirits in the dreamtimes to hear.

"*When you do not give away your personal Power Song vibration,*" Black Wolf told me, "*you are, let's say 'training' the spirit realm to know that when this particular vibration is felt it is you who comes. Your personal Power Song becomes your signature, your announcement into the dreamtimes.*"

It is important, however, to have Power Songs that can be used with groups, for they will aide in connecting all gathered by creating a sense of "wholeness" or "oneness," and elevating all energies to the same level.

Pima Moon-creation Song of the Earth Magician [9]

I am making the Moon, I am making the Moon!
Here I throw it to the directions.
Here I throw it to the directions.
Throw it to the east direction—there it comes up correctly.

Neesa, Neesa, Neesa

Neesa, Neesa, Neesa
Neesa, Neesa, Neesa,
Neesa, Neesa, Neesa
    Guy-we-oh, guy-we-oh.

Grandmother Moon,
Grandmother Moon,
Grandmother Moon,
    I honor you, I honor you.

My Power

I take back my power
my sacred, sacred power
I take back my blood
from the torment of mankind.

I take back my power
my red, flowing power
I take back my blood
and flow with love and honor.

I take back my power
my wise, wise power
I take back my blood
from the molestation of man's mind.

I take back my power
my rich, fertile power
I take back my blood
and honor my lava flow each Moon.

Herstory Myth Songs

A most wondrous experience is the sharing of Goddess mythology and herstory during woman gatherings, or sacred circle. The telling of stories becomes a living reality. Moral reasoning of the highest good becomes an inner vitality; no longer an abstract force outside our own being. Through songs of this type, a wholeness is created; the wholeness of our humanity in relation to the Earth and the cosmos. The Goddess emerges to guide us.

Cumulipo Chant [10]

Hina-who-worked-in-the-Moon floated as a Bailer,
She was taken into a canoe and called Hina-the-bailer,
She was carried to the shore and put by the fire,
Coral insects were born, the eel was born,
The sea-urchin was born, the volcanic stone was born,
So she was called Hina-from-whose-womb-came various forms.

Navajo Creation Chant [11]

The first woman holds it in her hands,
She holds the Moon in her hands,
In the center of the sky she holds it in her hands.
As she holds it in her hands, it starts upward.

Japanese Kubuki [12]

The Moon came out and it is round,
full and pure,
like a mirror without clouds,
shining and protective like the essence of the Buddha.

Woman Power [13]

It is to the Sisterhood we return at last
Always propelled by Woman Power.
It is the Goddess we at last ask in our hearts
Always compelled by Woman Power.

To the depths of our soul we wander as if lost
seeking a grandeur side of our life.
Standing at the threshold we see within our light
a beautiful Woman shining with power and might.

It is to the Earth we turn to connect with
Always encouraged by Woman Power.
It is to humanity we seek to hold and love
Always sustained by Woman Power.

Your Voice

Perform this journey during your next Moon time. Prepare for the experience by collecting a special incense, Goddess figurine, and a rattle or drum. Light the incense and use the smoke to purify the figurine and rattle or drum by passing the item through the smoke. With a feather or your hands draw the smoke to your heart, third eye, and crown of head in an act of purification. End by fanning the smoke in a circle around where you will sit during the journey. You have just created the boundary for your sacred space by "smudging."

Sit very erect, but be as comfortable as possible. Begin rattling or drumming, and as you do so chant "MaMa." You are shifting the vibrational level around you. Spirit requires tone to activate it, and when we rattle, drum and chant we create the vibration that is necessary to achieve this effect. The vibration also centers and grounds us. Continue until you feel a shift (no matter how subtle).

When the shift is felt discontinue rattling/drumming. Pick up the Goddess figurine and hold it to your belly. Gently press in until you feel your heartbeat. Focus on the heartbeat until your breathing seems to pulse with it (this may take about ten minutes).

As your breath and heartbeat become one, raise the figurine to your heart, then to your lips and kiss it. Raise it over your head and speak out a prayer such as:

> *Great Goddess, woman power,*
> *Mother of all life,*
> *this day as I bleed,*
> *I come to you.*
>
> *May your beauty surround me,*
> *May your strength protect me,*
> *May your blessings fill me.*
> *Ho. Blessed Be.*

Lower the figurine to the ground. Close your eyes and follow your breath in. Allow your focus to drop to your womb where the blood now flows. Acknowledge your guide, the Moon Goddess, by speaking her name three times.

Now is the time to listen to your aliveness. To honor it by getting back in touch with it. Aliveness. Listen to this aliveness. Do not let your mind wander. Do not zone out. If you start to do either, then be aware of it and breathe the distraction out of your body returning your attention to your aliveness.

By listening to your aliveness you can share with the oneness of all life. The quiet time helps us to create new songs that help express our aliveness. Now is the time of spirit activation. We no longer have the time to waste in long, drawn-out apprenticeships. We must begin being spiritual. We must begin activating shaman woman now. Tone vibration awakens shaman woman.

We can use the quiet time to gather the new words, the new tones and birth them back into the world. Our songs do not need to be intricate. Sometimes the most effective and beautiful song is a few sentences long. I have found that tones repeated over and over again in a certain arrangement can be as effective if not more than actual words. This is because, tones are part of a universal language, as evidenced in the elemental creation chant of Kali as discussed earlier, and when sung with the emotion behind creation they will continue to communicate their true meaning. When shared with others, Power Chants can be very effective.

So listen to your aliveness and birth the song, chant, tone vibration of your shaman woman. When it comes, sing it out. Add the support of the rattle or drum. Then stand and move with it; dancing the blood power. Birth it fully alive; joining the aliveness.

Slowly, stop moving, stop playing an instrument, and let only your voice vibrate the room. Sing the song three more times.

Return to your seat and bring the Goddess figurine to your heart. Give a prayer of thanksgiving to the Great Mother. Lower the figurine to your belly and give thanks to your Moon Goddess. Now give a prayer of thanksgiving to shaman woman.

Close your eyes. Breath gently, naturally. Return your focus to the blood flow. Acknowledge your blood power by saying:

> *The river is flowing,*
> *flowing and growing.*
> *The river is flowing,*
> *down to the sea.*

> *Mother, your child*
> *I will always be.*
> *Mother, I am your child,*
> *bless me.*

This format can be coupled with the Psychic Moon Lodge given in Chapter Eight. Experiment, and use this process for birthing stories, new art-forms, ideas, or to receive answers to questions, etc.

Song/Chant/Tone received:

Comments:

● ◐ ○ ◑

My Truth

I come from a place of the heart that speaks truth, and wisdom, and directs my own shaman woman to take advantage of the awakened state my consciousness moves in and out of. It is a place that has been made sacred by my own efforts at leading a spiritual life and walking the beauty path of Goddess worshipper and active feminist. The sacredness continues to grow as my own divinity each month is celebrated. I ebb and flow within this divinity; some days feeling less a shaman woman than on others, but ultimately always feeling the greatness of the life creative energy contained within.

Though I have not chosen to conceive a spirit-child, I rejoice each month for the ability to use this energy by channeling it to create my world around me. This life energy that spills out of me as red blood, sometimes with black lumps, and always mixed with the whiteness of vaginal mucus, builds the context found in the chapters of my writing or is the deepest meaning of whatever artistry I may be working on.

I have come to this place through the celebration of my femininity; honoring the blood, acknowledging this divinity, reclaiming my body as sacred. I have come to this place through the support of other women who have and are rethinking their own divinity, and are willing to celebrate it. I have come to this place through the quiet stirring felt in my womb each month before the blood flows. I have come to this place through the thrilling dreams that explode in the dark time and shed light on the obscure. I have come to this place through the making of tools which focus me on the female wisdom. I have come to this place through the repetitive words chanted to my own face reflected in a mirror. I have come to this place through crawling into the womb of the Moon Lodge and isolating myself from the rest of the world. I have come to this place through sharing my thoughts and beliefs with my lover and having him acknowledge my flow by rubbing my belly. I have come to this place through the eyes of Kisma—shaman woman.

Through exploration and experimentation, through challenge and willingness, through fear and joy, I have joined the feminine energy of Grandmother Moon and MaMa Earth and Great Mother and Goddess to arrive at the place where I truly stand in balance and am able to openingly and self-assuredly join the dance of highest female power. I ever continue to seek out new teachers and am in turn always sought as a teacher. Often I learn from the very women who were at one time my apprentices. I ebb and I flow. I give and I take. I am quiet and I am active. My body temple speaks to me. I listen to its messages, then I in turn give back to it the ease and comfort it requires to maintain the feminine energy balance.

The celebration of the feminine never ends but continues each phase of every cycle. It is a way of life. It is the life of a female enlightened. It is the ability of shaman woman. It is the living wisdom of Goddess.

The celebration of the feminine is liberating and self-prescribed; as unique as each one of us. Every woman contains the mechanism required for celebrating the feminine. All we need in addition to this mechanism is the willingness to delve deep within on a regular basis for the rest of our living days.

● ◗ ○ ◗

NOTES

1. The following books contain some beautiful ceremonies that can be perused for ideas in creating your own rituals:
   The Holy Book of Women's Mysteries—Z. Budapest
   The Grandmother of Time—Z. Budapest
   The P.M.S. Conspiracy—Felicity Artemis Flowers
   Home is the Heart—Roberta Gibson
   Moon, Moon—Anne Kent Rush
   An Act of Woman Power—Kisma K. Stepanich
   The Gaia Tradition—Kisma K. Stepanich
   Red Flower—Dena Taylor

2. Luisah Teish, *Jambalaya* (Harper and Row, 1985), p. 35

3. This elemental chant was said to be used by the Goddess Sara Kali Ma when she imposed order on primal chaos by forming the elements out of her magic syllables.

4. Anne Kent Rush, *Moon, Moon* (Random House, 1976), p. 111 (originally printed in Wood, *The Hollering Sun*).

5. Ibid., p. 177.

6. Felicity Artemis Flowers, *The P.M.S. Conspiracy*, p. 12.

7. Brooke Medicine Eagle, *Moon Lodge* (Cassette tape).

8. Brooke Medicine Eagle, *A Gift of Song* (Cassette tape).

9. Rush, *Moon, Moon*, p. 183.

10. Ibid., p. 161.

11. Ibid., p. 183.

12. Author unknown.

13. Stepanich, *An Act of Woman Power* (Whitford Press, 1989), p. 50.

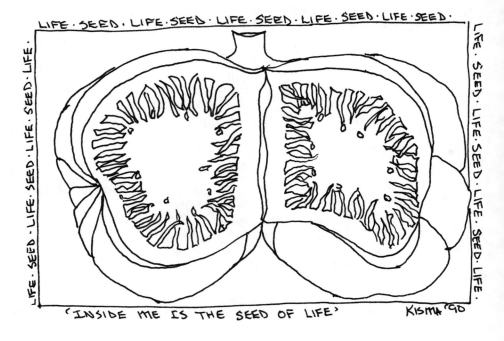

LIFE · SEED · LIFE · SEED · LIFE · SEED · LIFE · SEED · LIFE · SEED ·

LIFE · SEED · LIFE · SEED · LIFE · SEED · LIFE · SEED · LIFE ·

LIFE · SEED · LIFE · SEED · LIFE · SEED · LIFE · SEED · LIFE ·

'INSIDE ME IS THE SEED OF LIFE'   KISMA '90

Chapter Seven

The Wise Shaman Woman Herbs

Weeds! Let us reclaim this word. Weeds are wonderful; each one precious in its own way!

—Mary K. Greer

The energy of MaMa Earth flows up through every living thing upon her body. Her breath whispers through the soil, rocks, and mountains. Her wisdom quivers through the trees and bushes. Her strength flows through the streams, rivers, and oceans. Her healing is essenced in the flowers and herbs that dress her body with beauty.

The healing essences of flowers and herbs are used by shaman women. The healing wisdom is part of herstory, and as long as there are flowers and herbs growing on MaMa Earth, the female wisdom will never be lost. As with any craft, herblore is rich and diversified. Common herbs grow along side every road even in the most congested cities. Many are weeds which, once identified, become the most useful commodities in a shaman woman's healing cabinet.

When I made the decision to work with herbs in a holistic attempt at maintaining the equilibrium between body and mind, I started out very slowly. I bought as many books on herbs as I could afford (and continue to add to my collection yearly) and focused on three herbs that I could purchase from a local health food store: Black Cohosh (*Cimicifuga racemosa*) in capsule form; Red Raspberry (*Rubus idaeus*) in bulk leaf; and Dong Quai (a Chinese herb similar to the North American Angelica, *Angelica atropurpurea*) also in capsule form.

I experimented with these three herbs and found that of the three Red Raspberry was the most beneficial to use on a regular basis throughout the month. Although Black Cohosh and Dong Quai have healing properties that at the time I required, I found that both were "potentially toxic" (or poisonous) herbs.

Potentially toxic herbs are taken for only short durations of time because if over-used (overdosed) they will almost always cause a toxic side-effect. They are potent medicines that are to be used when powerful healing and releasing in the body is required.

Though the usage of Black Cohosh and Dong Quai allowed me to achieve the vibrational changes that I desired, I used them only after carefully researching their properties. When I was sure they were the herbs I needed, I took them in small quantities, monitored my body functions/symptoms closely, and used them for a short period of time. Afterwards I documented my findings and put the herbs away.

As holistic and homeopathic health care has become more popular, many of our local health food stores carry a wide range of commercially packaged herbs. However, the labels that are attached to commercially marketed herbs do not give adequate information and are often misleading, such as Black Cohosh and Dong Quai which labels suggest they are harmless but in reality are toxic if misused.

Many of us hear a calling to understand the craft of herb healing and so, to assist in your learning, I highly recommend Susun S. Weed's book *Wise Woman Herbal: For the Childbearing Year* as a place to begin your research. It is a valuable book and more inclusive than it sounds.

In her book, Susun speaks of the shaman woman:

> In Europe, five hundred years ago, men tortured and burned the wise women who healed with herbs, the midwives, the ones who celebrated the cyclical ways. Calling them witches, they burned them in millions and broke the flow of mother to daughter transmission. In the Americas, their sons down the way killed the medicine women and curanderas, the wise women in history.
>
> Without our connections to each other and the Earth, without our mother's wisdom, we forgot our power. When we were told that we had no souls, and no minds, and no sisters, we believed it was true. When they told us that child-

bearing was too dangerous and difficult for women, mid-
wives, and herbs, we believed it was true.

But the wise women live in our dreams, our visions, our
deepest memories. We hear their whispers and we listen.[1]

Susun is a wise shaman woman who has brought new knowledge into my realm of consciousness regarding herbal remedies.
When I first made contact with Susun (seeking her advice on the information I had originally planned to present in this chapter on the
"woman herbs"), I did so thinking I knew something about herbs.
After all, I had been working with them for years and had started
growing my own. However, Susun suggested to me that both the
format I was intending to use in this chapter presented incomplete
research on this subject that could possibly be misused by others.
She was, however, sympathetic with my goal of constructing a comprehensive "woman herbs reference list" which would allow
women to activate the Healer within.

The format I had originally intended to use was listing *any and
all* published herbal information I could find on the following areas:

1. Emmenagogues

2. Temporary Birth Control

3. Permanent Sterility

4. Balancers & Toners

5. Coming off the Pill

6. Cycle Regulators

7. Menstrual Conditions

8. Soothers

9. Abortives

In researching this subject, I gathered all my herbal books together, some of them dating centuries back. A foolish trap I had
fallen into was in thinking that just because an herbal book was written centuries ago that it contained reliable information and was,
therefore, the basis of modern herbals. In part I was right. Many
modern herbals simply borrow information from these older books,
which—Susun pointed out to me—are not necessarily correct.

"Did you ever wonder why these books were written by men?" Susun asked, and quite frankly, even though the thought had crossed my mind I had never really bothered to pursue it further.

"No," I answered. "Although the thought has crossed my mind. I just know that I don't always agree with the information that's printed in them. Something doesn't feel quite right. I mean, when I begin working with an herb, I use all the books I can find to examine the literal information resulting from research, but when I begin intuiting the usage of certain herbs, I do disagree sometimes with what is written."

"Well think about this," she said. "If you were being tortured or burned at the stake what herbs would you tell these men, who were torturing you, to use for healing?"

I was dumb-struck. Her question completely threw me off guard. "Well, I don't know," I began. "I guess anything they wanted to hear."

Susun retorted, "I would tell them to put cayenne in their eyes!"

At first I laughed. Then I understood.

"Herbals books from the thirteenth and fourteenth centuries," she confided, "were written while our sisters were being tortured for their herbal wisdom."

"We aren't encouraged to think about it," Susun finished.

Shaman woman gathers knowledge together little by little; she cannot take for granted those instructions that sometimes so blatantly reek of ignorance from the herbals of yesteryear. She does not assume she knows the sweet garden of herbs, if only book-learned.

Let us begin slowly, gently, using one herb at a time, experimenting and reading, sharing our information with other users, respecting the power of the plant—the individual effects it may cause in humans while recognizing at the same time that our constitutions differ and therefore different effects will spring forth from the usage of the same herb. Let us begin categorizing the herbs as "nourishing herbs," "tonic herbs," "cleansing herbs," and "toxic herbs" as the wise shaman woman, Susun S. Weed, suggests we follow.[2]

Let us hearken unto our wise shaman woman within, bring forth her voice and relearn the wonderful gift of MaMa Earth: the Wise Shaman Woman Herbs.

Herbal Remedies

Wise shaman women such as Susun suggest that our tradition be one centered around nourishment; that we do not "fix or cure or balance,"[3] and that our goals be to simply maintain the body/mind energy flow by nourishing our bodies, focusing on wholeness and allowing holiness to prevail in soul.

The tradition of the Wise Shaman Woman has not existed for most women, and so we have arrived at varying stages of toxicity and imbalance, discomfort and disease. These varying stages of toxicity directly effect our menstrual cycles; throwing our cycles into the realm of irregularity, PMS, or too profuse a flow. The time for women to once more turn to the plant allies has come. Through the usage of these allies, we can begin to nourish our bodies, find our wholeness and walk our beauty path in holiness once again. Let us begin by acquainting ourselves with just a few herbal remedies.

There is a word that is frequently used by herbalist and healers that describes an agent that when used promotes a menstrual flow. These agents are formally referred to as *emmenagogues* (em-men-a-gogues).

When your menses is a few days late an emmenagogue may bring it on. When there is a possibility of pregnancy and your normal period is a week away and you want to make sure you get it, using an emmenagogue for a good week before the expected menstrual flow is often effective. An emmenagogue, however, should not be relied on as a regular form of birth control because many emmenagogues can cause strong side effects, and as a wise shaman woman this type of attitude is one of irresponsibility and disrespect for life as well as the divine nature of our biology. However, it is important to contain this knowledge for reference or times of emergency.

The list of emmenagogues is both lengthy and varied (depending on the source). The following is a sampling of the various herbs that when researched in literature are identified as having emmenagogous properties (bold face herbs are the most commonly listed emmenagogues).

Aloe, **Angelica, Balm** (Fresh Lemon Balm), **Basil,** Bay Laurel, Bethroot, Beets, Birthwort, **Black Cohosh, Blue Cohosh,** Blue Vervain, Brigham Tea (which is very addicting), **Camomile** (or **Chamomile**), Camphor, **Catnip,** Cinnamon, Cimifuga Root, Corydalis, **Cotton Root** (Bark), Cramp Bark (same as Brigham Tea), Creeping Thyme (or Thyme), Dill, Dittany of Crete, Double Tansy (or Tansy), Elecampane, European Vervain (or Vervain), Ergot Fungus, **Fennel, Ginger Root,** Gensing, Horsetail, Hyssop, Larkspur, Lavender (which one woman I know feels can be addicting), Licorice Root, **Life Root,** Little Mallow, Lovage, **Marigold,** Marijuana, Marjoran, Masterwort, Mexican Tea, Mint, Mistletoe (leaves and berries), Montana Totentosa, **Motherwort,** Mugwort, Origanum, Osha Root, **Parsley** (fresh), **Pennyroyal,** Peruvian Bark, Purple Stem Angelica (or Angelica), Ragwort, Red Cedar (Eastern), Red Sage (or Sage), Rosemary, **Rue** (Common), Russian Thistle (or Thistle), Safflower, Saffron, **Sage,** Sagebrush (Big), Skullcap, Squaw Vine (which is an erroneous patriarchal name—the word "squaw" basically means "dick"), St. John's Wort, **Sumac Berries,** Summer Savory, Sweet Flag Root, **Tansy,** Thyme, Valerian (which is very addicting), Verbena, Water Avens, Water Pepper, Wild Carrot, Wild Ginger (or Ginger), Wild Yam, Wintergreen, Wood Sorrel (fresh), Yarrow, and Yew.

A list as extensive and varied as the one above can be very confusing when choosing which herb to work with, and often misleading. Several of the herbs above are also classified as being abortifacient (Cotton Root, Pennyroyal, Rue, Tansy), some are aromatics (stimulants), others are aperients (laxatives), some are considered potentially toxic herbs that if overdosed have toxic effects (Black Cohosh, Blue Cohosh, Cotton Root, Licorice, Mistletoe, Tansy) and others are poisonous with fatal side-effects (Larkspur, Pennyroyal oil, Rue). Therefore, it becomes vitally important for us to understand what the facts are surrounding each and every herb we decide to work with.

For those women who are interested in working with the Wise Shaman Woman Herbs but are not interested in doing research, the following herbal recipes are highly recommended as emmenagogues and have been tried and found to be true.

Teas

Ginger Root *(Zingiber)*: Put one teaspoon of the powdered root into a cup and pour boiling water over it. Allow mixture to sit for three to five minutes (or until water has cooled) before drinking. Drink no more than four cups per day for no more than five days. (I have read that there is a strong indication you are pregnant if you get nauseated from drinking ginger tea. If this should occur seek the advice of your midwife, healer, doctor, etc.)

Basil *(Ocimum minimum or Ocium Basilicum)* "Sweet Basil": Use one tablespoon of the fresh leaves per cup of boiling water. Steep from three to five minutes (or until water is cool before drinking. Drink no more than four cups per day for no more than five days.

Try using **Chamomile** *(Matricaria chamomilla or Anthemis Nobilis)*. Use in the same way as described above.

Herbal Capsules

As with any medication, drug-like herbal remedies are taken in very small quantities. To give an idea of the scale we are looking at: 1000 milligrams (mg) are equivalent to 1 gram (g). One g is equivalent to 1.5 grains, and 80 grains is equivalent to 1 teaspoon (tsp), whereas nourishing herbs are best eaten and drunk in quantity.

Aloe *(Aloe fruticosa)*: 50-200 milligrams (mg) for a tonic effect, and 300 mg to one gram (g) for a purgative effect. Take one to two capsules a day for no more than five days.

Black Cohosh *(Cimicifuga racemosa)* and **Blue Cohosh** *(Caulophyllum thalictroides)*: 300-500 mg. Take one to two capsules a day for no more than five days. Watch body for sensitive side-effects such as nausea, nervous trembling, vertigo and change in heart pulse. If one or more of these symptoms appear, discontinue use immediately.

Emmenagogue Combination[4]

20 drops Blue Cohosh tincture
20 drops Black Cohosh tincture
20 drops American Pennyroyal tincture

Measure tinctures into a cup of warm water and drink slowly. Repeat every four hours for no more than five days. Continue for one full day after bleeding starts, to ensure complete expulsion of all fetal material.

Blue Cohosh tincture stimulates the production of oxytoxin, the hormone responsible for uterine contraction. Black Cohosh tincture enhances and supplements the action of the Blue Cohosh. Pennyroyal tincture is an old favorite for "suppressed menstruation."

On a final note, vitamin C (ascorbic acid), is known as a very safe and effective emmenagogue that can be used after the menses is considered late. Take 500 mg every hour for 12 hours per day for up to six days. (It has been reported that approximately six grams of vitamin C [6000 mg] is the daily dosage needed to abort. Note that this dosage may produce loose stools.)

As a wise shaman woman, the addition of Burdock (Arctium lappa) and Seaweed to our diets will not only nourish the body but help ensure that the menses is regular. The properties of these two allies are well worth the investigation and usage. (For these and other recipes, refer to Susun S. Weed's *Healing Wise: The Second Wise Woman Herbal*.)

Many of us often experience menstrual cramps. Aside from relaxing and taking it easy, soaking in a nice warm bath, or massaging our bellies, sipping a steaming cup of either Red Raspberry *(Rubus idaeus)* or Peppermint *(Mentha piperita)* tea is extremely soothing. Use the tea recipe given above and drink a cupful up to four times a day until cramps subside (usually within a 24 hour period). A wise shaman woman regularly eats Dandelion *(Taraxacum officnale)* to help nourish her body and prevent the possibility of menstrual cramps.

Many women experience a heavier flow. Drinking tea made from Comfrey *(Symphytum officinale)* root or Red Raspberry *(Rubus idaeus)* leaves will help to strengthen the uterus and the entire reproductive system, aiding in the regulation of menstrual bleeding. I was once told that eating lentils will help to "singularly stay the menses"; I eat lentils on a regular basis and have never been a heavy bleeder. A wise shaman woman would also include Nettle *(Urtica dioica)* in her diet, for this ally is known to help heal a woman with profuse menses.

It is important to note here that should you begin having profuse bleeding it would be wise to seek the advice of your doctor or healer as profuse bleeding may indicate a severe problem such as uterine fibroids or cancer.

Both uterine fibroids and uterine cancer cause heavy bleeding. However uterine fibroids are almost never cancerous, they are an irregular enlargement of the uterine muscle known as fibroids and are also referred to as myomas or fibromyomas. Their growth is stimulated by ovarian hormones and generally diminish in the late forties as hormonal levels drop. Fibroids will actually shrink after the menopause and rarely create further problems.[5] If you do have a uterine fibroid and your doctor is advising you to have your uterus removed, please seek a second opinion. The uterus will shrink significantly in size after menopause.

Cancer of the uterine lining and cervix also cause profuse bleeding. Most doctors will perform a Dilation and Cauterization (D&C). A D&C is the removal of the uterine lining by a suction or a scraping technique. Most often cancer is not diagnosed, although an abnormality might exist. Hyperplasia is the more common abnormality of the uterine lining that causes heavy bleeding but is not cancerous. This condition can usually be easily cleared up by the treatment of progestins and does not require a hysterectomy. Also, cancer of the cervix can be treated in many ways. In all cases when hysterectomy is prescribed seek a second opinion. A rule to follow is: if an operation is not truly medically necessary, don't have it.

I would like to share my views on cancer of the uterus. I believe that women are generating cancer in this area of the body today because of the disassociation we have had from our sacredness and divinity. Desecration always creates disease. When we are ashamed of something we hide it or pretend it does not exist. We have been told that "pussy" is evil; the temptation of man which caused the falling away from his righteousness. The vagina has become an object of vulgarity. The scent has been joked about and equated with the smell of tuna fish. It is exploited in pornographic magazines, and has even become a trophy: "Did you get any pussy? Did you fuck her?"

The epidemic of vaginal disease is a result of woman's sorrow. It is time we put an end to this desecration of our female signature—the vagina. Let us speak out in support of our sacredness. We can begin by creating a personal affirmation. My personal affirmation is as follows.

● ◗ ○ ◗

I honor my cunt. It is divine—sacred. The tissues of my vagina are healthy and pure. When my blood flows, I honor my divinity, my woman power and rejoice in its creative potentials. This is the house of all life. Through me, all humankind is born; male and female alike. I will not allow anyone to desecrate this holy temple. They must knock at its door with respect. Before they are permitted entrance, they must show me that they honor this creative womb, this great gift of future generations. When the egg merges with chosen sperm and life is permitted to grow within, I become the Great Mother of Life. When birthing is at hand, I journey to the realm between life and death to bring back a spirit to incarnate in the body of my flesh and my blood. When the blood no longer flows, I will hold it; absorbing its power.

I hear the voice of the Grandmothers proclaim: "Honor this place now, or my wrath will be upon you. I will not tolerate the degradation of my daughters any longer. I will not tolerate the abuse of my sisters any further. I will not tolerate disrespect toward the Wise Shaman Women. I am creation. Man and woman may join this honoring with love and respect and in partnership."

Ho. Blessed be.

Shaman Woman Affirmation

In the space provided below, create your personal affirmation. Be as strong and powerful as you want, as short or long as it needs to be. Rewrite it as many times as it takes until it rings true in your heart. When your personal affirmation is complete, stand naked before a full length mirror and speak first to your own image and then send that reflection out to the rest of the world.

Personal Shaman Woman Affirmation:

Vibration works on all levels. Whether we speak the vibration through our affirmations, chants and instruments, or whether we work with the life force vibration through herbs and flowers, we can effect change into our minds, bodies and souls.

Working with the Wise Shaman Woman Herbs

When you begin working with the wise woman herbs it is important to keep a journal of which ones you use, the reasons you chose the herb (for what symptoms, etc.), the manner in which the herb is used (tea, tincture, brew, etc) dosage, length of time remedy used and during what phase of your Moon cycle. Note any changes detected, as well as any side-effects after the use of the herbal remedy.

Work with an herb or remedy for at least three months to clarify its effect. If ineffective, discontinue, and begin working with a different herb/remedy.

Premenstrual Herbs

Symptom:

Herb:

Remedial use (recipe, dosage, duration):

Month One (describe changes and/or side-effects observed):

Month Two (describe changes and/or side-effects observed):

Month Three (describe changes and/or side-effects observed):

Premenstrual Herbs—continued

Symptom:

Herb:

Remedial use:

Month One:

Month Two:

Month Three:

Premenstrual Herbs—continued

Symptom:

Herb:

Remedial use:

Month One:

Month Two:

Month Three:

Try to grow one or two herbs yourself making sure you do enough research to know the best times to harvest to obtain the full potency of the Devas (allies) of the herb. Store bought herbs generally have a shelf-life of six months. Their labels rarely indicate how long they have already been sitting on the shelf.

Fully research the herbs you choose and remember that exercise (walking/yoga), and massage can help during times of discomfort and can easily be implemented in your regime.

Comments:

The Plant Devas

Some of us contain the innate ability to befriend the Plant Devas. I am one who is bestowed with this gift and can hear their angelic voices whisper to me as I lovingly work the soil around my precious plants. Sometimes late at night the Devas, in their rejoicing, pull me out of dreamtime. I peek out at them through the lacy curtains of my bedchamber. They are magical beings who easily lure me into their inner kingdom and enhance my gardening abilities.

In *The Holy Books of the Devas* (Rowan Tree Publications, 1986), written by Rev. Paul V. Beyerl, the magical story of the Devas is told. The book begins:

> The song of herbs is written in the heart of Nature. Herbs recall the origins of all birth, for their source of life was the sea, that great, tumultuous ocean that gave birth, the origin of life upon our planet. In the annals of plant life it is written:
>
> "In the beginning was the soil, the Earth of life, which fed the waters of time out of which sprang all being. And thus did the Earth Goddess, the Mother of all Nature, bring into being the element Verda, the essences of being, the being of all life..."

It is the Devas of the plant kingdom that contain this essences of being, the being of all life. The Devas are our allies, and once befriended they can teach us the secrets of life. Many herbalists agree that it is better to have just 10 plant allies to work with than to try to know them all. I would like to add that the process required to befriend a Deva is very sensitive in nature.

● ◐ ○ ◑

The summer Sun warms my skin; pulls forth the moisture of my skin until tiny beads of perspiration form on my upper lip and forehead. Jumbo size Bumble Bees dance about the garden and then attach themselves to a basil or rue blossom. On my knees, I firmly break-up the soil around the trunk of the basil with gloved hands.

I love the rich, pungent scent this plant emits at the slightest touch. Without thinking of the Bee's stinger, I push my face into the middle of the bush and inhale the fragrance deeply. I am in love with basil. Suddenly the bush shimmers as if a light breeze has ruffled it. I withdraw my head and check the surrounding plants for movement. They are still.

Suddenly I sense a presence in the yard. I glance around, but there is no one. I turn my attention back to the basil. Automatically I slip the gloves off my hands and touch the nearest leaves. They are soft, fragrant. I smell the tips of my fingers, they too are fragrant. As if being directed, I pull a leaf off and stick it in my mouth. I begin to chew slowly. From habit, when using a sense other than sight, I close my eyes.

Again, there is a presence. Calmly, I barely open my eyes and focus on the basil. It seems to be shimmering in the still afternoon, but around the bush is a very distinct yellowish-green glow. I am being introduced to the Deva of basil.

● ◐ ○ ◑

As time passed, the Deva guided me in its care. The result is an extremely healthy and abundant bush two feet high and about two feet in diameter. I have found that I hear the Devas' verda when I am in the kitchen cooking. ("To the plant kingdom, chlorophyll is one of the sacred elements often written as verda, but not pronounced. It is a holy sound, Sung by all the plants as the whispering breeze, the tidal song of the ocean."—The Holy Books of the Devas.) Without thinking further, I walk out to the garden and stick my face in the bush, inhale deeply and choose a few choice leafs to use in the meal. Off and on, when out working in the garden in other areas, I am pulled to the bush and after inhaling the fragrance, break off the top of one of the branches and chew on it as I go about my business. Though I have not seen an apparition around the bush, nor actually received distinct information regarding the medicinal properties of the herb, I sense that I am being directed to use it when my vibrational rate requires it.

In the past I have also poured the water from my Blood Jar around its trunk and I believe that this act has created a psychic bond and that through this bond I automatically care for the plant properly. The reason I say this is because I have never read any books on growing herbs and am a complete novice in this area. Yet, only a few of my plants have died on me, and I must confess they were ones I simply did not give attention to.

To date, I am only allied with three Devas, and just recently have begun to hear the verda of a fourth; that of the giant Sunflowers that have not yet opened their faces to me. For the first time I am growing them! Wow, what amazing beings within themselves. I am growing the Helianthus Annuus, Linn. variety; the ones that grow up to 18 feet high with leaves as broad as 8 inches and flower-heads as large as 12 inches. It is a native of America and once planted will grow annually.

The Hopi Indians believe the Sunflowers are beings of a sacred species, and now that I have ten Sunflowers growing in my yard, ranging from 3 feet to a little over 7 feet in height, I understand why. It seems as if the Devas of this plant automatically made their presence known as soon as a four inch sprout was visible.

When I walk in my yard there seems to be a tribe of people standing there. The spirit of this plant is that strong. I find myself walking up to them and softly speaking to the Devas; anxiously awaiting the blossoming of the flower-heads that are still covered with green. During the early morning, in the grey dusk of dawn, I find myself looking out at them. Within the time lapse of an hour, I witness their bodies turning to face the Sun. When I go into the garden and stand next to them I feel dwarfed and humbled, and I know there is much to learn from the Devas once the face of the flower is revealed.

Whether we are aware of them or not, the Devas are there, patiently waiting for us to tune in to their sensitive and exalted vibration and receive their guidance toward our own healing, and then the healing of others. This connection with the Plant Devas can easily be achieved by taking the time to listen to the energy of each herb when worked with. Intuiting your healing is what I call "core healing" because you are picking up the base messages and receiving guidance toward focusing on what the real problem is rather than administering remedies to the effects, or symptoms, of your diseases/dis-comfort. Happy healing sisters—wise shaman woman! Follow your hearts, and listen to the whispering Devas.

NOTES

1. Susun S. Weed, *Wise Woman Herbal: For the Child Bearing Year* (Ash Tree Publishing, 1985), p. xiii.

2. Ibid, p. xviii

3. Susun S. Weed, *Healing Wise: The Second Wise Woman Herbal* (Ash Tree Publishing, 1989), p. 5.

4. Weed, (CBY), p. 149.

5. Sadja Greenwood, M.D., *Menopause Naturally, Preparing for the Second Half of Life* (Volcano Press, 1984/1989), pp. 13-16.

Celebration of the Female   Kisma '90

Chapter Eight

Sister Moon Lodge

Grandmothers, tell me what it is I should know myself now in order to serve myself, to serve my people, and to create a beautiful world?"

—Brooke Medicine Eagle

We cannot apologize for having this innate ability; this rightful title of shaman. We cannot apologize for being able to own, in the most abstract sense, the mysteries of birth-death-and-rebirth. But we must reclaim it. Our shamanic duty to life, to Great Mother, is to live our essence fully.

To live our essence fully requires us to live and work together collectively. Women are born into this world as carriers of beauty; the deep, inner beauty where spirit is alive. One of our most sacred responsibilities is to create this beauty in our environments, so that the light of spirit shines. In this changing tide of wisdom, women are being called to bring forth into reality what is waiting there for us, to awaken ourselves in the dream. This dream is seen in the cycles of Grandmother Moon and the women who join force with other women and together acknowledge Grandmother Moon's cycle in the monthly cycles, who come together and share in the woman ways, who connect with each other and ovulate and bleed together. This dream is seen in the sisters of the Moon Lodge.

The Moon Lodge is a woman's place, where we choose to retreat to during our bleeding time. It is a quiet place. A place of beauty, of restfulness. The quality of the environment is so that women delight in drawing ourselves away from the mundane world and take refuge in such a warm, nurturing, healing place.

It is through our monthly call to power that we receive the most vital information; the information about woman's ways. This knowledge lives within us, and it is during our Moon time that we can receive direction of what it is we need to do on Earth. Devotion toward disciplining self to be available when the veil is thin, enables us to listen to the deep parts of inner self; for the woman's ways is part of our cells, our DNA; our body that MaMa Earth has given us; the knowledge of our minds; Grandmother Moon's cycle within us. We must be willing to connect with all life, and be willing not to know. In our willingness not to know we must listen. We must retreat to a place of quiet in silence, and during the most receptive phase of our cycle receive the information that is there waiting to express itself and awaken our visions, our dreams, into this world of action.

In this time when vision is so important for us and for the healing of MaMa Earth, I would like to believe that it is the women who will bring forth the new way. Each of us have a dream. So often this dream seems disconnected, an indifferent part of the larger dream. Through the Moon Lodge women are finding that each of our dreams, though different pictures, are in some intrinsic way the same thing. As we share our dreams, our visions, and weave together the tapestry, we create the larger dream.

Brooke Medicine Eagle once said something that really made me stop and think. She was speaking about letting our eyes be triggered by Moonlight so that our inner Moon is triggered and our cycles became natural, in sync with the lunation cycle. She was marveling at the power of women and imagining all women bleeding in cycle during the New Moon and then coming out into full activity at the Full Moon, and how all women of the world would be praying and having vision together at the same time, and that if this were the new way, then women would literally change the world.

Now I turn to you, sister, who reads my words. Perhaps you have heard the call for honoring the deep function of MaMa Earth's gift of life blood within to bring your vision forth and connect with those of us who are weaving the tapestry. Know that the deeper function of the Moon Lodge is to participate in the visioning cycle naturally given women through the menstrual time; the vision of information that speaks to the feminine, the nurturing and renewing power within all. The time has come for you to create your own Sister Moon Lodge.

Creating The Womb

The first step to building your Lodge is to decide where the most appropriate place/or space available is. Perhaps you have an extra room that has been used as a "junk" room, or a guest room which houses a guest once in a great while. This room could be devoted as your Moon Lodge. A garage can easily be converted. How about a tool shed that is not being used. Or a small tent. Perhaps you know of a retreat cabin that is not too far away. You can build a Lodge either out of wood, or create a Lodge teepee, like mine.

Roberta Gibson in her book *Home is the Heart* (Bear & Co., 1989) gives directions on building a traditional Lodge. She tells us that "building a Lodge is, obviously, time-consuming. If constructing it out of wood and mud, the project can involve your men which will turn the event into a community/family oriented experience rather than totally segregated." (It is important to remember this as we create our Moon Lodge and retreat to them on a monthly basis; our intent is not to exclude men from our lives, but to honor the feminine, and that through our retreating we can bring back to our families a greater vision that can ultimately be manifested for the beauty of healing all relations and MaMa Earth.) Depending on the amount of space you have (whether you live on open land or have a large backyard) an average size structure would be approximately 10 to 12 feet in diameter and 4 to 5 feet high. Ideally, the structure would be a six-sided interlocked log structure. The side facing the east should be left open for an entrance. The roof can be cone-shaped and shingled, with an opening in the center for smoke to escape. (This structure resembles a yurt.)

Gibson goes on to explain that a mixture of clay, sand, and lime can be used to fill in the cracks between the interior logs to block out light and moisture (however, an expert should be consulted for the mixture proper for your bioregion). When packing the mixture between the logs make sure it is firm. It is best to do this type of work on a warm sunny day. Frost and moisture can crack a hardening adobe. When the adobe has hardened, you can patch any cracks with wet mixture. A large blanket can be hung over the entrance. In a Lodge of this type, you may want to dig a firepit in the center, about 1 foot deep and 2 feet in diameter. Place rocks on the bottom of the pit to help keep the fire going.

A teepee style Lodge (such as the one I have built in my back-yard) creates a very womb-like effect. Since I am not of Native American ancestry I had no idea what I was doing, but I was so very pulled to creating a Lodge that I allowed the Grandmothers to speak and guide me. In my garden (known in the community as "The Gar-den of the Goddess") I have a patio area that contains a brick fire-pit. The patio has a cement floor and a lattice roof, and occupies a space approximately 6' x 15'. The cement floor, however, is only about 10' long. At one end of the lattice covering grows huge honeysuckle vines that have created a natural wall. It is at this end of the patio that a plot 5' x 6' of dirt stretches out from the cement. I originally turned the patio into a temple where I worship Goddess and woman power and so had already hung venetian blinds to create an enclosed structure. From the beginning I knew I wanted to create a Moon Lodge in the backyard but I wasn't sure where. After using the temple for a few months it became acutely apparent that the Lodge was to be built inside the temple over the dirt floor and that it would be constructed as a teepee.

One late winter day I gathered pieces of wood from an old pi-geon coop. I found four long pieces of wood the same length, three small pieces the same length and two medium size pieces the same length. Since the four pieces where the longest I used them as the corner poles and buried one end in the dirt, leaned them together in the center, and bound the center ends together with leather thongs. The two medium length pieces were used to create a ground frame on both sides of the Lodge. With one piece in the east and one in the west, I dug a trench in front of the corner poles, placed the founda-tion sticks down in the trench and packed the dirt around them. Since I only buried them half-way a lip sticks up in front of the cor-ner poles. To finish the structure, I took the remaining three pieces and stuck one between the east and south pole; the south and west pole; and, the west and north pole. Because of the lay-out of the patio, I had to put the entrance in the north. Though I would rather have used hide (an expensive luxury at the time), I covered the out-side with blue and green tarps (bought at a local backpacking equip-ment store). Once the tarps were securely tied down, I crawled in-side to make any adjustments that needed to be made to the frame, and to behold the manifestation of my Lodge.

Creating A Personal Moon Lodge

If you are interested in creating your own Lodge, take a moment to evaluate where your Lodge will be (extra room, converted garage, tool shed, tent, etc.). List the possibilities and then circle the one that is most realistic for you at this time.

Make a list of the items you will need to create the structure and/or convert a space into a Lodge.

It is important to also be practical with finances, so estimate the material costs.

Start out slowly, don't over–burden yourself so that creating your Lodge becomes a hassle. Plan its birth over several months. I believe, that as is true with a Medicine Shield, a Moon Lodge is never perfect and never complete, but continually evolves to meet your spiritual needs.

● ◐ ○ ◐

A Nurturing Environment

When decorating the Lodge, making it ready for ceremony, be aware of every aspect of the space. If you're using a room, a converted garage, or cabin, then begin by repainting the walls in colors that are pleasing to the eye or related to the four directions. Hang sculptures and pictures that can be used as meditative mandalas. Re–carpet or cover wood floors with lush rugs. Add huge throw pillows for comfort.

In my Lodge I hung red material to create the walls. By doing this I hid the blue and green tarps that are the outside covering. In each of the directions I tied medicine bundles made out of cloth and string the color of the direction.

Medicine bundles can be made out of any type of material (e.g. cotton, wool, velvet, leather). When I make mine I like to use a man's handkerchief. For the Moon Lodge I chose four herbs to place in the bundle: sage for sacredness, Mormon tea for menstruation, mugwort for vision, and tobacco for spirit. I added a Moonstone and a bloodstone for their feminine properties, a small hawk and owl feather to assist me in seeing in both the daylight and night–time the bigger vision. I folded the bundles up neatly and tied each with a ribbon. The medicine of these bundles was to help bring forth the Grandmothers' voices of each quarter and assist me to receive the wisdom of the women's ways.

For the door, I hung lace so I could see into the temple where the main altar is. On the dirt floor I laid plastic first, then grass mats and topped it with red rugs. There are pillows to sit on and enough space to stretch out in.

It is important to make the environment beautiful, but not cluttered. The main reason for our retreat is to listen, not be encumbered by physical objects. However, it is important to keep certain items in the Lodge that are used in connection with bleeding ceremonies.

Candles

I have found that white, red, and black candles are the best colors for the Moon Lodge. White for our connection to Grandmother Moon. Red for our connection to woman power. Black for our connection to wisdom. These three colors also represent the three phases/faces of a woman's life. White: the virginal maiden. Red: the time of mothering. Black: the wisdom of the croning years. White: menarche. Red: menstruation. Black: menopause. White: vaginal mucus. Red: blood. Black: endometrium clotting. White: past. Red: present. Black: future. Get the idea?

Incenses

Most useful are those that are connected to the Moon, solitude, peace, vision, relaxation, healing, beauty, purification, dreaming, creativity. I suggest the following herbs for use as natural incenses. Some of the them, if dry enough, will continue to smoke by themselves if lit then blown out. Some will require special incense charcoal that can be purchased at most metaphysical bookstores.

Chamomile – peace and relaxation
Lavender – birthing energy
Myrrh – rejuvenation
Mugwort – visions
Orris – Moon connecting
Pine – centering
Rosemary – beauty
Sage – purification and sacredness
Sandalwood – to stabilize and bring energy to new
    beginnings
Sweetgrass – for spirit

Instruments

A drum and rattles can be kept in the Lodge. It is important to always bring forth the vibration of the Mother's heartbeat before beginning any ceremony in the Lodge.

Record book

A blank book in which each woman can write her thoughts, inspirations, dreams, visions, chants, or draw and paint her emotions. Writing instruments, and basic art supplies such as water colors, crayons, etc. can be stored next to the book. This book will help each woman touch the bigger vision.

Divination tools

Tarot deck for the Lodge is a powerful tool (I keep Vicki Nobel's *Mother Peace* in my Lodge); also I–Ching coins, rune stones, lunar and/or astrological calendar.

Misc. items

I keep a red shawl in my Lodge so I can pull it over my shoulders or head and embrace my shaman woman with the red power. A jar of red ochre is nice for painting your face or body. Clay or sculpting materials can be kept in the Lodge for creating Goddess figurines.

It is important for us to remember that the environment of our Moon Lodges need to instill beauty, restfulness, and quiet. The atmosphere that surrounds us during our bleeding is reflected back out to the world, so we must strive to touch closer to spirit during our Moon time, pull closer to the veil between us and the great mystery, the great voices to emerge into life in our fullest. We carry forth the energy planted in us at this time, so let us create loving energy, beautiful surroundings in which to retreat.

The central idea of the Moon Lodge, as told by Brooke Medicine Eagle, is to come together to dedicate ourselves to spiritual action for our people. The bleeding time and retreat to the Lodge is, in essence, a vision quest.

Decorating Your
Moon Lodge Environment

The environment of your Moon Lodge is very important. Take some time to visualize how you would like to decorate it. Get carried away and dream. Make it as elaborate or simplistic as you desire. Write down your ideas.

Take a moment to read over your ideas and make any changes. Close your eyes and visualize what you've written down. Did you leave anything out? If so, add it to your description. Is something not right? If so, change it and make it better. When you are sure the vision fits your needs, list the materials you will need, taking into account the finances that will be required:

Again, don't over-burden yourself with this project. Take a few months to decorate your Lodge. From the conception of my Lodge to the day of the actual Dedication Ceremony, nine months elapsed. This project for me was like a pregnancy. Some things just cannot be rushed.

The Blood Altar

Within the Lodge is an altar, preferably a *Blood Altar*. Whether the altar be in the center of the Lodge or off to one side, it will reflect the beauty of the feminine nature, the power of the blood, and the healing medicine that is enacted during this time. This altar is personal, and contains sacred objects. Blood Jar, Goddess figurines, magical tools, candles, incense, flowers, mirrors, seasonal symbols etc., are placed on exhibit in a pleasing way.

I believe that extra special attention should be given to the altar each time the Lodge is going to be used. As your Moon time approaches, pay closer attention to where you allow yourself to be. Follow this vision and collect the items that will adorn your altar. Take a few days to create it so that when the blood releases and you choose to immerse yourself in the nurturing environment of your Lodge, you will already be magnifying yourself through the objects on your altar. If forethought is given each and every time, your altar will become a mandala that can be gazed upon in meditation as you *listen* to the deep inner wells of wisdom.

Your Altar

Envision what your basic altar will look like. Either describe it, or draw a sketch of it below.

Make a list of the materials required to make the altar itself (include financial aspects).

Make a list of the basic items that will always be on the altar (include financial aspects).

● ◗ ○ ◗

Dedication

Once you have created the structure and adorned the environment of your Moon Lodge give thought to performing a Dedication ceremony before actually using it for sacred time. When I performed my Dedication I chose a day during the waxing phase of the Moon when the astrological influence of Taurus was hitting the Earth plane. I chose this influence because Taurus is the symbol of the Heavenly Goddess, and Taurus is ruled by Venus, the planet of love. I wanted to have the feminine energy of heaven showering down upon the Lodge with the feminine energy support of MaMa Earth.

On this day, as the noon hour struck, I gathered together my Blood Jar, Woman Power Shield and materials to make bundles for each of the directions and a Moon Bag (Refer to Chapter Nine—"Blood Gifts and Moon Tools" for details.) for the center of the Lodge. After entering the beautified Lodge, I sat very quietly in the center and breathed very deeply for a few minutes. As my breathing took on a natural rhythm I picked up my drum and allowed the Mother's heartbeat to radiate. I began praying. With a mixture of sage, cedar and lavender, I fumigated the Lodge. I tied the red shawl around my shoulders, lit the altar candles, and smudged. (Smudging is a Native American Indian form of purification using smoldering sage, cedar, and/or sweetgrass.) a new Menstrual Goddess figurine. (See Appendix A for details on where to purchase figurines/or perhaps you could make your own.)

As I made each bundle I called upon the wisdom of the Grandmothers. Each bundle was made out of a handkerchief that contained herbs such as: sweetgrass, sage, rue, Mormon tea, lavender and tobacco, and anointed them with blood from the Blood Jar. The material was nicely folded into an envelope and tied with colored ribbon. Each bundle was smudged and tied into place in one of the four quarters. Using my deer medicine rattle, I activated each of the directions and bundles with prayers.

I ended by singing chants of power, speaking out the intent of the Lodge, with the request that the name of my Lodge would be revealed to me during the next bleeding time.

Each Dedication ceremony will be different, unique to the woman, or women, holding it. The main importance is to allow your creativity and inspiration to flow spontaneously. Try not to be regimented in this ceremony. Remember to activate the energies, call in the powers of the Grandmothers of each direction, initiate the vibration of the heartbeat, and set an intention for the Lodge. One of your vows can be to use the transparent veil in calling vision for your people by praying, "Not for myself alone, Great Spirit, do I ask this vision, but that all the peoples may live."

Moon Lodge Dedication Ceremony

When your Lodge is constructed, your environment complete, and the blood altar set-up, the time has come for you to perform a Dedication Ceremony. It is important to plan this ceremony as it will set the intent of the Lodge.

Day and time of ceremony:

Intent being set:

Special items required for ceremony:

Chants being used:

Ceremony outline:

Code of Divinity

If you are working with a core group, it is important to develop a Code (see Appendix C for the Code of Divinity used in my Moon Lodge circle). The code is very simple and might consist of what the maximum number of women in the group will be. (I have heard that eight women is ideal, as eight is the sign representing infinity.) Perhaps your code might contain the decision to use the Lodge not only at New Moon, the bleeding time, but also at Full Moon. At New Moon the atmosphere would be one of quiet meditation performed in silence. A time to nurture each other with massage, the washing of feet before entering. A sleep–over might happen during this time to explore and share dreams. Dream work in the Lodge will become vitally important because it will help build the ability for you to remember; strengthening the memory muscle so that you can bring your dreams and visions into real life. The foundation of dreaming is the left–side of the brain, the feminine. Through this wonderful vehicle of remembering we not only bring forth the voices of the greater mystery from the past, but also the direction for future healing. The time of Full Moon would be more energetic. A time of letting go, of drumming, of meditating to join with the fullness of life. A time when ceremony is performed to make all visions a reality. However, in this decision of when and how often the Lodge will be put in use, thought can be given to when, if at any time, the Lodge will remain quiet and empty of human energy.

When we make the decision to come to a Lodge, we must prepare ourselves by beginning slowly. If you know of an already existing Lodge then contact is the first step. Meet with the sisters of the Lodge and sense the energies of each woman present. Ask about the Code of the Lodge, the intention of the Lodge. If all feels right, then attend one of their ceremonies before committing yourself to being a part of the Lodge.

Some women have very busy schedules, especially if a housemate, mother and/or working woman. Where does a woman of this caliber find the time to participate in the woman's ways? Women set the tone and the laws for women; that is how it has always been in herstory. Unless we begin setting the tone and law in our personal lives for our own time of retreat of beauty, nurturing, rest, and healing, we cannot expect others to allow us to do so. We require retreating time in our lives.

It is our responsibility to teach the men when they are young how to cook, help around the house, and to be part of the nurturing for all peoples of the household. Women are, after all, in charge of the male children. By setting this precedent in the young lives of children, healthy adults grow from this foundation. Unless we honor ourselves and require that others around us respect this requirement, no one will. I also believe that it is never too late to begin honoring self and initiating these changes in our households.

Regardless of your social status, begin slowly. Make the dedication to self to create this new discipline of honoring your Moon time. If need be, begin by spending only a few hours the evening after your blood begins to flow at the Lodge. Slowly advance to spending an entire night, and eventually taking a "wellness" day off from your busy schedule and retreating to it. Ultimately, spending all the days of your bleeding in the Lodge is something to strive for, but for many is not a realistic idealism.

If the above steps seem to be too much of a commitment at this point in your life, then acknowledge your Moon time by taking a 15 minute break at work to meditate and ask for guidance on how you can fully honor yourself. Start slowly, allow the Grandmothers to speak to you, and find the time that is best for your schedule.

Not everyone will be fortunate enough to be involved with a "physical" Moon Lodge. Yet, we can have our very own "psychic" Moon Lodge. This form of Moon Lodge is entered through mediation. The following guided visualization can be used for accessing the psychic Moon Lodge.

Psychic Moon Lodge

Find a place that is quiet, where you can be alone. Make yourself comfortable by either sitting or lying. Focus on your breath. As you exhale visualize all stress and tension leaving your body. Continue focusing on releasing negative thoughts as well. As the tension begins to leave your body, take three deep breaths and firmly release the air out of your lungs assertively pushing any residue that might still be there.

Relax. Breathe in and draw in the rich and powerful healing vibration of life. Visualize this rich, powerful healing vibration filling your lungs, flowing through your body, entering every major organs, absorbed into your bones, saturating every cell of your being until this rich, powerful healing vibration radiates out of the pores of your skin like a pure golden light.

Drop your attention to your first chakra (vagina) and imagine roots emerging and reaching down into the soil of MaMa Earth. Allow these roots to delve deep into the center of the Earth where at last they plunge into her core.

With three deep breaths, draw the powerful, regenerating energy of MaMa Earth into your vagina. Visualize this energy rising up through each chakra (womb, solar plexus, heart, throat, third eye, crown of head). As it moves through each chakra it is imbuing your system with renewed strength.

Relax. Place your hands over your belly and focus on your womb chakra; the female center. Allow your awareness to deepen and move into the activity of your womb. Your awareness deepens as you count backwards from 10 to 1.

10...be aware of your womb

9...sense the activity that is going on in it

8...the endometrium as it pulls away from the wall

7...the blood as it flows out

6...your body is cleansing itself

5 ... renewal

4 ... the Kundalini is activated

3 ... your power is awake

2 ... you are divine

1 ... shaman woman, step forward

Deep within your womb resides a very private and personal Moon Lodge. Visualize this Lodge as housing you now. You sit within its interior. The walls are covered with variegated shades of red cloth. The floor is covered with red rugs. You recline against huge, fluffy, red throw pillows. You are very, very comfortable.

As you rest in your chosen seclusion you notice herbs smoldering in a pot. You also hear the distinct sound of a drum beating out the heartbeat of the Mother. Listen to this heartbeat. Close your eyes and listen. This heartbeat is calling the Grandmothers to you. Through the heartbeat you can hear their voices. They wish to tell you about the woman's ways.

Listen and receive their wisdom.

(allow ten to fifteen minutes for meditation)

The Grandmothers have communicated their wisdom to you and are departing. Thank them.

Focus again on the heartbeat of the Mother and allow it to bring you back to the awareness of your body. Breathe deeply. Inhaling into the here and now; exhaling out of your inner Moon Lodge.

Feel the belly under your hands. Focus on the power of your blood. Speak out an affirmation of your divinity. Very gently, when you are ready, open your eyes and return to the physical.

> *Honoring this cycle within you will be more than empty form and words; it will be given new life by men and women alike. And wonderfully, we will notice healthier, more comfortable menstrual cycles and birthing.*
>
> —Brooke Medicine Eagle

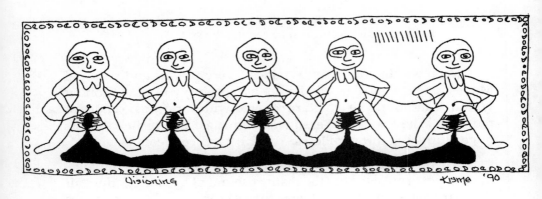

Visioning   Krsma '90

The new *Anima* as envisioned and created by Amber Dawn Noland.

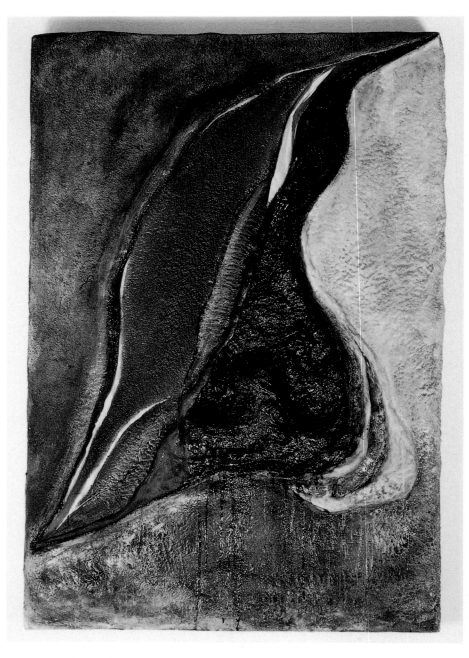

Artist Amber Dawn Noland brings forth the essence of the *Sacred Menstruating Vulva* in this 10' x 8' wall sculpture.

The Dark or New Moon Phase: During this phase I am my most serious and approach my spirituality from a very powerful base. I adorn my body with rich, dark colors. I am the medieval witch; the Great Goddess whose power knows no bounds.

The Waxing Moon Phase: I suddenly find myself wearing clothes that are more formfitting. I am on the go and don't want to be bothered with anything. I am the Virgin Goddess; one-in-herself.

The Full Moon Phase: As I celebrate this phase of my cycle, and usually because I am ovulating, I tend to reveal my body a little more. I like to use my hair to add a touch of sensuality and softness to my face. I am Ishtar, Oshun, Aphrodite; lover of life.

The Waning Moon Phase: "Red is beautiful, red is powerful, I am bleeding, I am in my woman way!" I am in touch with my body. Yemaya; powerful and ferocious.

Chapter Nine

Blood Gifts and Moon Tools

The giving of a Blood Gift to either a woman-child undergoing her menarcheal rites of passage ceremony, or a woman who has been bleeding for years but has chosen to undergo a rite of passage, is a sharing that truly comes from deep within. These are the gifts that are sacred and powerful. They touch upon the very essence of a woman's life, and act as reminders of our desire to honor self by reclaiming the divinity that is rightfully ours.

With all the resources available today, and the exploding creative inspiration pouring out of women, the following list of Blood Gifts are simply suggestions and are in no way complete. We must remember that the ceremony, and our participation in such a ceremony, is the greatest Blood Gift we can give a sister, however, physical items keep that initial gift alive.

When choosing a gift, let it come from the heart, and let it be as creative as possible. Remember we can give these gifts to ourselves!

Blood Gifts

Feminine Lingerie

As discussed in Chapter Three, we must become conscious of using supplies that honor the flow by using products which enhance the experience of menstruation for women. Whether you make the absorbers or buy them (see Appendix A for a listing of companies), giving an assortment of pad sizes as well as sponges is a healthy way to nurture self, while initiating the demystification of touching the blood.

Tote Bag for Feminine Lingerie

If one woman is going to give an assortment of absorbers, then perhaps another woman will want to give a tote bag made out of canvas, velvet, or corduroy to store the feminine supplies in. A smaller pouch that would fit in a purse could also be made to hold clean and used absorbers when away from home.

Blood Jar

To make the above gift ideas complete, a third woman could devise a Blood Jar (as described in Chapter Six) in which to soak the absorbers.

Performance

Theatrical presentations are also gifts. A short play of myth, comedy or personal saga possibly with song and dance performed to the female who is being honored. Pictures could be taken during the performance and then created into a book. Better yet, make a video tape of the entire ceremony as your gift.

Song

Songs can be written and sung to the woman, or recorded or written on parchment and framed.

Artistry

Poetry, illustrations, paintings and sculptures of a blood theme, woman power theme, feminine energy theme, make wonderful gifts. An expression of inner self in this way can be savored forever.

Jewelry

Vulva necklaces made out of cowrie shells represent the female signature. Moonstone rings represent our connection with Grandmother Moon. Anklets and bracelets made with white, red, and black beads are representative of the three phases of a woman's life: menarche, menstruation and menopause.

Clothing

Red gowns are the best gift in this department. Perhaps the seamstress in the group may want to make a very simple gown that the sister can wear during her bleeding when she visits the Moon Lodge.

Reading Materials

Any book (such as this one) that enhances a woman's knowledge on the feminine power can be given. To help a sister start her woman's studies library is a very wealthy gift to give.

Moon Journal

A blank book can either be made or bought. This is one of the more necessary gifts. This is perhaps the gift that the Crone of the circle would give the sister. It is important for each woman to keep a journal in which she records her dreams and visions, and information received from the Grandmothers because when each woman shares her collected wisdom with the others, the larger tapestry gets woven.

Lunar Calendar

I feel that this is a mother's gift to give her daughter. A mother who encourages her daughter to have fertility awareness and chart her cycle bridges one of the most devastatingly evident problems in todays society—teenage pregnancy.

Tarot Cards

Each woman can have at least one deck of Tarot cards to use during her bleeding time. There are so many beautiful decks created by women, that choosing the best deck might take hours. However, the favorite seems to be Vicki Noble's *Mother Peace* deck. Other decks to consider are: *Daughters of the Moon, The Cat People,* and *The Rose Deck,* all of which are very feminine.

Goddess Figurines

The more Goddess figurines the better, and especially the Menstrual Goddess (see Appendix A for purchasing information). In my collection I have over 20 figurines and still want more. The newest addition to my collection is the statue of Inanna/Ishtar (who is my main deity). Making a Goddess icon can be a very spiritual experience and a special gift.

Candles

A supply of white, red, and black candles is a wonderful gift to receive. A candelabra would make a nice addition to this idea and would actually complete the gift.

As you can see from the list above, there are numerous ideas available. Masks can be made, baskets of Woman Herbs collected and displayed, a Moon drum, a basket in which to store Blood Gifts and Moon Tools can be given. You see there is no end to the possibilities.

Your Blood Gift Idea List

List any additional Blood Gift ideas that came to mind when reading over the above lists.

● ◗ ○ ◗

Moon Tools

Moon Tools are quite different from Blood Gifts, although some can be classified as both. Moon Tools are the power tools that a woman either makes herself or purchases and then consecrates to use only during her bleeding time. Again, the list of tools could go on and on, so I shall only mention those ones which I feel are most valuable to focus on in the beginning of your Moon time celebrations. Also, my goal is not to give directions on how to make the tools. What I hope to accomplish by mentioning them, is to inspire within you the desire to create your own in the way you are guided to do so. There is no right or wrong way to make tools. Herstory tells us not to be afraid to not know, but to simply echo out into the real living our vision.

Prayer Bundles

These are placed in each of the four directions of the Moon Lodge. They are filled with herbs, crystals, feathers, stones, fetishes, etc. The cloth and ribbon used in the construction of the bundles are best when color coordinated with the direction it will be placed in. The intent of the bundle is infused with prayers while you make it. Smudging the bundle upon completion and rattling over it after placed in its direction will activate the energy.

Menses Incense

Making your own power incense helps to transform your atmosphere. When making your own incense, collect the herbs that you are drawn to. Whether store bought or harvested, make sure they are completely dry before using. Most herbs can be ground easily in a kitchen blender. To help the mixture burn, a pinch of Salt Peter (purchased through herbal supply companies) can be added. Most dried herb mixtures will burn easily on the charcoal made especially for incense which can be purchased through most metaphysical stores. (For suggested herbs, refer to Chapter Seven.)

Woman Power Shield

Whether you make your shield out of leather and willow, or canvas and grapevine hoops, or cardboard, this power shield becomes the symbol of where you stand in your Spirit Lodge at this time. Be aware of astrological impacts when creating your shield. I have found the day of Summer Solstice to be the most auspicious for this work because it is the day of inner fire. Inner fire transforms us. The Woman Power Shield aids us as a tool in this transformation. The elements connected to south and west are taken into consideration and worked with; south for fire and the place of innocence and spirit; west for water and the place of woman power and nurturance.

Dream Pillow

As we work with our power, our dreams become vitally important. Dreams are a wonderful resource to use for they are continually developing and aid us. Whether you choose to make an elaborate pillow or one simply filled with mugwort (a visioning herb), once you have used a dream pillow you will never sleep without it: (For a more in-depth study on Dream Pillows and the Dream-Catcher Ceremony, refer to my book *The Gaia Tradition: Celebrating The Earth in Her Seasons*, Llewellyn Publications, 1991.)

Belly Stone

Any stone or rock that you are drawn to can be used as the Belly Stone. This stone is used during your bleeding time. To use it is simple. First you stretch out on your back and place the stone over your power center (which for women is usually somewhere between the navel and vagina). This creates belly center awareness and connects you to the Mother's mind that lives within.

Moon Crystal

As many of us know, crystals are powerful transmitters of energy that can be set with intention. By consecrating a crystal for use only during the bleeding time with the intention of peace, creativity, dreaming, healing, etc., we can enhance our environment; the atmosphere we will echo back to the world once we emerge from our retreat. It is best to use this crystal only for the bleeding time and left in the Lodge. Try using stones that are red such as garnet, ruby, jasper, lava rock, or bloodstone (green & red). Crystals also make good Blood Gifts.

Moon Bags

These are personal power bags that are made by each woman to be placed on her own altar during the bleeding time. I have found that if the bags are imbued with a commitment or vow of some sort, they help the woman achieve her goal. (For instructions on making a traditional Moon Bag, and for a ceremony that can be used in conjunction with the creation of the bag, refer to my book, *An Act of Woman Power*, Whitford Press, 1989.)

Mirrors

It is important to have at least one mirror in your Lodge. It is very empowering to look at your face during affirmations, chanting, or during trance work. When we look at our face in the mirror we see the womanly face of Goddess alive.

I believe that body paints, jars of ochre, and of course, the Moon Lodge Record Book are important tools to have. Since Moon Tools are usually made by the woman who uses them, in most cases it is better not to give them as Blood Gifts. However, if you are really drawn to create a Moon Tool for another woman, my suggestion to you is to follow that desire.

Your Blood Tool Idea List

Make a list of any additional Blood Tool ideas that came to mind when reading over the above lists.

May your celebrations be filled with power, inspiration, creativity and rejoicing.

AFTER THE FLOW

After The Flow

In herstory we look forward to the days when we will no longer drop the blood from our vaginas, but hold it; for we realize that the time *after the flow* is a time of great power. As we leave behind the time of menstrual cycling, we move into a creative, expressive, wonderful time of true freedom.

> *There is a secret one inside,*
> *all the stars and all the galaxies,*
> *run through her hands like beads.*[1]

With the dignity of aged wisdom gained through not only direct experience, but the inner mind of MaMa Earth as a result from our years of listening to the inner voice speak to us, we are able to stand tall and firm in our beliefs. We become very powerful shaman women who stand for nurturing, renewal and beauty. It is not just for personal self that this stance is taken, but the whole of Earth's children.

As young women we begin by understanding the charge we come into this living with; the charge to understand nurturing and relationships. With the gift of caring, we learn about cyclical renewal and healing. When this cycling begins with menarche, we pass into the status of womanhood. We begin to understand the great mystery's gift of creation in our womb, and begin rejoicing in this divine aspect of our bodies. During our bleeding time the inner voice is consulted for direction. This direction is usually for self, or for family and friends; those people who are intimately connected to us. We catch our blood give-away and cycle it back to MaMa Earth by pouring it on her body, or use it as an offering in our chalices. We can honor our divinity by using the blood as paint on our own skin and sacred objects, thus demonstrating the full power of shaman woman.

Some women decide to become impregnated. When this happens the blood is held in order to create the house that the unborn baby requires for nourishment. With this event, women pass into the status of motherhood; the second major phase of a woman's life. In this phase we begin, remotely, to understand the full power of the blood.

During a natural course of a female's life, the ovaries eventually stop releasing eggs, and one day the last drop of blood passes the lips of the vulva. The period of menopause is worn like a cloak. We become the Grandmother, the acquirer of wisdom.

Then the time of Croning arrives; a time of honor and acknowledgement. The third and, I believe, most important phase of a woman's life is entered—the status of Wise One, Crone, is achieved.

Each phase is just as important as the next. Each passage deserves acknowledgement and celebration. And so, menopause is also a time of honoring, for we are now preparing to enter the third major phase of our womanhood—the Cronehood that will come after the second Saturn return, usually between the age of 58 and 60.

It is important to note that the time of menopause is not a definitive event but takes place over several years. Therefore whether we are premenopausal, well into it, or postmenopausal a celebration is in order.

Take the time to remember your menopause (just as you did your menarche). For the woman who has not entered this phase, it is important to look forward to menopause and begin creating new beliefs about what the menopause experience can mean; this change can be looked at as a gift that significes the accumulation of wisdom. Menopause can be a very positive experience.

I provide the following journey outline in the form of "already having experienced menopause." However, in parentheses I provide suggestions of how to experience the journey if you are a younger woman, or pre-menopausal.

Menopause Journey

Go to a special place where you will not be interrupted for at least an hour. Put the phone off the hook, a *Do Not Disturb* sign on the door and sit back and relax.

Focus on breathing smoothly, fully. With each *out* breath, release the stresses of the body/mind and the strains of day-to-day living. Release fully with each breath, visualizing that your body is also becoming completely relaxed.

With each *inhale*, draw in a very pure and healing vibration. Breath this vibration into every organ in your body; visualize it circulating through each of the seven chakra (energy) centers in your body (e.g. vagina, womb, solar plexus, heart, throat, third eye, and crown of head). Draw this vibration so fully into your body that every cell is saturated with pureness and healing energy. Now, let your breathing resume its natural flow.

Turn your awareness to your womb center. Place your hands over your belly and concentrate on the feminine energy (the secret one inside) that is housed in the womb center. Allow your focus to drop deeper and deeper into this center. Begin counting backwards from 10 to 1.

> 10 . . . you are aware of your body
> 9 . . . falling deeper into your womb
> 8 . . . connecting to your woman power
> 7 . . . surrounded by woman power
> 6 . . . re-awakening your memory
> (awakening to willingness)
> 5 . . . going back in time (opening to the future)
> 4 . . . back to the time of your last blood
> (to the time of your last blood)
> 3 . . . the last drop of blood
> 2 . . . to your time of Changing Woman
> 1 . . . it is the time of your menopause

Allow the memory of this experience to be re-awakened fully. (Allow the vision of this experience to awaken.)

Remember how you felt—whether it was positive/negative/indifferent. (Now is the time to create a new belief about the menopause.)

How did you face the body messages of menopause such as hot flashes, vaginal dryness, skin and hair changes, etc? (How can you work with the physical changes you will undergo during menopause?)

Who were the other people involved in your menopause—husband, lover, daughters, sons, sister, brothers, girlfriends, or other relatives. How did they respond to you at this time? (Who would you like to share your menopause with? How can you encourage them to celebrate this event with you; that it is a positive time?)

Remember everything you can. Remember the last blood. How you felt when it no longer flowed—did you notice the pause immediately, or did it take several months? When you did finally notice, did you acknowledge that your bleeding days had ended? Did you let your memory take you back to the last blood? How did you feel when you realized you had passed through the BIG change of life? (Visualize how you would like to experience your last blood. Do you want to be aware of the pause? When you are sure that the blood no longer flows, how would you like to celebrate this change?)

Now it is time to reclaim the titles of Grandmother, Wise One, Crone. These titles are empowering. Let us reach into the very center of the wisdom that supports these titles, for they are the "crowns" once worn by the matriarchs, the leaders of the woman's ways. Examine each of the three titles and come to understand the energy that supports it. *Grandmother* means you are a woman who is experiencing the time of menopause or one who holds the blood power, one who focuses on right relations and is not afraid to say "no." *Wise One* means you are a woman who is very close to the Croning, a Grandmother who prepares to enter the third and most powerful phase of a woman's life, one who easily lives her age with beauty and wisdom, no pretensions. *Crone* means you are a woman who has undergone her second Saturn Return and has arrived at her 60th birthday, as a Wise One. As a crone, you continue to work with spirit and continue to usher forth the Grandmothers' voice of right relationships. Of the three titles, which one fits you? Understand why this title fits you. Now claim it and publicly wear this title.

Very gently, bring your hands to your heart and slowly open your eyes. Now, carefully record the memory of your menopause experience (the vision of menopause) on the following pages and the title you claim as your own.

Menopause—My Last Blood

Currently I am age:

I started menopause at age:

Today's date is:

I claim the title:

Memory:

Let us begin changing our beliefs about menopause. Let us honor this stage of our lives. Let us celebrate the last blood. Let us affirm the power of the matriarchal crowns. Let us reclaim our wisdom. Now!

● ◗ ○ ◑

NOTES

1. Sufi song inspired by Rumi, given by Zuleikha.

TA YU

the great possessions have now been acquired—
knowledge and wisdom.
the wise one is now in the spotlight.

Six in the 5th line:
the spiritual woman uses her gifts wisely and her
sisters recongnize her integrity.
thus a truthful relationship exists.

CH'IEN

the wise one is like a dragon rising to its zenith;
the propitious, who is now dedicated to the
betterment of society.
the creative power is now held and is
directed to develop order and peace.

Chapter Ten

Menopause

meno-pause \men- ə-póz\ *n* (F mēnopause, fr. *mēno-* men- +*pause*): the period of natural cessation of menstruation occurring usually between the ages of 45 and 50—**meno-paus-al**\ men- ə-pó-z əl*adj*
— *Webster's New Collegiate Dictionary*

I am standing in a crowded room. An intense wave of heat rushes through my body. I am inflamed with its power. Automatically I start fanning my face with my hand. My body is burning!

Glancing around, I check the crowd in the room to see if anyone is watching. Everyone is involved in their own discussions except for one woman. A very old woman, who is sitting very quietly on a chair in the corner. So quietly that I had not noticed her before.

Our eyes meet. My hand stops furiously flapping. This very old woman nods her head ever so slightly. She smiles and motions with her hand that I should come to her. I do.

"Pull up a chair," she speaks to me. I am surprised at the strength in her voice. After finding a chair and moving it next to hers, I sit and face her.

"Hot flash," she comments after I sit down.

"What?" I ask.

She smiles at me. "The fire that just rushed through your body was a hot flash."

"Oh." I glance around the room suddenly aware that the crowd is gone and just the old woman and me remain. Before I can comment on the disappearance of the crowd she speaks again.

"You must be in your mid-40s I would say." I nod my head but she doesn't see it and continues talking. *"Welcome to the passage of time, you're preparing for the time of pausing when the flow will cease and you'll hold the blood."*

"Menopause," I mumble under my breath. This comment stops her and for the first time since I sat down she turns and eyeballs me.

"Shame on you Kisma," she scolds. *"I thought you were more conscious than that. All this talk you've been doing over the years about honoring the blood and claiming your womb divinity and honoring the Grandmothers and trying to organize a 'Grandmother revolution' and all, well I would have expected something else to come sputtering out of your throat chakra. Why you sound like one of those sleeping sisters out there who are still under the influence of the patriarchal enforced stupidity."*

"Wait a minute," I interrupt. *"I'm only dreaming. I'm not even a mother yet!"*

Laughter explodes from this old woman and with it another wave of fire rushes through my body. My hand starts furiously flapping again, searching for the coolness I hope to find; coolness and relief.

"You are such a silly girl! Of course you're 'only dreaming.' We're all only dreaming—why should you be any different?" She doesn't wait for my response. *"Ride the fire flash, Kisma! Feel the Kundali as she rises within you. Yes, don't look so surprised. This heat, this fire, these commonly referred to 'hot flashes' we women undergo are the gracing, or blessing I should say, of Goddess Kundali. She's now preparing you to hold the power! This happens when you cease to flow, or menopause. Goddess Kundali is preparing you to really receive the woman S'akti (power) at the time you pass through the third knot into Cronehood."*

I shake my head. *"Whew, what a mind-blow."* We look at each other and start laughing.

A very soft, wisdom-lined hand touches mine. I look down at it and hear her say, *"Think about the fire."*

I wake.

● ◑ ○ ◑

Menopause literally translates into men: "Moon month"; an ancient and universal measure of time, with the celestial body that measures it, and pause: to stop, to rest. The ending of the Moon month; the last blood.

The time of menopause is known as the BIG change of life, but can be more positive than women are lead to believe through the current dictates of the media. In herstory, the Change is a time in a woman's life to be celebrated. Like the previous two phases, menopause is not without its own physical symptoms: the sporadic bleeding, the hot flashes, vaginal dryness, a seeming decrease in sexual drive, and possible osteoporosis with the on-set of the croning years. Each woman's experience is so different; for some, menopause is traumatic and hot flashes, etc., may seem intolerable.

The term menopause actually refers to the last blood, but is used broadly to describe a transitional time from a few years before the last menses to a year after it. The average age of menopause is between 48 and 52, but can range from 42 through 55.

Menopause takes place as the hormone output from the ovaries declines. As this occurs the menses will first become irregular and then eventually stop. Like menstruation, as mentioned above, menopause has its own unique messages such as hot flashes, night sweats, and vaginal dryness. These three messages are experienced by four out of five women.

We can begin noticing changes in our menstrual cycles in our mid-40s. It is at this time that ovulation becomes less regular. When this happens we may bleed an average of every 21 to 25 days rather than the standard cycle that occurs every 28 days. As our cycles change, we may also notice a change in the blood flow, sometimes it will be much lighter than what once was considered normal and occasionally very heavy. It is not unusual to begin skipping a month. After skipping a period, prolonged spotting or erratic bleeding may be experienced. At any time ovulation may recur and normal periods are resumed.

During menopause there are only a few bleeding patterns that we want to watch for, especially repeated periods that tend to be very heavy; irregular. The most common cause for this type of bleeding is lack of ovulation and a result of hormonal imbalance due to the production of too much estrogen and too little progesterone. However, it may also be caused by uterine fibroids, or cancer (refer to Chapter Seven).

As we near the age 50, our menses will get further apart and lighter. When this happens, we can take it as a sign that soon our periods will stop entirely. This is the menopause; the last blood. Occasionally some women will experience this before 50, some after.

However, very few women still menstruate at the age of 55. When we no longer bleed we have gone through menopause and officially entered a new phase of our womanhood. But until the menopause actually takes place, we have many new experiences to undergo.

● ◗ ○ ◐

"Think about the fire," old woman tells me.

"Okay," I begin slowly. "Fire is Dipa (Sanskrit)—light. It is red. It is menstrual blood. I guess its equated to "will." Fire is the name or that action which builds and destroys shapes. Fire is what is seen and touched, I mean, that is felt as temperature—in space, although air is what is so felt in space. I don't know. I mean, it is a compound that makes up the material universe in one sense and is considered an element in a magical sense." I was lost in my abstract thinking.

"Fire is manifold, its a great mystery being. It is the only element, during all these years of evolutionary apprenticeship, that I have not been able to quite understand. Hard as I try, fire, has always ended up burning me even when I've tried to ally it."

I looked at old woman who seemed to be sleeping. So I continued my musing. "Okay, fire was the element of fear I had when I really began working with the chakra system of my body and striving to understand the basics of the Kundalini. I never stopped to think that I would so intimately experience the fire, and Kundali for that matter, through hot flashes of all things!

"Hot flashes! Wow, I've mis-read them all along. I mean we are so taught to believe that they are a symptom, a negative condition attached to menopause. After all, we are taught to believe that menopause is a horrible aspect of life and when we go through the BIG change in life, that life is basically over.

"How many times have I been conditioned to think that menopause is a disease?"

Old woman startled me. "That's it!" she all but yelled out. "The BIG disease—menopause." I was staring at her. She had become so animated.

"Old woman, how old are you?"

She chuckled. "Old enough to know," was all she would say. I couldn't accept her evasiveness.

"Wait," I whined. "I know you're old enough to know. Goodness-gracious! What I mean is, how old are you?"

"Old," she clicked her teeth together. "Okay, think about this in terms of age: one-celled."

I couldn't help but laugh, which seemed to make her angry. Realizing that this old woman was probably the Great Goddess herself intruding—or rather **visiting**—my dreaming, I stifled my laughter, bit my tongue and said, "Hot flashes."

This time old woman asked "What?"

"Hot flashes," I said. "Hot flashes are a gift, aren't they?"

"Yep."

"The hot flash originates from the seat of the Source, I mean the base chakra where Kundali rests. So, let me ask you this old woman—by the way do you have a name?" I asked.

"Call me Mahakundali."

"Mahakundali?"

"Mahakundali."

"Wait a minute," as I said this Mahakundali looked at me.

"Okay," she responded. "What?"

"Mahakundali basically means 'the great coiled power' in Sanskrit!"

"My you are a smart one," she toyed. "Apparently you have done your homework. If you don't like that name you can call me Maya-S'akti—she who alternates between phases of potentiality and phases of explication!"

I was admonished. "No, I am sorry," I apologized. "It is just that I have never talked to pure consciousness before. I thought you were a Grandmother maybe, or a guide?"

Mahakundali shifted positions, lifting her nose a little as if I had just issued further insult. "Well," came out in a huff. "Who do you think the Grandmothers are? Or guides for that matter?"

"I, I, I . . ."

"These Grandmothers, these guides are merely Mahakundali as Kundali-S'akti while abiding in the human body's Earth center the Muladhara-Chakra. Maya, darling!"

"Ahhh," I screamed. "This is too much for me." Fire raged through my body. The heat swirled inside. I looked down at the flushing of my skin and felt the parchment take place. At that moment I felt wetness between my legs. I was spotting again.

"Ride the fire, Kisma," Mahakundali sang to me.

"Ride the fire, feel her climb, higher and higher.

"Ride the fire, feel her life, taking you higher and higher.

"Ride the fire, the S'akti rises, contracting the veil of consciousness.

"Ride the fire, back to Samkhya, the marvelous seat of memory.

"Ride the fire, Kisma and become Akasa, the force of Primordial Power."

My body temperature returned to its normal state. My flushed face was still tinged with the residue of the heat. I opened my eyes and looked at Mahakundali. "Did I ride the fire?" I asked.

A warm smile spread across her face. "Dear child," she began. "You are only dreaming. You have not even become a mother yet. Menopause is still years away. No, you have not ridden the fire yet." Her warm hand patted mine. She continued. "When you wake you will have wonderful new insights to help prepare yourself for the menopause as well as to share with other women, especially those of menopausal age.

"You see, the gift of S'akti (power) that women are offered as they undergo this transitionary point of their lives, have long been forgotten. It is time for women to begin receiving this gift; preparing their whole lives for the gift of such potent power.

"As has been true with many other natural gifts of womanhood, the kundalini power and the chakra systems have been stolen from women; the knowledge of this gift strangled and hoarded by men who strive to receive this power. Why, there are so many forms of practice in the Eastern part of this world that focus on opening the energy points of the body and raising the coiled serpent from her rest; raising her 'fire' to unite with the Siva of the crown, and through this achievement, attaining the supreme state of Bliss—there are more forms of this practice then you can imagine. These yogis have denied women the right to practice this form of yoga until just recently.

"Men are funny creatures. They desire power so intensely and yet are more in need of the S'akti of a woman; this is the great secret of life." She elbowed me and winked.

"Riding the fire is breathing in the S'akti, the power of woman, of creation, the divine current of life. For you see it is the great and Supreme S'akti that is the creative energy, who is the cause of the universe and Consciousness itself.

"So, hot flashes, in one sense, are the kinetic aspect of S'akti's movement within; her force of the body. Hot flashes are the natural act of receiving wisdom; the lifting of the veil.

You see, during the other phases of your life your attention has been elsewhere. As a young girl approaching menarche, your thoughts were on the appearance of the blood. During your bleeding times, your thoughts have been on your physical body and hooking up with the divine Grandmother's voice within. During motherhood, your thoughts will be on your child. As the blood flow begins to slow and you begin to hold it, and if you don't get caught-up in thinking you're going through a terrible event, then finally your thoughts can rest on the power, the S'akti.

"With your focused energy and the power of the held blood, my essence can rise inside. As I rise, I cause heat. As the hot flashes come, and if you ride them—close your eyes and experience the great stirring of power inside—you open yourself up and can receive my gift, my blessing.

"The changes you'll notice in your skin and vagina, the dryness, well ... will only remind you that the thermal temperatures of your body are still in the raging process. Many a powerful woman in yesteryear has birthed through menopause after having rode me completely. Those women became the matriarches of the land—the real Crones of power."

Mahakundali shifted in her seat. Her eyes closed for a minute. I thought she might be falling a sleep, but then she opened one eye and grinned.

"See," she said as if proving her point. "Just because I decided to rest for a moment you think I am going to sleep and leaving you. Remember, power continually sleeps inside. When it wakes, yawns and stretches itself, and then rises— well, you've just got to be aware enough to hear its calling and wake-up with it; ride the fire.

"Tell the women. Tell them to listen for the messages that I give them. When that blood begins to stop flowing and the fire rises inside— tell them they better hear the message, wake-up and hop on. Eventually, I'll need to rest, and when I do, when I coil back up and take a nap, if they didn't ride with me, if they didn't receive my gift of S'akti, then they missed out on the most powerful natural gift I decided to bless them with at the birthing of their consciousness."

Mahakundali looked at me closely. "That goes for you too, young lady!"

Okay, sisters, did you hear what Mahakundali said? Now is the time to begin preparing for the menopause by exercising our minds and reconditioning them to view this phase as an extremely powerful time.

Riding The Fire

If you are presently undergoing the body changes that take place pre-menopause, begin observing your cycle and listening to the messages Mahakundali is giving. Remember that though you will eventually no longer bleed it is important to maintain your relationship with Grandmother Moon, so continue to Moon-watch, but focus on your body.

Compare what you once considered as your normal Moon's cycle to the menopausal changes now taking place. Focus on the messages that occur spontaneously throughout the month to see if they occur in conjunction with your bleeding cycle and/or the Moon cycle.

When hot flashes flare, try focusing on them by relaxing, breathing deep and evenly, opening your mind to receive the S'akti (power) as you ride the fire. Chart your journey with the fire and see how your values and ideas might be affected by this experience.

Ending Date of Moon Time:

First week following:

Riding the fire:

How often does it occur?

How long does it last?

Describe your body cycle (water retention, swelling, slender, ovulation, bleeding, etc.).

What is your mental attitude?

Your emotional attitude?

Your spiritual attitude?

Moon phase:

Second week:

Riding the fire:

How often does it occur?

How long does it last?

Describe your body cycle (water retention, swelling, slender, ovulation, bleeding, etc.).

What is your mental attitude?

Your emotional attitude?

Your spiritual attitude?

Moon phase:

Third week:

Riding the fire:

How often does it occur?

How long does it last?

Describe your body cycle (water retention, swelling, slender, ovulation, bleeding, etc.).

What is your mental attitude?

Your emotional attitude?

Your spiritual attitude?

Moon phase:

Fourth week:

Riding the fire:

How often does it occur?

How long does it last?

Describe your body cycle (water retention, swelling, slender, ovulation, bleeding, etc.).

What is your mental attitude?

Your emotional attitude?

Your spiritual attitude?

Moon phase:

Comments:

Nourishing Ourselves

If we face the transitions of our lives (menarche, menstruation, motherhood) as stages that prepare us for the golden years when we receive the power and thus become fully empowered, we nourish our minds, our bodies and our souls.

Through this nourishment we strengthen the tight-bond between mind and body so the channel remains open and receptive, allowing the energy of change to steadily flow through.

Nourishing our minds is done through the reconditioning of the fertile soil and planting of positive seeds towards the natural physiological occurrences of our bodies and the understanding of the power we truly hold; the deepening of that power as we are initiated into each level of the matrix.

As we reclaim our bodies, strive to understand the biology of them and begin working in cooperation with them, we become aware of the wonderful wisdom of the woman's ways—the strength, the power, the connection with creativity.

The blood ceremonies we performed during our bleeding times can now be transformed into internal power-evoking ceremonies wherein we call upon Kundali and request her fiery presence to aid us in reaching potent levels of awareness, contracting the veil so we can look at wisdom, and rise up with her into that wisdom and unite with our inner male twin and thus become the supreme bliss of balanced energy.

When our ceremonies are complete and Kundali rests once more—closing the veil for the time being—we can bring forth the new knowledge received and become a physical manifestation of the Grandmothers, the guide.

Nourishing our bodies is done through the remembrance that our body is an ecology system. We know what happens when man-made chemicals are indiscriminately added to our natural resources, so it is the same with our bodies. When we indiscriminately fill them with synthetics, or empty foods, we do not nourish them. Rather, we encourage discomfort and dis-ease, which becomes manifested as symptoms surrounding naturally occurring changes in our bodies.

Just as there are *Wise Shaman Woman Herbs* that assist us during menstruation, so there are *Wise Shaman Woman Herbs* that assist us throughout the menopause. (A little further in the text we will take a look at these allies.)

Nourishing our souls is done through affirming our holiness by chanting and singing, or simply gazing at our changing face in a mirror. As we accept the importance of our life, the changes we physically undergo, new levels of consciousness are awakened and we remain balanced.

Meditation and quiet walks, communing with nature, cooing to a soft, warm pet, listening to the excited babble of a grandchild, encouraging our adult children through difficulties and their life changes is the substance that life perpetuates itself on. The golden years are the pleasure years when we've already been through it and can now sit back, relax and simply enjoy it as a holy part of living.

Wise Shaman Woman Herbs

The messages of menopause are indeed conditions that accost our attention when they arise. They are part of the package, the speaking of our body, the instructions of the supreme divinity of creation. Rather than ignore them, let us face them and read them, as if divining their appearance to gain insight into future days. The following are a few herbal remedies that can assist us during this phase.

Teas

Damiana *(Turnera aphrodisiaca)*—place 1 teaspoon of the leaves into a cup and pour boiling water over it. Allow mixture to sit for three to five minutes (or until water has cooled) before drinking. Drink no more than one cup per day. Damiana is recognized as being good for females generally, and helps to balance female hormones. It also helps to stimulate the pelvic organs. Increases sexual desire.[1]

Passion Flower *(Passiflora incarnata)*—place 1 teaspoon of the herb into a cup and pour boiling water over it. Allow mixture to sit for three to five minutes (or until water has cooled) before drinking. Very beneficial for hot flashes. Drink no more than one cup per day. Headaches that are caused from nervousness can be soothed with this herb.

Red Raspberry *(Rubus idaeus)*—use 1 tablespoon of the leaves per cup of boiling water. Steep from 3 to 5 minutes (or until water cool) before drinking. Drink no more than one cup per day. Red Raspberry helps to strengthen the uterus and entire reproductive system. This is an herb that benefits every woman no matter what phase she currently resides in.

Capsules

Black Cohosh *(Cimicifuga racemosa)* and **Blue Cohosh** *(Caulophyllum thalictroides)*—300-500 mg. Take one to two capsules a day of each for no more than 5 days a month. Watch body for sensitive side-effects such as nausea, nervous trembling, vertigo and change in heart pulse. If one or more of these symptoms appear, discontinue use immediately. These herbs supply a natural estrogen.

Dong Quai (a Chinese root, *Angelica sinensis*, similar to the North American Angelica, *Angelica atropurpurea*)—take one to two capsules per day for not more than five days per month. This herb acts as a mild laxative as it lubricates the intestines. It has been helpful in eliminating dry skin problems by moistening and softening the skin. Helps to dissolve blood clots. Gives nourishment to the brain cells. It is found to be high in vitamin E, and B_{12}.

Though Dong Quai is claimed to be one of the most effective uterine tonics and hormonal regulators, its action is considered very potent and can cause stomach distress when ingested alone. Using Dong Quai in conjunction with Comfrey root tea will help protect the stomach and will enhance the effect of Dong Quai on the reproductive system. If taken with Licorice tea, the combination will guard against digestive disruption but still function in this formula as precursor to the needed hormone, enabling the body to balance and adjust its hormone production.

Dong Quai is also effective if taken as a tincture. The usual dose would be 5-25 drops a day taken in a glass of water.[2]

Ginseng *(Panax quinquefolium)*—take one to two capsules per day for not more than 5 days a month. The Ginseng root strengthens the endocrine glands which include the metabolism of vitamins and minerals. It builds vitality and resistance. It contains steroids similar to estrogen.

Herbal Brew

1 tablespoon Rosemary *(Rosmarinus officinalis)*
1 tablespoon Mint *(Mentha spicata)*
1 tablespoon Elecampane *(Inula helenium)*
1 tablespoon Mugwort *(Artemisia vulgaris)*
1 tablespoon St. John's Wort *(Hypericum perforatum)*
1 tablespoon Shepherd's Purse *(Capsules bursa pastoris, Medik)*
1 tablespoon Vervain *(Verbena officinalis)*

Bring one quart of water to a boil. Place herbs into a one quart jar. When water comes to a boil pour into jar over herbs. Put on a tight lid and let steep for at least 30 minutes. Strain out herbs and store in tightly capped jar.

When using mixture, drink one cupful of reheated brew a day to treat sudden hot flashes. Or if high blood pressure persists drink one cupful every four hours per day for up to five days or until pulse returns to normal.

As wise shaman women who nourish the body, it is important for us to eat foods that are high in calcium or take a calcium supplement. The Recommended Daily Allowance (RDA) for calcium is 800 milligrams (mg). Women of all ages may want to take 1,000 to 1,500 mg daily. Calcium carbonate or calcium citrate are the common forms found in health food stores. It is important to note that vitamin D must be present in the body to allow absorption of calcium from the intestines. A natural form of vitamin D is formed on our bare skin when we are outdoors in the Sun and is stored in the liver until needed. Vitamin D can also be found in many dairy products. It is best to get about 400 IU (International Units) of vitamin D daily to ensure optimum calcium absorption. However, excessive vitamin D is not advisable. The easiest way to take vitamin D is in a daily multivitamin supplement.

Some dairy foods high in calcium are:

> 1/4 cup (400 mg) skim milk power
> 1 cup (350 mg) low-fat milk
> 1 cup (300 mg) yogurt
> 1 cup (120 mg) low-fat cottage cheese
> 4 ounces (150 mg) tofu

We can also add calcium rich foods to our diets. Collard greens, sardines, kale, salmon, broccoli, corn tortillas, dandelion greens, lamb's quarter greens and blackstrap molasses are very beneficial.

Two other plant allies that are very beneficial to women during the menopausal years are nettle leaves and stalks, and seaweed. (For recipes on preparing these two plant allies for eating, refer to Susun Weed's *Wise Woman Herbal: Healing Wise*.)

Experimenting With The Wise Shaman Woman Herbs

As you work with the Wise Shaman Woman Herbs, keep track of the specific manner in which you use them (e.g. tea, capsule form, in foods, etc), and the quantity used as well as the preparation process. Note any changes in your physical condition after the use of the herb, or remedy. Use only one herb, or remedy for at least 3 months to clarify its effect. If ineffective, discontinue, and begin working with a different herb or remedy.

Remember that exercise (walking/yoga), and diet will greatly assist you at this time.

Symptom:

Herb:

Remedial use (form, quantity, process):

Month One:

Month Two:

Month Three:

Symptom:

Herb:

Remedial use:

Month One:

Month Two:

Month Three:

Comments:

I am sitting quietly in my garden sipping a steaming cup of tea. I am feeling very free. My flow has all but stopped. I know the day of menopause has all but come and gone. I ride the hot flashes and have gotten use to the flushed parchment the fire leaves on my skin and hair. I embrace these residual effects of menopause as symbols of my new attired wisdom.

Mahakundali has not been back to speak with me in my dreaming. Rather, she seems to appear in the plant allies that I work with in my garden.

This lack of communication tends to make me think that I am enjoying my BIG change in life and working in cooperation with my body, not fighting it the way so many women have been taught to do.

Suddenly a mockingbird imitates the many tribes of its species with a medley as if it were a pianist showcasing various composers. I sigh and close my eyes. As I lift the cup of tea to my lips I deeply inhale the steam.

"PMZ!"

My eyes open and I look around. I am sure that that was the voice of Mahakundali. Deep within the surging of the fire rises.

"PMZ!"

"Okay," I respond. "PMZ."

Laughter rises within. Heat and warmth and wisdom and suddenly the veil lifts and I see the world anew. I remember the meaning of the term PMZ; I once read it long ago before the time of mothering. PMZ: post-menopausal zest (a phrase coined by Margaret Mead). This time it is my laughter that explodes into the quiet afternoon. "Yes," I whisper as if responding to someone sitting next to me. "We can live our lives with PMZ. May every woman who is pre-, menopausal, and post-, be blessed with PMZ!"

As if I have just blessed the world, the mockingbird takes up its medley again. I go back to the wonderful tea I am drinking. Lift the cup to my lips, inhale deeply and then sip the fragrance into my inner sanctum. I close my eyes and allow the essence of the herb to spread throughout my mind and body. Gently its vibration radiates out through the pores of my skin. I am shining. A shining light filling with eternal wisdom.

Someone gently nudges me. I hear, "Kis, wake-up. You're gonna be late for work" whispered close to my ear. I pry open a sleep-encrusted eye, look at Jack's face. I smile and say:
   "Boy, was I dreaming."

● ◑ ○ ◐

NOTES

1. Penny C. Royal, *Herbally Yours* (Sound Nutrition, 1976), p. 23.

2. Susun S. Weed, *Wise Woman Herbal: The Childbearing Year* (Ash Tree Publishing, 1987), p. 148.

Chapter Eleven

The Voice of the Grandmothers

We practiced guiding and showing the way during the days of our bleeding in anticipation for menopause. We have passed through the time of bleeding which we openly embraced. Now we have become guides for the planet.

Often, as I sit alone, I wonder what it would be like if my Grandmothers had lived until now. I want to sit and listen to their stories. Learn from them. Share my experiences with them even if only to hear their chuckles at my youthful ignorance. Only in the spirit world have I been visited by their essence, and then only by my father's mother (a little Polish woman; white haired and wrinkled), whom I knew as a child. She spoke wisdoms that then I did not quite understand. It has been in her honor that I have lit the ancestral flame at Samhain (October 31), and prepared the dumb supper plate. My mother's mother I never knew.

Yet, I feel as if both Grandmothers guide me, their woman blood running through my veins. And five years ago during a Samhain ritual, I feel as if they both spoke when telling me I would never go hungry, that there would always be food in my home.

I have heard my own mother's tears, and wonder what my Grandmothers' tears would be like.

"My son is dead," the wails of a grey-haired woman shatter the hearts of all who gather round her. She is bent over the body of her son; young, handsome, in uniform, splattered with blood.

This old woman raises her face to look in our eyes. Tears run down her face. I think to myself that she is much too old a woman to be this son's mother. Her eyes fix on mine, and the tears run like streams down her withering face.

She is beauty in the most elegant way, for suddenly she is the epitome of all the grieving mothers that have lived and died and lived and died. I see the anguish behind her eyes; the scorn of the wars of death. The anger flashes out from behind the waterfall of tears, flashing out the fire of dejection. The flames dissipate into the air. Her eyes close as her lips part to issue forth another forlorn cry.

I realize this woman's heart has finally broken. She can no longer mend it. Her body sobs against the bloody body beneath her. She cradles this lifeless form in her arms. She seems so weak, so helpless.

"They took my husband this way!" she screams into the death. "They took my son and my daughter's husband. They took my sister's loved ones, and the village men; those who were old enough to carry arms. But now? Why must they continue to take our men? Why must they continue to kill each other? Why must we women continue to dance with ghosts?"

I notice the older women in the crowd begin to shuffle on their feet and mumble. There is anger forming in this group. Impassioned anger. I watch as they begin holding hands, and feel mine grabbed up in the forming bond. Slowly we create a circle around this old woman who still sits cradling another offering to MaMa Earth.

"We will not stand for war any longer!" a voice yells.

"Yes," begins the woman to my left. "Our voices have been denied too long. We will speak out."

A murmur goes through the circle, rippling through our hearts. The old woman lays the death back on the ground and places her shawl over the agonized face. She stands. Slowly, she stands. Her face is hard and cold looking. Her mouth is drawn tight. Her eyes are sharp with years of repression and pain. She raises clinched fists over her head and turns in a circle looking each of us in the eyes.

"There was a time," she begins. "When women were honored. We kept the peace. We kept the unity of the village together. There was a time when we gathered together and allowed our musings to be heard and discussed. There was a time that our voices were sought. Our words guided *the welfare of the people. We lived in the women's ways of power and nurturance.*

"But in the past men grew jealous of this natural gift of power that we held. They joined together seeking to overpower it. They had a long fight on their hands!"

The crowd cheered. The old woman continued.

"Yes, they had a long fight on their hands. In fact, in order for them to be victorious they had to murder us!" Silence. Eyes closed. Tears flowed. Moans of sorrow.

"Why?" the old woman beseeched the sky. "Why would a mighty god allow his people to be so brutal? What would they gain from throwing the partnership off balance?

"These men, these tribes did not stop and ask themselves these questions. But the Grandmothers were given the answers, and as we came forward to give warning of such actions, our voices were silenced. Now, we have become weak, separated, ignorant.

"Well, I will not remain weak any longer. I will not stand alone. I am not ignorant. I call to my sisters. I call to the virgins, the mothers, the Grandmothers, the Crones, all women of every age, wake-up. Wake-up and stand strong and firm in your power. Our voice is needed. Our experience and understanding of relationships and the partnership of life, the balance of the two primal energies of life—female and male—are gravely needed.

"We must stand up and shout at the top of our lungs: We will not have things killed. We will not have the forests cut down. We will not have our waters polluted. We will not let our people go homeless; our children starve. We will not stand for war. These are unacceptable now! Let us change the world. Let us enact the world vision of peace and unity and balance and healing. Let us begin now.

I say: "Let us form the GRANDMOTHER REVOLUTION!"

The Grandmother Revolution

The Grandmother Revolution must begin and must be supported by women of every color, age and walk of life. This revolution is not one of hostility, but of rationality, of bringing forth the full power of the feminine energy back into balance.

In the Grandmother Revolution we must begin looking forward to the day when we will travel through the menopause and eventually step into the Grandmothers' Lodge, beginning our reign as Wise Ones, Crones. Through the wisdoms gained during our years of bleeding, let us stand as shaman women and actively speak out against those things that continue to inflict harm on women of age.

In my life, I have truly known few Crones, and the ones that I have known have either been filled with disease or were senile. Gone, it seems, are many of the wise ones from our society. I wonder how this has hurt us as a whole people? Myths often say most of the important inventions of early civilization were made by women in their "years of wisdom."[1] These women wore the title of "Crone" which related to the word crown, and represented the power of the ancient tribal matriarch who made the moral and legal decisions for her subjects and descendants.[2] The original Crones of the matriarchal community were women past the age of menopause, in whom the wise blood no longer flowed. The Crone therefore was considered to be the "wisest of mortals."[3]

At one time cultures honored the Crones, they did not reject them. They were rejected at the time when the newly dominant patriarchy transformed these gray-haired high priestesses, into minions of the devil. In the 12th to the 19th century (primarily from the 15th to the 18th), this rejection developed into a frenzy that legally murdered millions of wise women.[4]

However, today the law does not murder witches any longer, but the Grandmothers are still eliminated from society for they are made invisible. Rarely do they appear on movie and television screens. Yet, men who are in middle or late-middle age can be seen frequently on screens and are usually paired with younger women. It has become socially acceptable for men to leave their wives for younger women.

Through the media and multi-million dollar cosmetic companies women are encouraged to hide our age; to wash the grey out of our hair; smooth away wrinkles with ointments or surgery; and are constantly being told that the youthful, lean body is beautiful. Men, on the other hand, are considered to be distinguished and mature looking when middleage is upon them. Women of all ages are negated by this propaganda.

Let us take the first steps in reinstating the status of women of age to a level of dignity and respect by supporting the grey color of hair and honoring the mature figures of the matron. Let us seek out these wise ones and listen to their stories and encourage them to join our circles and form their own. By doing this we can help restore the Grandmothers' Lodge that eventually all women enter.

The following visualization is designed for women who have already gone through menopause. However, younger women can greatly benefit from this visualization by envisioning what we might look like when we are older.

The Beauty of Age and Wisdom

Take a moment to stand before a mirror. Look at your face. Look at the color of your hair. Really see the Grandmother, the wise one, the Crone that rests in your face. Look into your eyes and see the light, the wisdom. Smile at yourself. Hug yourself with your eyes. Then physically hug yourself.

Look at this act of love. See the wisdom from this self-acceptance; the empowerment. Now close your eyes and allow an affirmation about beauty of age and wisdom to come into your heart. This affirmation is about you and all women who enter into this phase of womanhood. Take a moment to write the affirmation down.

Now, look at your beautiful, wise face. Look into your eyes. Smile at yourself. Hug yourself again. Light a candle and hold it up to your image in the mirror and speak your affirmation loud and clear. Say it as many times as you would like.

When you can tear yourself away from the beautiful woman in the mirror, tell yourself thank-you for loving yourself so much. Find a quiet place where you can reflect on the emotions that were conjured up by this act. How did this make you feel?

Try and perform this act once a week for a month. Then perform it every month at New Moon for the rest of your life.

● ◗ ○ ◖

Let us stop and think about the day when we will be considered a woman of age, a Grandmother, a Wise One, a Crone. What kind of a world will it be for us then? For those of us who are actively working with woman spirituality and reclaiming and recreating the women's ways, how can we work so hard on supporting women without empowering the future days of our lives?

Barbara G. Walker, whose work I draw from for this chapter, has written perhaps the most important book for women of age to read, *The Crone: Woman of Age, Wisdom, and Power*. She speaks to the current Grandmothers and tells us that:

> The real solution to this problem is not to assume the protective coloring of sweet-little-old-ladyism in the hopes of escaping notice. Not being sadistic as a rule, women often fail to understand the basic fact about sadistic behavior. It is not allayed but stimulated by appearance of vulnerability in the prospective victim. It would be better for old women to as-

sert their right to judge, to be bolder in questioning male authority, to demand the respect due them as mothers and as decent, caring citizens.

Walker also speaks to the younger women, urging us to "uphold the ideals of feminine authority" so that when our own Cronehood has come we will "not be blighted by fear or contempt" to speak out for what is right.

As a whole, people we have been weakened because of analytical thinking that separates us from the realms of psychological and social forces. The Grandmother Revolution can help remind and put us back in touch with these realms of psychological and social forces: relationships. Women have intuitively known what is needed in interpersonal behavior patterns and moral codes to encourage the optimum quality of life. It has been the male-dominated culture that has suppressed our formal expression which might have further developed into an ethic.

Our civilization needs more of the gut wisdom women achieve simply by living as women. We are the birth givers, the comforters, the observers of human nature. We are frequently the sole nourishment of warmth and pleasure that gives stimulation and meaning to the lives of men. Old men are supposed to have acquired enough wisdom to run corporations and governments, yet, I believe, older women acquire even more wisdom especially when we work in cooperation with the natural powers that are acquired through each transition of our physiological functioning; perhaps enough wisdom to establish better moral standards for the world.

As we look around and see the polluted environment we live in, see the housing problem, the hungry people, let us acknowledge that this is the harm that has resulted from denying the voice of the Grandmothers, of women being heard. Had our voices not been silenced, we would have said "no" a long time ago to such atrocities.

Our voices under the tutelage of the Grandmother Revolution is gravely needed. "No," needs to be uttered against the "power-over" attitude that engulfs our world. We need to stop forgiving and excusing the male misbehavior on the grounds that men are like little boys and can not be expected to assume truly mature responsibility for their actions. It is this excused male behavior that in its most sadistic nature accused women of evil and tortured thousands of witches which more often than not resulted in their death.

Yes, history has dealt a hard blow to women of age. The truth of the matter is, that the balance of power on MaMa Earth depends on the empowered wisdom of our postmenopausal women; the true psychic, spirit-empowered healers.

The occult power of women, inextricably bound to our hormonal life, is very great and for the postmenopausal woman it is made even greater for the mere fact that the blood is now held and the internal flame can be fully experienced. We are far indeed from being the weaker sex, and it is time for us to prove this. Though we have been robbed in the past of our dignity to age gracefully and naturally by the media induction to believe that beauty and youth are the tools of power, we no longer need be victim to that mind-set. The real power is in our ability to become fully activated with the menopause.

As younger women, through the Grandmother Revolution we can take a stance as shaman women and support our Grandmothers, remembering that we too shall one day be a Grandmother. In this vein of action we will help create the "voice" of the Grandmothers and birth forth the acceptance and honor that is our birthright.

Let Your Voice Be Heard

As a woman of any age, now is the time to begin exercising your right to be heard; your right to voice your opinion.

As a Grandmother, as a Wise One, as Crone, take a few minutes to examine different aspects of society. What are the issues you disagree with? What do you want to say "no" to? Write these issues down.

Look at these issues a second time. Pick one issue that really stands out. Circle it. How can you make your voice heard? Outline the steps you need to take to have your voice heard.

Make a commitment to yourself to make your voice be heard. Write an affirmation for this commitment.

Now take the necessary steps and do it—let your voice be heard.

Date:

The issue you are speaking out on:

The method you are using to be heard:

How does it feel to speak out for the welfare of the planet and future generations?

I believe the Grandmother Revolution ultimately stands for our ability to be able to enact the vision that we dream of collectively or individually; taking the whole tapestry that women have been weaving and laying it over the physical world; inciting our vision, this tapestry to evaporate and be absorbed into the physical world thus changing everything it touches.

We can begin the Revolution in our own homes by seeking the advice of the elder women in our family. Taking the time to hear what they have to say. Listening to their suggestions. Allowing them to help us in projects; asking for their help with projects. We must also take a firm stance in allowing their voice to be heard by other family members by supporting them; encouraging them to speak up and out.

Becoming A Grandmother

Take a moment to think about how the older women in your family are treated. Think about how you treat them. Do you make time for them? Do you seek their advice? Do you ask them to help you with a project? When the entire family is gathered together and they want to speak, does the family listen? Think about how they must feel being overlooked.

Now visualize yourself as being older. Visualize that you are now the Grandmother of the family. Think about being treated in this manner. How do you feel? Do you feel weak, powerless?

Envision how you want to experience your time of age. How you want others to treat you.

See yourself as strong. How are you strong? From where do you draw your strength?

Now think about what you, as a younger woman, can do to start creating an atmosphere of respect and caring for your Grandmothers; what simple changes you can make in your own relationship with older women?

In doing the above exercise we take the time to really get in touch with how we are behaving toward the Grandmothers. By putting ourselves in their shoes we can begin to define how we do and do not want to be treated when we are in that phase of life. Asking the simple question "how can I now prepare society to be the kind of place where I can act, create, express with pride once I, myself, am a Grandmother" takes on significant importance.

● ◑ ○ ◑

I would like to share the wonderful thrill which can take place when we find a Crone to help guide us. Two years ago I attended a Summer Solstice Camp in Nevada City, California and came in contact with Jean Mountaingrove (co-founder and editor of *Woman-Spirit* magazine for the decade 1974-1984). We never spoke at that camp, but her essence went home with me. In doing research for this book I ordered a back issue of Woman of Power magazine and found an article written by Jean on the blood mysteries. The article provided an address for contacting Jean. I wrote Jean and introduced myself and asked if she would be willing to help review this manuscript. She agreed, even though she indicated her life was very busy at the time. I sent her the first section on menarche. When she returned the manuscript she wrote a note of encouragement.

"This is a very beautiful and loving gift to women," she began, and went on to say " . . . my comments, etc. are details. I think they may be too 'picky' . . . " She closed by saying, "I learned from and enjoyed your Grandmother Moon chapter especially."

I immediately sat down and read all her comments scribbled throughout the paper. I was amazed at the clarity she gave me. I respected her warnings about not "blaming the victims," but most importantly, when I saw her "No No No," written on one page where I had indicated that a female will bleed for the better part of her adult life, I had to smile and realized that I lacked the wisdom that comes through the experience of becoming a Grandmother. In fact, women sorely lack the wisdom of the Grandmothers. We need this wisdom not only for the welfare of the planet, but for the direction and encouragement required to grow old gracefully rather than fearfully.

The Guidance of a Crone

Take a moment to think about a Crone who has recently helped you, or who at one time may have helped you. Tell her story.

Paula Gunn Allen in her book *The Sacred Hoop*, reminds us of the importance of remembering our Grandmothers:

> We as feminists must be aware of our history on this continent (America). We need to recognize that the same forces that devastated the gynarchies of Britain and the Continent also devastated the ancient African civilizations, and we must know that those same materialistic, antispiritual forces are presently engaged in wiping out the same gynarchical values, along with the peoples who adhere to them, in Latin America. I am convinced that those wars were and continue to be about the imposition of patriarchal civilization over the holistic, pacifist, and spirit-based gynarchies they supplant. To that end the wars of imperial conquest have not been solely or even mostly waged over the land and its resources, but they have been fought within the bodies, minds, and hearts of the people of the Earth for dominion over them. I think this is the reason traditionals say we must remember our origins, our cultures, our histories (and herstory), our mothers and Grandmothers, for without that memory, which implies continuance rather than nostalgia, we are doomed to engulfment by a paradigm that is fundamentally inimical to the vitality, autonomy, and self-empowerment essential for satisfying high-quality life.

Yes, the time of the Grandmother Revolution is here. We must join together to create a better society for women to grow older in. The stance begins in our own minds and hearts, and then it needs to be enforced in our own families. This, after all, is where all change begins.

● ◑ ○ ◑

NOTES

1. Barbara G. Walker, *The Crone: Woman of Age, Wisdom, and Power* (Harper & Row-San Francisco,1985), p. 31.

2. Walker, Ibid, p. 14.

3. Walker, Ibid, p. 49.

4. Walker, Ibid, p. 30.

GRANDMOTHER

KISMA '90

Chapter Twelve

The Grandmothers' Lodge

We simply must recover this Grandmother's voice and the power of this stage in life as menopausal women. The first step in this reclaiming is women gathering together to share the experience of menopause, the taboo, and the wisdom.

—Sedonia Cahill

Writing the third section of this book has been much harder than anticipated. I so sincerely wish to touch the hearts of women, and yet, having not undergone my own menopause and entered the Grandmothers' Lodge, I seem at a loss for words. The greatest gift received, however, has been the encouragement received from the women who are postmenopausal.

During the past weekend I attended a retreat with the Core Sisters of Long Beach WomanSpirit. The retreat was held at the Crane's Nest in Long Beach. Iona Washburn is the owner of this beautiful Bed & Breakfast Inn. She is a Crone in the truest sense of the word. In a discussion we had over this book, I told her that I felt the attitude toward women of age would not entirely change until those of us who are now younger pass into that stage of life. Iona agreed. However, she impressed upon me that it *must* also begin with the current Grandmothers. She finished by saying, "I think it is time someone put on a Crone Festival!"

Through her words I realized that the need for festivals of this kind are desperately needed. For years we've been putting on seasonal celebrations, monthly Moon circles, women spirituality conferences, feminist retreats, yet we do not regularly honor the Crone.

Brooke Medicine Eagle (a very wise teacher on the wisdom of the women's ways) explains that:

> . . . when our elders step across the threshold of the Grandmother Lodge they become the Keepers of the Law. No longer is their attention consumed with the creation and rearing of their own family. In this sense, they have no children, and in our ways those who are not parent to any specific child are parents to ALL CHILDREN. Thus their attention turns to the children of All Our Relations—their own children, the children of their friends, their clan or tribe, and the children of all the hoops: the Two-Leggeds, the Four-Leggeds, the Wingeds, the Finned, the Green-Growing Ones, and all others. Our relationship with this great circle of Life rests ultimately in their hands. They must give-away this responsibility by modeling, teaching, and sharing the living of this law in everyday life—to men, women, children—that all might come into balance in this way.[1]

It is important that we honor these women, encouraging them to become the above models and teach us how to honor relationships again. Let us begin by sponsoring Croning Rituals. If it is not possible to put on a "community" Crone Festival, perhaps we can put on private ceremonies for ourselves and our friends. The following is the vision I have of the Crone Ritual I will go through when my time of Croning arrives:

> *The night is very dark. The Moon is obscured behind the clouds. It is chilly and so I have a very long, black cloak on that warms me from the night air.*
>
> *I stand at the edge of a cliff looking down upon the crashing waves. I have always loved the ocean. From this cauldron of regeneration, I draw my strength. The salty scent of the water reminds me of blood and I breath it in.*
>
> *Behind me, in the distance, a chorus of women's voices rise up like the lip of a forming wave. They are chanting into the night—calling me to come now. I am the Crone.*

Mother of the night.
Mother of all.
Bring forth your wisdom.
Grace us with your vision.

The heartbeat of the sacred drum joins with the voices. I turn and face the direction the sounds vibrate from. I close my eyes and open, allowing this calling to saturate my heart.

Crone of the light
we honor you this night.
Bring forth your wisdom.
Grace us with your vision.

As I open my eyes, I see a procession of candle light approaching. Two by two they come. Women of every age dressed in flowing red gowns. They are the symbols of the blood power. The reminder of the days of flowing. They are the symbols of the new order. The reminder of the women's ways.

They stop before me and step apart, creating a lined walkway of sparkling light. At the end of this twinkling path stands my daughter. She is dressed in white like I am. She too wears the red sash around her waist, a black cloak over her shoulders. We are reflections of the other; young and old.

My daughter holds her hand out to me. I smile. She smiles. I walk down between the singing women, the candlelight kissing my face.

Daughter of this life
your time has come
you are now a Grandmother
we give you the crown.

Sister of the Moon
this night we honor you
you are now a wise one
we give you the crown.

Mother of the light
this night we honor you
you are now a Crone
we give this crown to you.

Our warm hands take hold as we come together at the end of the procession. This reflection of yesterday embraces me in her arms. She whispers "I love you."

> Grandmother come,
> we take you to the Moon
> to celebrate this croning
> the passage of time comes soon.

Together we turn and walk, journey back to the sacred temple that has been decorated for this Rite that honors my entrance into Cronehood.

> Wise One for you,
> in honor of all you do,
> we sing the song of croning
> and pass the crown to you.

My daughter and I kneel at the threshold of the sacred temple. We touch our foreheads to the praying stone and send our blessings into MaMa Earth. A Handmaiden in waiting, brings forth a chalice of purified wine. I take the chalice from her hand and hold it to my heart. Then drinking full, I empty the chalice and sit it upside down beside the praying stone.

> It's time to go inside,
> the ritual now begins.
> This night the Crone shall emerge
> into your precious skin.

My daughter rises, and together she and the Handmaiden pull back the shimmering veil doorway. As the inner sanctuary—newly transformed—is revealed, my heart feels as if it has been blasted open. Tears begin to form.

The altar of the Lady is adorned with flickering light. Fringed fabric of red, black and white is draped everywhere. Deep, deep colored red roses are sprinkled across the floor and in the center of the room stands a magnificent golden sword.

> Mother of the night.
> Mother of all.
> Bring forth your wisdom.
> Grace us with your vision.

I stand and enter. I move to the altar and peer down upon the symbols of cowrie shells and spiraled shells, cauldrons of birth, masks of death, seeds of life, illustrations of women with grey hair dressed in silver. Behind me the rustling garments of the women entering the room remind me I am not alone in this new stage of life I now enter.

Tonight I turn 60. Tonight is my third rite of passage. Tonight I receive the crown. Tonight I become fully empowered as Wise One—the Crone.

> *Crone of the light*
> *we honor you this night.*
> *Bring forth your wisdom.*
> *Grace us with your vision.*

Let us create the ceremony honoring the special woman who is crossing this threshold. In doing so we give support to her as she enters into, perhaps, the greatest of all responsibilities.

When the Moon is full, let us come together in beauty and grace and heartfulness to shower the wise one with gifts and tell her what she has meant to us; the example her life has been for our community. Let us dance the circle dance around her and sing songs in honor of her.

As the rites of passage wanes to a closing, let the new Crone be reminded of the primary responsibility she is charged with; that of nurturing and renewing All Her Relations, and speaking forth when the need for change is at hand.

At the end of the rite, let us encourage her to speak as Crone and share a wisdom with us; making her personal affirmation of power.

A Croning Ritual

Ground and center all participants. Form a circle by holding hands. All breath together to establish a sense of oneness. Have someone play a drum, beating the heartbeat of MaMa Earth.

Purify the participants, altar and circle by burning a mixture of sage, cedar and sweetgrass and drawing the smoke over your body (this is known as smudging) with your hands or a feather. Use the feather to fan the smoke over the altar and then walk around the circle fanning the smoke to mark, or "cut" the boundary of the sacred circle.

Call in the directions (East, South, West, North), elements (Air, Fire, Water, Earth), elementals (sylphs, salamanders, undines, gnomes). End by acknowledging Father Sky and MaMa Earth (above and below).

Raise the energy of the circle by chanting and performing the Grandmother Dance (for description of the dance, see Chapter Six).

Have the woman being honored light the altar candles:

> *White* for the Virgin phase of her life. Encourage her to speak about a wisdom learned during this time.

> *Red* for the Mother phase of her life (or if never a mother for the bleeding years). Again, she shares a wisdom learned during this phase.

> *Black* for the Crone phase of her life that she is now in. Let her speak boldly about how she feels about entering this phase.

Invoke the Goddess/Crone aspect.

Sing and dance some more.

Have each woman stand before the Crone and give her a gift. Each woman speaks words of support, or words of honor, blessings, etc. to the Crone.

All gathered circle around the Crone, singing her name, acknowledging her as Grandmother, Wise One, Crone.

Crone declaration made by the woman being honored.

Sing and dance (optional).

Crone gives thanks to all women gathered.

Crone gives thanks to Goddess/Crone.

Crone dismisses directions/elements/elementals/Father Sky/ Mother Earth.

Crone opens circle, ending the rite.

● ◑ ○ ◐

Just as there is a special need for "flow-ers" to have a Moon Lodge, so it is important for the Grandmothers to have a Grandmothers' Lodge. Brooke Medicine Eagle explains that:

> What this (Grandmothers' Lodge) means for women, in very practical terms, is this: When you pass beyond menopause, you have the opportunity for a renewed and deeply power- ful experience of yourself. As you drop away from the still- ness and fear that has been generated by the "over the hill" cultural trance, and open yourself to the truth that lives within you, you will find an incredible challenge for which you are better equipped than any other two-legged. You have the opportunity to sit in council, and using the power of the blood held among you, create a harmonious world around you.[2]

I have visions of the Grandmothers' Lodge as being a group of older women sitting around a kitchen table drinking tea and dis- cussing life. Unlike my formally manifested Moon Lodge (which I hibernate in during my bleeding time and at New Moon), I believe the *physical* Grandmothers' Lodge is the "minds" of older women. Yet, the mind of a postmenopausal woman is virtually uncharted territory, for men have shown little inclination to explore it. In fact, more often then not, the wisdom of the Grandmothers' minds are ignored as nonsense, and so have therefore been denied as an ac- knowledged force in the welfare of our culture (as discussed in Chapter Eleven).

Barbara Walker in her book *The Crone* describes the wisdom of the Crone as being "that wonderful quality that men have described as the mysterious 'feminine intuition,' when in fact the real name of it is: intelligence." This intelligence is required in our culture to bring back the balance that Brooke Medicine Eagle describes.

This means can be achieved through the council of the Grandmothers. With the cumulative experience of many years of living, observing, and relating to others, women may routinely achieve higher levels of understanding the human condition than most men dream of. Therefore allowing us to reach deep insights as to what our community requires.

Walker's closing statement in *The Crone* states:

> . . . if the self-seeking power-lust of mature men were made subject to the 'intuitive' judgment of mature women, instead of the other way round, surely human life and society could be improved. The Earth might become a safer, kinder, healthier place. People might care more for the welfare of future generations. Instead of trying to escape inevitable death in futile fantasies, they might enrich life by honest work on their legacy to their posterity. Women, who have suffered so much at the hands of patriarchal mythmakers, need no longer pretend not to understand their motives. God can't, but woman can call man to account for his gynocidal, genocidal behavior.

Once again, we begin to see just how vitally important the voices of women can be.

Your Wisdom

If you could share an important wisdom gained through a life experience with younger women—this is an experience that has given you support and a positive attitude—what would it be?

Do you know a younger woman you can share this wisdom with? If so, make an appointment to speak with her. Share with her the power behind the women's ways, the power of the blood, the transitions of a woman's life, then issue forth the voice of wisdom. After you have done so, evaluate how empowered you feel, as well as the reaction of the younger woman.

● ◐ ○ ◑

As younger women, let us go to the Grandmothers, the Wise Ones, the Crones and ask for their wisdom. Let us sing the song of honor to them. Let us say:

> *Grandmothers, please show your face proudly*
> *and sing us your songs.*
> *Wise Ones, please teach us, the younger women*
> *how to mature;*

> *share with us the women's ways as you have*
> *experienced them.*
> *Crones, please help us say "no" to the atrocities of man.*

Not only can the Grandmothers help us reach balance in our living, they may be able to help us face death. When we begin honoring age and the wisdom of a long life, we can begin to face death once more with an open-mind.

We live in a society that refuses to accept the fact that death is inevitable. If we strive to eliminate this "fear of death" mentality and accept it as a natural status in life rather than deny its existence, we will be guided back to a state of balance and arrive at a place where we can embrace the life-death cycle, enriching our daily subsistence.

Like the Crone triple aspect of Goddess, our living Grandmothers can be recognized not only as nurturers of Earth's children but also as an embodiment of women's care for the dying and the dead. We must encourage women to face their aging with pride rather than with shame. We must have pride in them.

As shaman women, let us arrive back at the natural place where the cycles of life—birth, growth, decline, death, rebirth—are seen as a complete whole, a wonderfully evolving, enriching, empowering aspect of life. Just as there is power in living, there is power in death. It is the shaman woman who can once again become priestess of the final rite of passage: death, and assist others to cross over the threshold into the world beyond. Through her wisdom, when the time of death draws near, she is able to peacefully sing the Death Song[3] and pass into the invisible cycle through the tender hands of her sister Grandmothers, the wise ones, the Crone.

> *From the middle*
> *Of the great water*
> *I am called by the spirits.*

As we turn toward the women's ways in each phase of the matrix, we begin to remember unrecorded herstory. The beautiful tapestry of wisdom is mended. We arrive at that point of healing where, together, we walk in the sanctity of peace. As this occurs, we will wear—with dignity once more—and stronger than ever before, the title of "Woman."

The following, I believe, is another woman's "remembering" of herstory as it was in the beginning.

VISION[4]

> *She was an old woman, an old woman of the tribe, and her knees ached when she moved, and her body had fleshed out over the years but she was strong.*
>
> *She was the one who sat in the North; who sat in the jaws of the Serpent Mound. To her, the tribe brought their dead and she drummed while the tribe sang the spirit songs and gave honor to the dead. She drummed as grief and memory washed over the body which lay in the Mouth of the Serpent. She drummed as love's magick transformed the power of death; weaving death and life together into the spirit dreams of the tribe.*
>
> *Into the eyes of the living she looked, and when the waves of the voices had slowed, she drummed with their breath and drew their silence to the fire. Between the fire and the Mound, one of the tribe would stand to speak the choice of the Dead. To the chosen Guardian—air, fire, water, earth—the old one would release the spirit of the body as the flesh itself was returned to the cycles of life. She was wise in the ways of death and of sorrow. She was the Earth Drum Woman and the Wolf Star marked her path.*

● ◐ ○ ◑

With this vein of thought, let us consider the gains of forming this Lodge of wise shaman women. Whether or not you are a woman who has had the conscious opportunity to learn and deepen yourself in good relationship throughout your lifetime to better serve yourself in these later years, the time of menopause and croning can be highly productive. A time that can begin the change required in our culture.

Let us remember that change in social patterns produces change in the deity. Conversely, a change in the divine image can produce social change. The time has come for women to deny the angry and war-like male deity that supposedly cursed our sex. We must reject his demands for obedience, praise, service, and money. As we do this we automatically free ourselves from one of the most potent psychological traps power-hungry men ever set for us. It has been power-hungry men and their angry God who have told us we must serve and obey abusive husbands. It has been power-hungry men and their angry God who have ordered us to bear children we didn't want, and to furthermore, give them the lawful right of lineage. It has been power-hungry men and their angry God who have called us sinful for experiencing sexual pleasure.

As the need for new deity comes into full life in our hearts, we must also join together and reinstate a full three-dimensional feminine deity, with her own authentic theology, with her law of love and peaceful living, with her nurturance and beauty. Through the Grandmothers' Lodge, as well as during the previous stages of our lives, we can issue forth our voices, based on the wisdoms gained through the experience of refusing to be the scapegoat of all evil and become the upholders of the Law of Good Relationship.

If a leader is not leading the people in a way that is good for all people, let the shaman women be the voice of change. If the industrial companies continue to pollute and kill our environment, let the shaman women be the voice of change. These voices can automatically become part of our culture once acknowledged and encouraged to nurture and renew the people by taking action. Brooke Medicine Eagle sums up the above by saying:

> When I look about the world around me, I see that every critical issue facing us is an issue of relationship—whether it is with the Russian people, within our too-often dysfunctional family systems, or whether it is our alienation from each other and from nature, or our awakening willingness to relate to ourselves as co-creators with All That Is. These are the matters we are being asked to address and to take spiritual action within.[5]

Shaman women understand these relationships. The benefits gained from the re-entry of the Grandmothers' Lodge in our culture will be a shifting in relationships. The time of power has come for those who hold their blood, those who are very powerful shaman women who stand for nurturing and renewing and beauty. Let us support the women of age now, and prepare for the day when we, too, shall become a Crone.

Those of us who already gather in circles need to seek out the Crone and bring her into them. We need to honor her by acknowledging her Crone status. In our communities we need to sponsor Festivals of Croning so that these Grandmothers can come together and meet. Their meeting will begin the gatherings required for the development of Lodges. As the Grandmothers begin gathering together, they can determine the common interests, skills, and goals among themselves just as younger women do and "voice" these interests, skills and goals into our communities. I would like to believe that the Grandmothers will not meet only to increase their own learning and understanding, but to also open their Lodges to younger women; providing a place to go to for guidance in the women's ways.

May this most powerful, creative, expressive, and wonderful time of freedom expand into all aspects of our lives, and the consummation of the women's ways be solidified.

> *I live, but I will not live forever.*
> *Mysterious Moon, you only remain,*
> *Powerful Sun, you alone remain,*
> *Wonderful Earth, you remain forever.*
> *All of us (warriors) must die.*[6]

● ◑ ○ ◐

NOTES

1. Brooke Medicine Eagle, "Grandmother Lodge," *Shaman's Drum*, Spring, 1986.

2. Ibid.

3. Paula Gunn Allen, *The Sacred Hoop* (Beacon Press, 1986), p. 67.

4. Tasa (Reprinted with permission from *Spirited Women*, (August 1990/9990, Vol. 3, Is. 9).

5. Eagle, Ibid.

6. Allen, Ibid, p. 70.

Epilogue

I sit here reflecting on the previous chapters of this book and know that there is so much yet unsaid that needs to be shared, but I'm not sure what words those are.

From my experience as Goddess worshipper and feminist, I know in my heart that the woman's ways are just beginning to unfold and though there are diverse and wonderful books available on woman spirituality, they are but a particle of the wisdoms we have yet to explore.

As women become more politically active, and eventually gain higher seats in governmental office, the cultural arena of life will begin to shift; for the Grandmothers' voices will finally be heard.

Until that time, all women must begin rethinking and reclaiming those aspects of our lives that have been stolen from us and/or that we have been taught to hide in shame. In liberating our own minds we begin to liberate the minds and lives of future women.

The feminine energy is desperately needed to gain a balance in this living. This is not by any means a new thought to those of us who have been involved in Goddess and/or feminist communities. However, the general community still lacks this understanding. I believe it will be through women, that this understanding is achieved.

How do we become sponsors of such a message? The first step is getting in contact with our bodies; learning our biology, and then working in cooperation with its natural cycle. As the divinity in this cooperation is revealed, women blossom into a new outlook on life, and, above all else, femininity.

Practically all of history is based on change by force. I believe the new age, the new way of living will be brought about by nurturing and wellness; softly, tenderly, peacefully.

Yes, I may seem to be an idealist, but as a woman walking her path in this current age, I cannot accept this new way of living manifesting by any other means. The Grandmother voice inside of me is tired of war and hate and bigotry and hunger and housing problems and revolutionary rebels that advocate violence and polluted elements and financial instability and the current systems of government. I recognize the sickness that eats away at the core of this world's people, and I am saddened, but not hopeless.

Vision tells me there is a *better way*. Dreams show me this better way is attainable. Cycles bring me closer to the natural rhythms of this better way.

Each month as I bleed and honor my womanness, I gain deeper insights into world pain and suffering, as well as the possibilities where change can take place. I am shown the solutions that can be enacted in my own life to bring me one step closer to this better way.

I recognize that, as insignificant as my life may be, if each of us join together and take part in vision, we *can* change the world. This joining of forces must come from all peoples of every race.

Sitting here, I know that this better way of living will probably not take place in my lifetime. I can accept this however, and hope that at the very least the change will begin in my child's lifetime, and rest gracefully in the pleasant thought that it is the future generations who will ultimately benefit.

Though I am not sure whether reincarnation is a reality, I do feel that some part of me has always been alive and so, therefore, will continue to be. Whether this part of my aliveness is simply the organic nature of my essential beingness or not, I find strength in this concept. It is this strength that propels me into doing my part to ensure the safety and welfare of future generations.

I turn to the women in my writing because I truly know in my heart that women can make a difference in this concept. Though we have been denied and suppressed for thousands of years, the future is still ours.

This future is not one based on "power–over" or a mind–set of superiority, it is a future that is one of healed women and men *loving life!*

Loving Life. I think these two simple words are the epitome of what all my writing, and my life for that matter, is about.

To those of you who share my words, whether you be female or male, may your life incorporate the wisdom of loving life, and may this attitude change the very foundation upon which you now stand.

Let us all look forward to enjoying to the fullest our living, but let us be compassionate for the future generations that have as much right to experience life as we do.

Ho. Blessed Be.

LUNATION CALENDAR JOURNAL

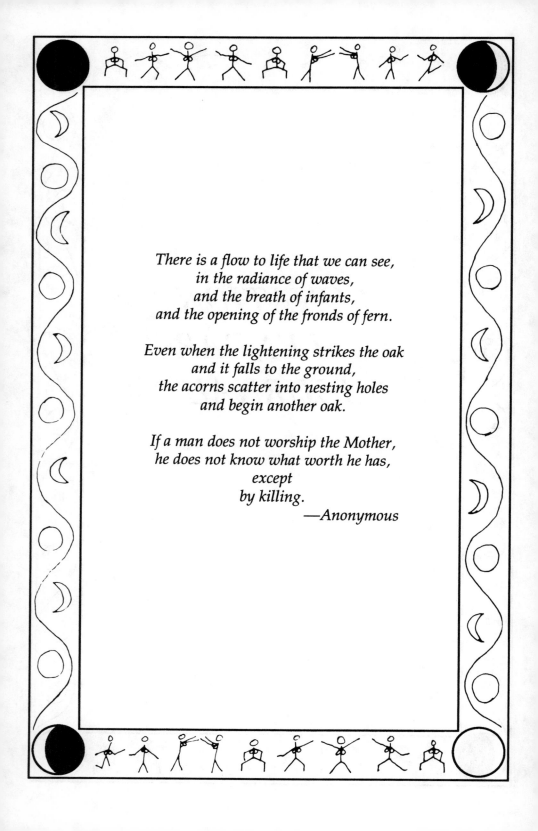

There is a flow to life that we can see,
in the radiance of waves,
and the breath of infants,
and the opening of the fronds of fern.

Even when the lightening strikes the oak
and it falls to the ground,
the acorns scatter into nesting holes
and begin another oak.

If a man does not worship the Mother,
he does not know what worth he has,
except
by killing.
—Anonymous

Lunation Calendar
Journal

When we make a conscious decision to work in co-operation with our bodies and our relationship with Grandmother Moon, charting the progress of our achievements is very empowering. *A Lunation Calendar Journal* roadmaps such progress; revealing the changes we have initiated in our lives and also allowing us to understand "self" better and better.

This book of "revelations" will encourage us to apply ourselves in other area's of our lives; for through reviewing the passage of time as charted in our journals and the achievements we've made, we come to embrace our magickal abilities. Through altering, changing drastically, or creating a more intimate world, we come to understand that magick gets quite ordinary when we live with it! In this ordinariness, we can continually fulfill our own needs.

The following is an excerpt from my own journal. This example of how to use this Lunar Calendar Journal, and how revealing your entries can be, is given in the hopes of inspiring you further to bring the magick into your ordinary life in a non–ordinary way!

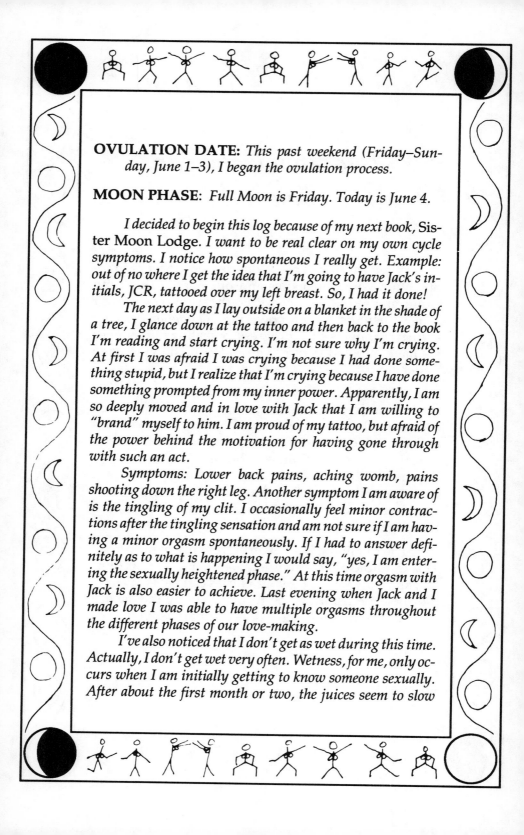

OVULATION DATE: *This past weekend (Friday–Sunday, June 1–3), I began the ovulation process.*

MOON PHASE: *Full Moon is Friday. Today is June 4.*

I decided to begin this log because of my next book, Sister Moon Lodge. *I want to be real clear on my own cycle symptoms. I notice how spontaneous I really get. Example: out of no where I get the idea that I'm going to have Jack's initials, JCR, tattooed over my left breast. So, I had it done!*

The next day as I lay outside on a blanket in the shade of a tree, I glance down at the tattoo and then back to the book I'm reading and start crying. I'm not sure why I'm crying. At first I was afraid I was crying because I had done something stupid, but I realize that I'm crying because I have done something prompted from my inner power. Apparently, I am so deeply moved and in love with Jack that I am willing to "brand" myself to him. I am proud of my tattoo, but afraid of the power behind the motivation for having gone through with such an act.

Symptoms: Lower back pains, aching womb, pains shooting down the right leg. Another symptom I am aware of is the tingling of my clit. I occasionally feel minor contractions after the tingling sensation and am not sure if I am having a minor orgasm spontaneously. If I had to answer definitely as to what is happening I would say, "yes, I am entering the sexually heightened phase." At this time orgasm with Jack is also easier to achieve. Last evening when Jack and I made love I was able to have multiple orgasms throughout the different phases of our love-making.

I've also noticed that I don't get as wet during this time. Actually, I don't get wet very often. Wetness, for me, only occurs when I am initially getting to know someone sexually. After about the first month or two, the juices seem to slow

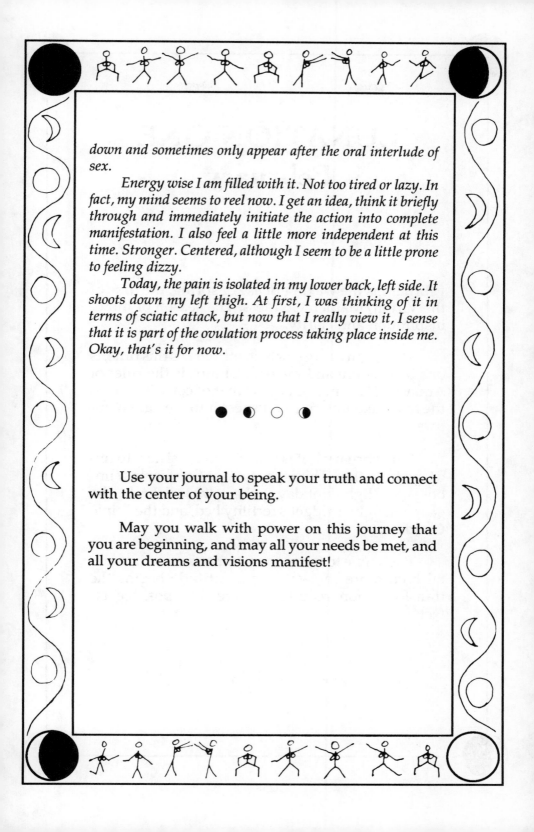

down and sometimes only appear after the oral interlude of sex.

Energy wise I am filled with it. Not too tired or lazy. In fact, my mind seems to reel now. I get an idea, think it briefly through and immediately initiate the action into complete manifestation. I also feel a little more independent at this time. Stronger. Centered, although I seem to be a little prone to feeling dizzy.

Today, the pain is isolated in my lower back, left side. It shoots down my left thigh. At first, I was thinking of it in terms of sciatic attack, but now that I really view it, I sense that it is part of the ovulation process taking place inside me. Okay, that's it for now.

Use your journal to speak your truth and connect with the center of your being.

May you walk with power on this journey that you are beginning, and may all your needs be met, and all your dreams and visions manifest!

LUNATION ONE
February

February is the waxing phase of spring, the time of the Virgin/Maiden Goddess. The season of mind, inspiration and clarity.

Aquarian energy, which influences this time, is one of freedom and magick. Uranus is the ruler of Aquarius. Uranian energy is that of consciousness, the re-awakening consciousness into the light of future life.

On February 2, it is traditional for sisters to undergo Initiation. This is the time of Candlemas/Imbolg—a High Holiday, when we celebrate the growing light, Bridget's fertility bed, and the Triple Goddess.

It is a time to focus on our attitudes as our mental bodies are re-awakening. Attitude begins the transformation required in creating positive effects.

The Crescent Moon is the most powerful time to work our magick during this month. Perform "seed planting" rituals at this time and watch your dreams manifest over the waxing year.

The Full Moon of February is known as the Chaste Moon or Sylph's Moon. Dance in the air at this time and receive clarity on your beauty path.

Pay attention to the rising Sun each morning. Face East, the guardian energy of the Spring, and open to receive the new rays of this power source by chanting:

> *Greetings Brightness,*
> *blessed be.*
> *Thy power unlocks*
> *the golden key.*
>
> *Make this day*
> *be good for me.*
> *As I do will*
> *so mote it be.*

The Goddesses that are celebrated around the world this month are: Bridget, Selene, Our Lady of Lourdes, Diana, Victoria, Caristia, Hygeia, Februa.

Ovulation Date:

Moon Phase:

Bleeding Time:

Moon Phase:

LUNATION TWO
March

March is the full phase of spring, the time of the Vernal Equinox, when Persephone rises from the underworld as Kore, the Virgin of Spring. The rebirthing of spring is the sign of Demeter's happiness at being rejoined with her daughter, Persephone.

The Vernal or Spring Equinox is a time of equilibrium when day and night are of equal length and the tide of the wheel of the year flows smoothly. We can use the energy of this seasonal shift by grounding into the deep core of MaMa Earth. This grounding will act as an anchor, holding us firmly as the energy moves forward turning the wheel into ever increasing action.

The fullness of spring surrounds us and, like the Pisces fishes, we can look in both directions with little effort. Neptune possessively presides over the energies and prods the subconscious mind with his trident, inspiring the intuitive facilities.

It is a time of inspiration. Intuition is re-emerging after a dark winter and all subtle bodies are re-aligning. We can use our intuition in conjunction with the Full Moon of March to delve to depths never thought possible. Our highest ideals can be looked at and scrutinized for realistic possibilities.

The Full Moon is of importance this month. It is known as the Seed Moon. We can use the Full Moon light as a "magick mirror" and view the progress of the seeds planted with the Crescent Moon of February.

> *Magick mirror of the night,*
> *glowing fully with soft, muted light.*
> *Guide my vision,*
> *help me to see,*
> *the progress of my seeds*
> *planted last month with thee.*

The Goddesses that are celebrated around the world this month are: Vesta, Rhiannon, Isis, Aphrodite, Artemis, Cybele, Anna Perenna, Astarte, Athena, Minerva, Eostara, Luna.

Ovulation Date:

Moon Phase:

Bleeding Time:

Moon Phase:

LUNATION THREE
April

April is the waning phase of spring; a contradiction to the term "waning" because we are moving into the most active season of the year.

Ruled by the Ram and Mars, gives us a burst of action; a sense of strength. The emphasis at this time, however, is on identity. Being in the season of spring and re-birth, renewal, etc., we can use this cycle to evaluate our current status and map out the transformation we wish to effect. The use of Tiger's eye can be very powerful at this time.

The Full Moon of April is known as the Just Moon.

The Waning Moon is the power powerful time of this month. Using Tiger's eye we can journey deep inside. Withdraw from society long enough to listen and receive.

The Goddesses that are celebrated around the world this month are: Venus, Cybele, Kwan Yin, Ceres, Hathor, Ishtar, Flora.

Grandmothers
I call to you this day,
do you hear me, Grandmothers?

Women from the living past,
my female ancestors,
I seek to honor you.

I surrender my little ego.
I surrender and
put it aside.

Like the snake,
I am hibernating,
ready to shed my skin.

As I do so,
Grandmothers,
I open to receive your wisdom.

Please help guide me
along my woman's path.
Please help me to heal.

Ovulation Date:

Moon Phase:

Bleeding Time:

Moon Phase:

LUNATION FOUR
May

May is the waxing phase of summer, the time of the Mother Goddess. This is the season of healing. Disease is the racing of the mind; mind exhaustion. We have now entered the phase of body action and/or awareness. The action of our internal fire roaring to life, engulfs and burns away the blockages of the mind.

I am a circle,
I am healing you.
You are a circle,
You are healing me.
Unite us, be as one.
Unite us, be as one.

May is the month of Taurus, ruled by the planet Venus. A month of love and sexuality; tenderness and values. May 1 is Beltane—a High Holiday when sexuality and fertility of all life is honored.

The element of Fire is most prominent during this time. Fire is the transforming element of nature—the spirit of life. *Igne Natura Renovatur Integra* (All Nature is Renewed by Fire). Think: INRI.

During this waxing month of summer, be conscious of your own fire and the flame of candle, bonfire, hearth fire, lightning, starlight and sunlight, becoming one with all fire and one with the illuminated spirit of Goddess.

Let us use the Crescent Moon to perform "pyromancy" (fire gazing), or dance around its spurting arms.

Fire spirits
dancing so bright,
show me the inner
world of my life.
Dancing and reaching
up toward the sky,
Fiery spirits
purge me
of all lies.

The Full Moon of May is known as the Lover's Moon. Dance with the fiery spirit of passion and receive the strength and encouragement to continue down your path.

The Goddesses that are celebrated around the world this month are: Bona Dea, Sheila Na Gig, Bendis, Artemis, Tao, Ceres, Virgin Mary, Proserpine, Maria.

Ovulation Date:

Moon Phase:

Bleeding Time:

Moon Phase:

LUNATION FIVE
June

June is the full phase of summer when communication becomes the focal point. Greatly influenced by Gemini and Mercury, June's energy is rich with the power of intellectual communication and awareness. We need not fear our words, but rejoicingly and actively seek to speak our truth, affirming our worthiness.

This is the month that affirmations, or personal chants become extremely potent, especially if combined with the usage of candle burning. The intellect has been inspired by the passion of fire. Now it is time to integrate that passion into our spirits.

Candle glimmer,
candle glow.
Take this wish
and make it so.

The longest day of the year, celebrated this month is known as the Summer Solstice—a High Holiday.

The Full Moon of June is known as the Mead or Honey Moon. We can dance under her luminous light and send forth our vibrations of love—love of life, love of others, love of self.

As we celebrate our universal sense of love, we can communicate the elusive quality of peace to our sisters and brothers, teaching our children the peace chant, and impregnating the Earth's vibration with our voices.

> *May peace prevail on Earth.*
> *May peace prevail in our minds,*
> *May peace prevail in our hearts,*
> *May peace prevail in our lives,*
> *May I know peace.*
> *May my ancestors know peace*
> *May my children's children*
> *   unto seven generations know peace,*
> *May peace prevail on Earth,*

As we sing forth our peace chants, we greatly help bring back a more balanced way of living. In doing so, we reform the partnership of polarities. Balance and Peace—two great goals for all of the human race to obtain!

The Goddesses that are celebrated around the world this month are: Carna, Juno, Pax, Vesta, Epona, Hera, Muses, Litha, Fors Fortuna.

Ovulation Date:

Moon Phase:

Bleeding Time:

Moon Phase:

LUNATION SIX
July

July is the waning phase of summer. Though the pace of life is in full action, the energy is at a mellow high. July is the time of Cancer, the Crab. It is the time of nurturing, touch and security. Ruled by the ever elusive Moon (the female principle), the home, the family and "self" become the center of focus.

This is the time when the emotional body is on fire. It is a time of preparing for the release that will be made in the upcoming months of Autumn. Life is at that standstill point like the sprinter at the moment before the gun goes off and the race begins and is over. This is the time of playfulness and tenderness. Although sexuality has been ignited, the Moon seems to shadow it and subdue the erotic by transforming it into the love of family.

Mother, hear me calling,
I am old, I am old.
Mother, hear me calling,
I must grow, I must grow.

In this season of summer, the Mother Goddess has been activated. The Mother remembers us to the sisterhood of all women. And in our remembering, we come face to face with the realization that this sisterhood has been shattered and scattered about the Earth far too long.

As the healing energy is native in the season of summer, women are now in a native season of healing. And as the fire is the power of the summer, so the blinding light of our healing can show us how to transform our lives.

As a woman choosing to heal herself, we must begin by turning the characteristics associated with mother (nurturance, love, compassion, understanding, protection, caretaking) onto ourselves. We must mother ourselves.

Let us use the magick of fire during our empowerment of Mother Goddesshood by remembering that first comes destruction, then creation, and that this is the way of the Goddess, of Shakti (feminine) energy. As fire burns through the old structures, eliminating them, transmuting their energies to a higher vibration level, then releasing the creative energy to allow the cure—so we too can use the Shakti power to transform our spirits and heal our souls!

The Full Moon of July is known as the Hearth Moon or Maiden Moon. We can use this energy to evoke playfulness into our lives.

The Goddesses that are celebrated around the world this month are: Cerridwen, Juno, Our Lady of Fatima, Demeter, Amaterasu-O-Me-Kami, Athena, Sekhmet, Bast.

Ovulation Date:

Moon Phase:

Bleeding Time:

Moon Phase:

LUNATION SEVEN
August

With the seventh lunation, the wheel turns into autumn. Autumn is the secret time, for it is the twilight of seasons when we are caught between life and death. The turning of the wheel takes us down into the center of woman power. If compared to a woman's Moon time, autumn is the waning Moon, the time of bleeding...the womb...the blood mysteries.

In this phase of introspection we come to that place of relationships: family, friends, lovers, co-workers, employers, employees, etc. We have become awakened with the spring and begun actively healing ourselves with the summer action.

August is the waxing phase of autumn, the time of the Crone Goddess. If during the season of the Crone we take the time to journey deep within our psyche, she will bring us face to face with our fears.

The phase of Leo, the male principle, is underway; ruled by the Sun, we are brought face to face with the identity of ego. We are constantly reminded that now is not the time to be selfish or possessive, but join together and form a clan; a working unit. It is a time to surrender to life's flow.

Medicine Woman where art thou?
Medicine Woman, come now.
I am right here.
I am right here, right here.
I am with you.
I am with you.
Deep, deep within you.

As shaman woman, the journey into darkness becomes an intense time. As power woman walks her path, she must be willing to release the extra baggage from her life, just as the womb releases the unnecessary endometrium during the bleeding time, and opens to the changes that are smoldering just beneath the surface. Being within her power and yet available to others is the balancing of Temperance. It is the wisdom of the Crone that teaches us how to endure and pass through the season of release most effectively.

The first day of August is the beginning of the Harvest and is referred to as Lammas, the time of gathering the foods that grow wild or are cultivated. We can acknowledge this High Holiday from the ego point of view and use it to "release" our ego just as MaMa Earth releases her hold on the food of her body, providing us with abundance so that our lives may continue.

The Full Moon of August is known as the Poet's Moon. Allow your own deep sonnets to surface. You might be surprised at the richness your words now hold.

The Goddesses that are celebrated around the world this month are: Virgin Mary, Hecate, Isis, Virgo, Ceres, Ops, Ilmatar.

Ovulation Date:

Moon Phase:

Bleeding Time:

Moon Phase:

LUNATION EIGHT
September

September is the full phase of autumn, the time of self-realizations and courage. We have traveled the wheel from rebirth (spring), through growth and healing (summer), and now into the very center of our self-realization (autumn).

The energy is influenced by Virgo; a time when we find we will respond to encouragement and appreciation, and have a deep hunger for sharing experiences and self-realization with others. The planet Mercury rules Virgo. Mercury represents reasoning ability, the mind and ways of communication. We can use these energies to go fully into our self-expression. We can travel, without fear or hesitation, into the center of our darkness; our shadow-self that we always blame for bringing the negative life-situations.

The Autumnal Equinox (September 21-23), the celebration of Mabon is the High Holiday. It is a time of balance between the dark and the light.

The full moon of September is known as the Harvest Moon. With the energy of the Full Moon, we can begin to harvest the changes of self into our inner sanctum. We can take the soft, muted light of the Crone in her fullness, and ask her to share with us the richness resulted from all our hard, interpersonal work we've been focusing on.

Harvest Moon,
up in the sky,
Smile down on me.
Oh Crone, you are
in full glory,
in this ripe time
of your season.
And I honor you,
will you show me,
will you help me,
will you honor me,
by mirroring back
the richness
of the changes
that have taken place
inside of me?

The Goddesses that are celebrated around the world this month are: Laskshmi, Radha, Artemis, Venus, Kore-Demeter-Iacchos, Libra.

Ovulation Date:

Moon Phase:

Bleeding Time:

Moon Phase:

LUNATION NINE
October

October is the waning phase of autumn, the most powerful time of the Crone energy. Through the Crone we can come to understand better the elements of love and wisdom, gaining a truer sense of balance in our lives.

We must look closely at the masks we have worn. Go with these masks and find new ones, new faces, bring them forth and examine them to see if the eye holes will reveal more truth than the old ones. We must be willing to come face to face with the monster masks as well as the beauty masks we each wear. It has often been said that "Beauty is in the eye of the beholder," and that sometimes the "Ugliest exterior can house a most beautiful Spirit." Find the balance between the two.

The Full Moon of October is known as the Hunter's Moon or Snow Moon.

The Waning Moon is the most powerful. We can use this time to go deeper than ever before, and make contact with the Shadow Queen that resides within. Once we travel through the shadow, many fears diminish, and we begin to really access our inner Goddess power.

The Feast of Hecate is celebrated at the time of Samhain, Hallowmas. This is the third and final harvest of the year. The veils are thin this night. As we participate in the feast of Hecate and honor our ancestors, the spirit world overlaps with the physical and we can commune with the universal mind.

> O, Hecate, tis Hallow's Eve,
> Set us free.
> Ancient Mother, Guardian Crone,
> Hear my call,
> Split the veil this night for me!

We can use this powerful time of Crone to honor the Crone within, prepare ourselves to one day become her. For the woman who is already in her Croning years, we can honor her by holding a special ceremony just for her.

> Crone of the light
> we honor you this night.
> Bring forth your wisdom.
> Grace us with your vision.

The Goddesses that are celebrated around the world this month are: Sophia, Demeter, Fortuna, Redix, Hecate.

Ovulation Date:

Moon Phase:

Bleeding Time:

Moon Phase:

LUNATION TEN
November

November is the waxing phase of winter, the time of the Great Goddess; it is the season of spirit, dreaming and death.

> *It is to the north I go,*
> *to touch the midnight hour.*
> *As the stag prances on high mountain tops,*
> *my strength bounds forth:*
> *Spirit—my friend,*
> *Enrich this circle I dance within.*

Ruled by the passionate sting of the scorpion's tail and the lord of the underworld, Pluto, we enter the realm of the subconscious; the occult. The deep intensity of our desires are penetrated. We can learn how to be temperate with our emotions, and aware of those feelings of vengefulness and sarcasm.

The Crescent Moon can begin to take u s into our dreams where many mysteries of the occult can be experienced.

Spirits of the dreamtime,
Ancient Ones I call to thee.
Come meet me in my dreams,
come to me
and set me free,
from the bonds of this physical body.
Set me free to walk with thee
in the realm beyond shadowland,
in the land between
waking and sleep.

The Full Moon of November is known as the Sylph's Moon or Philosopher's Moon. It at one time was also known as the Dark Moon because it lead us into the darkest time of life—the season of death and repose.

Full Moon magick can be coupled with the usage of smoldering herbs that help a trancing effect, such as wormwood, mugwort and valerian. The usage of a crystal provides a most powerful way to connect with the element of Earth, which is most powerful in the season of winter. Crystals speak to us and remind us of our deep ecology, for they are the bones of MaMa Earth.

The Goddesses that are celebrated around the world this month are: Kami, Hecate, Artemis, Gaia.

Ovulation Date:

Moon Phase:

Bleeding Time:

Moon Phase:

LUNATION ELEVEN
December

December is the full phase of winter. This is the time of higher mind. This is also the time of visualization, preparing to give birth to new plans for future manifestation. In the darkest time of the year, we can begin laying the foundation of optimism and enthusiasm toward our future. We can begin creating our new philosophy, aspiring to reach new levels of higher education—the education of internal wisdoms.

The Full Moon of December is known as the Yle Moon or Hecate Moon. The magic at this time is vibrating at an even level. We can use the energy to receive new aspirations for the new year. Visualization techniques become vitally important.

The Winter Solstice births forth the new Sun. At this time we can give-away to the darkness our negativity so that we can rebirth into our visualized persona with the new solar Sun of spring. This is the self-image that we have been working on over the previous seasons.

I am opening up in sweet surrender
to the illuminous love light of the one above.
I am opening up in sweet surrender
to the illuminous love light of the one above
I am opening, I am opening.

When we open up to receive the new energy being birthed and sent toward our Earth plane, we will receive an illumination in our centers, hearts, minds and body. This new illumination will help animate the new image of self that has been in transformation over the past lunations.

Once filled with the illumination of the new animated you, as the dawn arrives following the longest night of the year, this new self vision can also be birthed. The birthing of this new self vision becomes the foundation of who we are for the next entire turning of the wheel of the seasons. She becomes the self, who will bring forth the new level of lessons to be worked with, the new set of changes to be undergone. She becomes the new essence of our Higher Self, made a little more visible to ourselves and the world!

The Goddesses that are celebrated around the world this month are: Bona Dea, Athena, Ixchel, Tonantzin, Lucina, Ops, Acca, Larentia, Astarte, Demeter, Vesta, Hestia.

Ovulation Date:

Moon Phase:

Bleeding Time:

Moon Phase:

LUNATION TWELVE
January

January is the waning phase of winter, a time to take a look at death and reclaim it as part of the cycles of life.

Influenced by the scrupulous, yet practical qualities of the seagoat, Capricorn, and governed by the taskmaster of the zodiac, Saturn, January is the most abstruse energy to be used in making contact with the Earth element. This can be done through the very bones of our skeletal system which seems to depict the reality of death to our very immaterial minds.

It is a time of truth and wisdom. Working with Great Goddess to understand the cycles of life. Touching deeply our bones.

I am the wisdom of the Universe.
I am the death after birth.
I am the darkness of mysteries rich and deep,
that none living dare to speak.

Great Goddess moves with us through life, supporting the many roles we play, laying the foundation for making possible the manifestation we create, providing the structure needed to release and allow change and death to cycle in and through our minds, bodies and souls.

When we claim our power, or take back our power, it is the Great Goddess who we are portraying. When we stand up for our beliefs and the welfare of others, it is Great Goddess. She is the motivating factor behind the most magnificent strength portrayed through women of substance, who initiate change on a social/political/economical and ecological level.

Through the Moon Lodge, through the Grandmothers' voice we begin to realize the full potency of woman. In the Grandmothers' Lodge through the voice of the Grandmothers we can put into action the magnificent strength of woman. Together, women of all ages can create the changes and lay the new foundations of right relationship, and build the new way.

The Full Moon of January is known as the Cronus Moon.

The Waning Moon is most important during this time. We can trance into the deepest sense of our ecology and touch the bone structure of all life. We are in essence preparing for our rebirthing back into physical activity.

The Goddesses that are celebrated around the world this month are: Inanna, Kore, Justicia, Pax.

Ovulation Date:

Moon Phase:

Bleeding Time:

Moon Phase:

LUNATION THIRTEEN
Rebirth

The time of rebirthing is at hand. The great Wheel of the Year has turned one full turn of the solar year. Thirteen lunations consist in the solar year.

Throughout and about, transformation begins,
Within and without, the wheel doth spin.
White, red and black,
the center of Spirit
comes dancing and flowing
to my circle of life
once again!

This is the time of examining the progress made over the last year. By using the awareness of your potentialities you can pass through initiation into the phase of the "spiritual woman" who walks her life in balance, in harmony with nature and the seasons.

A time of celebration is at hand. Honor yourself. Honor your sisters. Honor your female ancestors. Honor MaMa Earth. Honor Grandmother Moon. Honor Great Goddess; the First Mother—Shaman Woman!

From the belly of the cauldron
from the inside of my womb
comes forth the secret elixir
the magickal blood of life.

Powerful, I stand,
face painted red.
Powerful, I dance,
inner thighs streaming red.
Powerful, I sing,
vibrations rippling red.

as the endometrium sheds,
I shed the veil of silence.
As the endometrium sheds,
I shed the veil of enforced shame.
As the endometrium sheds,
I shed the prison of patriarchy.

From the belly of the cauldron
from the inside of my womb
births forth the sacred divine,
the mighty pungent woman power!

MaMa Earth,
in honor, I share with you
my flowing, life blood!

Ovulation Date:

Moon Phase:

Bleeding Time:

Moon Phase:

Appendix A

Networking

Feminine Lingerie—woman owned, operated and manufactured companies:

New Cycle Products
P.O. Box 3248
Santa Rosa, CA 95402
707/571-2036 (Susan Gravelle answers the phone)

> New Cycle products are 100% cotton, washable menstrual pads available in three sizes: Mini, Midi and Maxi. Prices range from $3.95-5.95 per pad. T-shirts, tote bags, cycle charts and several publications by Tamara Slayton founder of New Cycle Products and The Menstrual Health Foundation. I have found these products to be of excellent quality.

MoonWit Menstrual Alternatives
R.R. #4, Lang's Road, C-21
Ganges, B.C., V0S 1E0
Canada
604/537-4683

> MoonWit pads & liners are 100% cotton flannel and terry cloth, and are offered in two sizes: regular and Goddess-size. The prices range from $3.75-5.00 per pad. Christina Budeweit is the Lady responsible for this wonderful business and has taken on the added fun of a newsletter entitled *The Rag* which will come out at the Solstices and Equinoxes. I advise the regular size for first time bleeders and for women who bleed lightly.

Many Moons
14-130 Dallas Road
Victoria, B.C. V8V 1A3
Canada
604/382-1588

> Many Moons products are made of 100% cotton flannel that contain a washable cotton core. One size pad is offered, but available with a belt or beltless and are sold in sets of 6 and 8 respectively. Prices range from $29.50-34.50, again respectively. Patterns can also be bought to make your own for $4.00. A wide material selection of colors and design patterns are offered. *These pads are extremely luxurious.*

Hazelbud Services
157 Wynchwood Avenue, Suite 6
Toronto, Ontario M6C 2T1
Canada

In Harmony
P.O. Box DD
Albuquerque, NM 87103

Seventh Generation
Colschester, VT 05403
800/456-1177

Sisterly Works
RR 3, Box 107
Port Lavaca, TX 77979
319/439-5451

Learning Centers/Organizations—that focus on menstruation and/or women's issues:

The Menstrual Health Foundation
P.O. Box 3248
Santa Rosa, CA 95402
707/571-2036

> Founded by Tamara Slayton author of *Reclaiming the Menstrual Matrix, Reclaiming Our Daughters, Food for Females,* and *The Ecology of Being Female* booklets. She offers a wide variety of classes and workshops as well as on-going support groups and individual consulting.

WEN—Women's Environmental Network
287 City Road
Islington Long EC1V 1LA
UK

P.A.D.S.—People Against Dioxins in Sanitary Products
c/o 5 Annesley Sy.
Leichardt 2040 NSW
Australia

The Wise Woman Center
c/o Susun S. Weed
P.O. Box 64
Woodstock, NY 12498
914/246-8081

Boston Women's Health Collective
246 Elm Street
Somerville, MA 02144
617/625-0271

Moonlodge Retreats
Nova Quest
Contemporary Wellness Education
Blomidon
Nova Scotia, B0P 1H0
Canada
902/582-7369

Reclaim the Moon Lodge—(classes and retreats)
Contact: Carole Shane
303/440-4164, or
Christina Nelson
P.O.Box 265
Villa Grove, CO 81155

Sky Lodge
Brooke Medicine Eagle
P.O.Box 121
Ovando, MT 59854
406/793-5730

Moon Lodge Circle Network—contact for those women who wish to be a part of the ever widening and awakening wisdom of woman who celebrate the blood mysteries. This network is organized by Brooke Medicine Eagle and Kisma K. Stepanich. For more information send SASE to:

> *Sisters Of The Moon Lodge*
> 204 1/2 E. Broadway
> Costa Mesa CA, 92627
> 714/548-0551

Lunar Calendars—charts and calanders for and about woman power:

> *The Lunar Calendar*
> Luna Press
> P.O. Box 511
> Kenmore Station
> Boston, MA 02215

> *Moon Calendar*
> S&S Optika
> 7174 South Broadway
> Englewood, CO 80110
> 303/789-1089

> *Cycles of Harmony Personal Moon Calendar*
> R.R. 1, Box 247
> Easton, KS 66020
> 913/773-8255

> *Ever' Woman's Calendar*
> Morning Glory Collective
> P.O. Box 1631
> Tallahassee, FL 32302
> 904/222-7028

> *MoonDance: A Woman's Fertility Awareness Calendar*
> Variena Publishing
> 3100 W. 71st Avenue
> Westminister, CO 80030
> 303/429-8888

We'Moon Almanac
Musawa
Mother Tongue Ink
37010 Southeast Snuffin Road
Estacada, OR 97023
503/630-7848

Menstrual Goddesses—figurines that can be used during the bleeding time in ritual or for personal altar.

Gaia Catalogue Company
1400 Shattuck Avenue #9
Berkeley, CA 94709
800/543-8431—outside California
415/548-4172—California orders

Star River Productions
P.O. Box 6254
North Brunswick, NJ 08902
800/232-1733
201/247-9875

Menstrual Cassette Tapes:

Brooke Medicine Eagle
  Moon Time
  Moon Lodge
  A Gift of Song

Order from: Harmony Network
P.O. Box 2550, Guerneville, CA 95446
707/869-989

Appendix B

A Woman's Survey Regarding Menstruation

This survey is being conducted for an up-coming book focusing on the menstrual matrix (menarche, menstruation, menopause). Your time and consideration will be most helpful.

(Please use a separate piece of paper for long answers.)

1. How old were you when you had your menarche (first bleeding)?

2. Was menarche a positive or negative experience (elaborate as much as you would like on this?

3. How did menstruation change your views on life?

4. Do you experience symptoms labelled as PMS (PreMenstrual Syndrome), and if so, which?

5. Do you cycle regularly?

   If so, what is your cycle (ex. every 21 days, sporadic, etc.)?

6. What form of birth control do you use?

   Why do you choose this form?

7. Do you use sanitary napkins? If so, why?

8. Do you use tampons? If so, why?

9. How do you feel about this biological function as a woman?

10. Are you more sexual around your menses? If so, do you have intercourse during your cycle? If not, why?

11. How old are you?

12. Are you aware of the Moon phase during which you menstruate?

13. I view my menstrual blood as (check one):

_____ evil/curse

_____ dirty/something to be ashamed of

_____ inconvenient

_____ sacred/something to be proud of

14. If you have undergone menopause what was your experience?

15. Do you have any daughters?

    How did (or will) you handle their first bleeding?

16. Do you believe that Eve ruined it for women? If so, why?

17. Do you understand physiologically what is happening in your body pre- and during menstruation? Please describe.

18. What is a Moon Lodge?

19. Are you familiar with, and do you use a lunar calendar?

20. What are your views on menstruation and the work-place?

21. Have you ever willingly touched, smelled, and/or tasted your menstrual blood?

22. Would you be interested in learning more about PMS?

    Have you undergone a hysterectomy, if so, complete or partial?

    How has it changed your life?

    Why did you have to have one?

24. Do you celebrate your cycle, if so how?

    If not, why?

25. Please check one of the following:
    ____ Student ____ High-school ____ College

    ____ Professional/profession:

    _____

    ____ Job/housepartner/job title:

    _____

    ____ Job/housepartner/mother/job title:

    _____

    ____ housepartner/mother

    ____ housepartner

_____ single mother

_____ single

_____ other

26. Would you be interested in learning more about the blood mysteries and how a woman can become self-empowered by rethinking her ability to bleed cyclically (if yes, please write name, address, and telephone number below)?

27. Do you consider yourself to be a feminist?

Appendix C

Sisters of the Moon Lodge

Welcome Sister, and bless you for listening to your inner voice and allowing it to direct you to connecting with the women's ways. The act of honoring your own divinity is one of personal power. In this honoring you come into contact with the full scope of your energy as experienced through the guidance of your inner Medicine Woman, Spirit Woman, and Goddess. When acquaintance with these three levels of Higher Self has been made, and you pass through the integration of them, you begin to draw upon the rich and diverse aspects of your power and that of all life. The sweet and tender umbilical cord with MaMa Earth is re-connected, and the inner mind of the Great Mother is activated. Once the Mother's mind is inaugurated, the great wisdom can begin to flow. This wisdom is the voice of the Grandmothers; the women who have walked before us, who exist with us, who dwell in the future. It is the wisdom of the Grandmothers that aide us in re-creating the women's ways as needed today.

If you are a woman who wishes to become involved in my Moon Lodge, it is important that I share with you the conceptualization of the Lodge as received through the voices of the Grandmothers. Once you have reviewed the following and acknowledge that this foundation will meet your spiritual needs, then may we walk this part of our individual spiritual journeys together.

Background

The vision to create a Moon Lodge was prompted after having attended a Summer Solstice Woman's Camp in Nevada City, California during June, 1989. It was in the beautiful foothills of the Northern Sierras that I was able to celebrate my own understanding in the solitude of a beautiful hut constructed out of willow. There I read material by Mary Greer (author of several books on Tarot; the first book entitled *Tarot For Yourself*) and Jean Mountaingrove (she was co-founder and co-editor of *WomanSpirit*, a quarterly journal of feminist spirituality for the decade 1974-1984). I was ecstatic at the thought of being able to take shelter in this womb-like hut even though I was not bleeding. My own awareness of the blood mysteries had been flourishing for well over three years at that time. I had been performing my "Women Who Bleed For Life Ceremony" a little over a year, and at one time had offered an on-going waning Moon gathering focusing on menstruation (which, unfortunately, never got off the ground). Nevertheless, I left Nevada City with the vision of one day having my very own Moon Lodge.

In December of 1989 I moved into a house with a beautiful little backyard. Immediately I set about turning the backyard into a garden befitting an audience by the Goddess, and transformed a dilapidated brick-fireplace patio (in a corner of the yard) into an outside temple. As the solar wheel turned another year, 1990, my backyard became publicly acknowledged as *The Garden of the Goddess*. Women Spirit Rising (my spiritual organization alive at that time) held all our events in the Garden. By the end of the first month in 1990, I began to realize that my Moon Lodge would be a reality. Winter waned and Spring waxed. As the rains slowed to a stop, I began the construction of the Moon Lodge. The foundation of the Lodge was laid in the month of April. WSR's Beltane ceremony partially centered around the Moon Lodge and the creation of a "fertility circle" in the west corner of the Lodge.

I spent the next several months creating a womb-like environment inside. On July 15th WSR died. On July 25th I sent out a letter to all our members notifying them of this death. On Lammas (August 1st), the members of my private coven (Rose Moon) and the core sisters of WSR held a burial service for both WSR and Rose Moon. I was releasing both of these spiritual outlets from my life. I was no longer to be committed to teaching women on a regular basis. I was now free to begin nourishing "me" once again. However, previous to the death of WSR two events had been scheduled. The first was the "Moon Lodge Dedication Ceremony" on Sunday, July

29th, and the second was a "Women Who Bleed For Life Ceremony" on August 18th. I knew that both these events would take place.

The first event, the "Moon Lodge Dedication Ceremony," was enacted by myself. No one showed. I didn't really expect anyone to since I had sent out the letter informing all the members of the death of WSR, but I had verbally told four other women that I would still be holding this ceremony regardless of WSR's status. The ceremony was very spontaneous. I smudged the heck out of the Lodge to purify it. I centered and grounded the Lodge energy by beating the Mother's heartbeat out on my ritual drum (which has now become the Lodge drum). I invoked the four directions by calling on the voices of the Grandmothers. I acknowledged Father Sky and Mother Earth. I sang to the Goddess; female wisdom and energy of the Lodge.

Next I created woman medicine bundles for each of the four directions, tied them into place on their post and activated the prayers of each bundle by smudging it and rattling. Lastly, I created the altar space next to the "fertility circle" in the west corner of the Lodge. I chanted and sang songs and laid out an outrageous Tarot spread for my own direction. I sat in silence before ending the ceremony to allow the Grandmothers to give me information regarding the Lodge. They did. The first direction I received was on the up-keep of the Lodge. Once a week it was important to feather dust the material of cob-webs and sweep out the rugs. It was important to keep the flap always closed, and human energy was to be active inside the Lodge only during the waning phase of the Moon cycle; in other words, from Full Moon to New (or Dark) Moon. The only human activity within the Lodge during the waxing phase (New Moon to Full Moon) was the weekly cleaning. The Lodge was finally ready for active use. I couldn't wait 'til my next bleeding to retreat to the Lodge.

On Sunday, August 12th, I entered the Lodge during my bleeding time. I performed my first Moon ritual within the Lodge. It was during this ritual that the conceptualization of the Lodge was established. I will present that information next, but first I would like to end this section by saying that on Saturday, August 18th, the first group of sisters will be entering the sanctum of the newly dedicated Lodge during the "Women Who Bleed For Life Ceremony." I greatly look forward to being the one to introduce them to this woman's place.

Sisters Of The Moon Lodge
Code Of Divinity

August 12, 1990

Naming of the Lodge

The name of my Lodge was conceived to be *Sisters of the Moon Lodge*. A long-legged spider conveyed this name to me as I lay on my back staring up into the conical ceiling of the Lodge.

I had just taken a moment to stretch out and massage my belly in an attempt to help ease the cramping. During this massage session I asked for a name to come. After closing my eyes and counting from 10 to 1 and going deeper within, I truly received nothing and was distracted by another cramp. I opened my eyes and began singing a chant I wrote in 1987 for a "Little Sister Ceremony" entitled Sisters of the Moon. As I lay there singing this chant, massaging my belly, and looking at the center point of the ceiling, a long-legged spider crawled out from a fold in the red material walls.

"Listen to your words," the spider communicated to me. So I did as I was told.

> *Sisters of the Moon*
> *we gather once more*
> *to celebrate the bloom*
> *of love and life and mother Earth.*
>
> *Let us weave the circle*
> *as in ancient times*
> *singing, sharing side by side*
> *holding hands,*
> *becoming one.*

The Lodge Chant

Obviously, the best suited chant was immediately acknowledged to be: "Sisters of the Moon." Simple and straight-forward, wouldn't you agree?

As I lay there singing the words, the full message of this chant was revealed to me. I began to dissect each line. "Sisters of the Moon"—was the call to all females; virgin, mother, Crone. "We gather once more"—the re-emerging of the women's ways as exemplified through the forming circles of the women's spirituality movement. "To celebrate the bloom"—the vagina is often refereed to as flower. When the bleeding comes upon females, she has come full flower; blossomed into the office of womanhood. In the Moon Lodge we celebrate this office during our bleeding time. "Of love and life and Mother Earth"—women understand the intrinsic nature of love and relationships as this is the Charge we are born into this life with; the great mysteries gift of life given to our wombs; and, our intimate connection to Mother Earth.

"Let us weave the circle as in ancient times"—in honor of our Grandmothers, today we can once again honor the divinity of female by weaving the great vision's tapestry that all women have access to during the bleeding time. "Singing, sharing side by side"—our voices will radiate together and we shall share our visions as we sit next to each other; it will be through this tool that the world can, and will, be changed. "Holding hands, becoming one"—as we join forces and connect our power, the female energy is rebirthed into this physical plane. It is in this oneness that we can accomplish anything!

Sisters of the Moon

Sisters of the Moon
we gather once more
to celebrate the bloom
of love and life and mother Earth.

Let us weave the circle as in ancient times
singing, sharing side by side
holding hands
becoming one.

The Medicine/Energy of the Lodge

The Lodge's energy is that of Deer Medicine.

When preparing to celebrate my first Moon Ritual in the Lodge and I was gathering power tools to take with me, I was very drawn to all my Deer Medicine tools. (In the winter of 1989 it was revealed to me that my personal medicine was the deer.) And so, as I created the first "active" altar in the Lodge it contained a picture of a deer I had taken while on a journey in Utah, my Deer Medicine rattle, my south power tool which is an obsidian blade knife with a deer antler as the handle. It is important for me to tell you that this power tool was one of the original power tools given to me in the dreamtime by my Medicine Woman preceding my Shaman's Death/Initiation. It took almost two years to receive the various parts that would make-up the tool. Again, when I received the deer antler, it was from the same sister (Deborah in Vermont), who had given me the first sign, or revelation, that my medicine was Deer (even if she was unaware of what she was doing at the time). I constructed the tool in the waning winter of 1990 and used it for the first time in a power ceremony inside the Garden of the Goddess temple. (I wrote about this ceremony in one of the last chapters of my second book *The Gaia Tradition* (Llewellyn Publications, 1991.)

To get back to the altar . . . The other items were: Medicine Woman Crystal, Spirit Woman Agate, Ishtar/Inanna figurine, Menstrual Goddess figurine, the lunar beads, ochre, and female peacock smudge feather.

After I had called in the quarters, Father Sky, Mother Earth, and Ishtar/Inanna, I automatically picked up the deer rattle and began shaking the rattle round and round, over my head, spiraling it up to the center point of the ceiling. As I did so, I heard my voice say, "The medicine of this Lodge is Deer. Come gentleness. Come peacefulness. Come safety. Come nurturing. Come kindness."

To the Native American Indians it is the deer that teaches us to use the power of gentleness to touch the hearts and minds of wounded beings who are trying to keep us from Sacred Mountain. Like the dappling of a fawn's coat, both the light and the dark may be loved to create gentleness and safety for those who are seeking peace. Thus the medicine of the Lodge was to be Deer, and this medicine, I suddenly knew would ground and center the Lodge by creating a place of serenity.

Because of this great message received, I have generously placed my deer medicine rattle and south power tool permanently in the Lodge. This was a big step for me, as both these tools have been used by no one but me, and were considered very personal. I gladly share them with you dear sister, if this is the medicine you are seeking. If not, it is better your hands do not touch such gentle tools at this time, unless you are willing to experience your life as that of the Tower Tarot card.

Lodge Insignia

I had no idea the Lodge would have an insignia, but it came immediately following the evocation of the medicine. The Otter is the sigil of the Lodge.

The Otter is the medicine of woman; the realized dream. Otter's lesson is in female energy. It lives on land, but always has its home in the water. The elements of Earth and Water are the female elements, which is interesting because when I sit in the Lodge I position myself so I face the northwest. Native American Indians again tell us that Otter teaches us that balanced female energy is not jealous or catty. It is sisterhood, content to enjoy and share the good fortune of others. Anchored in the understanding that all accomplishments are worthwhile for the whole tribe.

Woman energy without games or control is a beautiful experience. Through this symbol, the women who partake in the energy of the Lodge shall become Otter and move gently into the river of life; flowing with the waters of the Universe; for this is the way of balanced female-receptive energy. By honoring this symbol we shall discover the power of woman.

The Intent of the Lodge

The original intent of the Moon Lodge is solely for the purpose of creating the women's ways for use today. We must leave behind the past, not rely on recreating the past, but work on creating the new ways with the roots still in the past; never forgetting history and its horrors. The women's ways shall be etched deeply in herstory.

I placed myself into a trance state before seeking an audience with the voices of the Grandmothers. I wanted to go into that deep inner space where my most sacred direction comes from. I also wanted to go deeper than I ever had because I wanted to receive the guidance necessary to nurture all women, not just me. I received a very distinct message on the intent of this particular Lodge at this time, however, it was also expressed that Lodge intent should evolve as the established or original intent is fulfilled and as the needs of the participants change. The changing and establishing of new intent is to be done through a special ceremony focused solely on this specific purpose, but original intent must be completely fulfilled, in other words, completely and utterly exhausted. If one woman feels there is more information and need for the original intent, an agreed upon time limit shall be set, and in that remaining time, original intent must be intensely focused on. At the ending of the agreed time boundary, a new evaluation of original intent will be examined.

As the women who partake in the Moon Lodge come together it is not for individual purpose but for all women. We shall be vehicles for the voices of the Grandmothers to speak through. These voices will give us the wisdoms required for us to actively take part in the new ways of this world. We shall record the new laws and the needed ceremonies to help shift the planet energy and the consciousness worldwide. We shall receive the lessons that are needed large scale, and how to implement those lessons into our societies in a gentle manner. Through this intent, each of the women involved in the Lodge will receive the guidance and direction she individually requires, but will not approach the Lodge with selfish motivations in solving personal problems. When approaching the Lodge, each woman will do so with an open and receptive mind to receiving the wisdom from the Grandmothers' voices for nurturance of all relations. Because of this intent and purpose, the Lodge shall be open to being a mixed group of bleeding women, menopausal women, and post-menopausal women. However, it must be understood that this Lodge is not a Grandmothers' Lodge, and is not indefinitely established with the intent for nurturing all peoples. As previously described, the intent can and will eventually evolve and may move into a place for bleeding women to benefit by, or become one for personal growth only, at which time the menopausal and post-menopausal women may feel it necessary to begin their own Lodge.

The main emphasis of the original intent is to establish and create the women's ways as needed today.

Meeting Times

The Lodge is open to active energy in the waning phase of the Moon cycle; from Full Moon to New/Dark Moon. The women of the Lodge can use the Lodge for personal use during this phase, and are encouraged to do so especially when they are flowing. I would like to express here one concern that might be raised by individuals regarding bleeding times that occur other than the waning phase of the Moon. I believe that if a woman feels she has a regular cycle and does not care whether she is bleeding in accordance with the Moon cycle, fine, however, because the Moon Lodge is dedicated to the natural cycles of Moon, Earth, and woman (in the ultimate or most balanced sense). The women who bleed during the waxing phase should celebrate and honor their bleeding in their own way at home or elsewhere. The Lodge must be reserved for bleeding women only during the waning phase in order to keep the energy balance we are seeking in the wisdom of the women's ways. Therefore, if a woman does not bleed in the waning phase, it would probably be better if she did not come to the Lodge individually, but only during the meeting time of the core. [Ed. note: In her book, *An Act of Woman Power*, Kisma gives complete instructions for how women can "naturalize" their menses, i.e., get themselves to bleed in accordance with the lunar cycle, through use of certain herbs and adopting a proper mind-set. Thus, it is not inevitable that a woman who does not bleed during the waning phase will always be precluded from the community of the Moon Lodge.]

The core of women will meet only once a month on the evening of the New/Dark Moon. This monthly Moon Lodge meeting will be for the purpose of working on the established intent of the Lodge (original or otherwise if evolved). There will be no reminder telephone calls as to meeting dates and times.

Core of Women

The core of women was received to be a maximum of eight. My teacher, Brooke Medicine Eagle, has told me that eight is the sacred hoop of women; a symbol of infinity when turned on its side. So the core shall be a hoop. However, in my Lodge, each meeting is only open to three women, which means that we will not always be working together, and is the reason for the advance three day telephone reservation.

At first when I received this bit of information I was deeply concerned about having a core of eight, but a monthly meeting consisting of three only. I was quickly consoled and told that this format would create a more peaceful environment for the core. Not every woman wants to participate each month. Each of us, from time to time, have other obligations that will unfortunately fall on the New/Dark Moon. To establish a rule that one must be available every month for this meeting does not meet the needs of individuals in today's society. Those women who really want to be a part of the monthly meeting will take the initiative to telephone and make a reservation. Therefore, only those who hear the inner calling within a given month will attend. This is the way the Grandmothers choose it to be.

Another concern of mine was, if eight women make up the core, but only three can participate each month, what happens if one of the core women does not make an attempt to come to the monthly meeting for more than two to three months in a row, and there is another woman who really wants to be part of the core? "Very simple." I was told. "It shall be the understanding of each core member that they must attend at least two meetings each season. Therefore they will remain active." That was simple. So the seasons are:

> Spring: February—March—April
> Summer: May—June—July
> Autumn: August—September—October
> Winter: November—December—January

Admittance into the core will be based on: 1) if there is an opening; 2) agreement to the Code of Divinity; 3) acceptance by the existing core; and 4) comfortableness with the members of the existing core.

It is important to state here that there is no leaders in this Lodge. All members of the core are part of a coalition. All matters are put to a vote. At each meeting, the different parts of the ceremony will be divided by a volunteer basis. Though I may be the owner of the Lodge, I am not the leader!

Because of the original intent of the Lodge, women of all ages can make up the core: pre-menarcheal, menstruating, menopausal, post-menopausal. However, as discussed in the section on Lodge Intent, this Lodge is not a Grandmothers' Lodge, and if and when the original intent changes, the Lodge may become suitable only for bleeding women at which time the menopausal and post-menopausal women may wish to branch off and begin a Grandmothers' Lodge. For women who have undergone hysterectomies, or no longer bleed due to genetics, you are more than welcome to be part of the core.

Miscellaneous Items

The up-keep of the Lodge shall be shouldered by the core. Each month one of the women will volunteer to be the Lodge keeper and will assume the responsibility to feather-dust and sweep rugs once a week. Lodge keeper will also be responsible for opening the Lodge thirty minutes prior to the meeting, and preparing the space for the meeting (see Meeting Format for details on meeting set-up). As part of her service to the Lodge she will contribute the following items to the Lodge:

> candles: 1 white, 1 red, 1 black
> incense: either made or bought, or sweetgrass, cedar, lavender or sage for smudging
> matches or a lighter
> a package of incense charcoal
> notebook paper and pens
> art supplies

However, if the same woman volunteers to care for the Lodge twice in one season, she only needs to bring the above supplies only once during that season. It is also the responsibility of the Lodge keeper to make notes on any necessary repairs to the Lodge, e.g. material for the walls, plastics and rugs for the floor, tarp for the outside of the Lodge, which will naturally need to be done as the Lodge becomes weathered. Should the Lodge require complete renovation inside or out, all members of the core will financially contribute the monies needed to purchase the necessary supplies and will actively take part in the renovations on an agreed upon day. When this type of repair is needed, the Lodge keeper that month should bring it up at the meeting. (If I am not attending that meeting, she should telephone me and tell me of the needed repairs. I will make it my responsibility to contact all core members.) The Lodge keeper will go out and purchase the necessary supplies. She will turn the receipt over to me at which time I will calculate how much each member will need to contribute. Again, I will telephone the core and schedule a renovation date. On this date, all core members shall come together, reimburse the Lodge keeper and participate in the renovation.

Leaving the Core

Simply communicate your need to us. Out of respect, attend one last meeting to release your participation in the Lodge and receive a blessing from your sisters. If I am not present at this meeting, I would greatly appreciate receiving a telephone call by either the departing core member or someone who was at the meeting; the person who will be making the call should be chosen during the meeting.

Meeting Format

A very distinct format for each meeting ceremony was received. It is as follows:

I. All shoes are removed before entering the Lodge. All miscellaneous items are left outside the Lodge. The bathing of feet shall take place at the entrance. The Lodge keeper is responsible for preparing the foot bath water and shall bath the feet of the first woman who will bath the feet of the second woman who will bath the feet of the Lodge keeper.

II. Check-in. This is the time to express how you are feeling. This is not intended to be a gossip session, as this type of energy does not belong in the Lodge. Simply express how you have been and breath out, releasing this energy from you. This is also the time to indicate departure from the core, the need for renovations, or any other business at hand pertaining to the Lodge/core.

When business is complete, decide who will be responsible for each section of the evenings ceremony. This should be done by volunteering.

> A. Smudge the Lodge first. You may smudge the women, or pass the censor to allow each woman the time to smudge.

> B. Ground and Center. The heartbeat of the Mother will be sounded by using the ritual drum.

C. Invoking the Grandmothers in each direction using the knife power tool:

East: *I call upon the Grandmothers of the East.*

Bring forth your wisdom of clarity, of farsightedness. Allow your light to fill this Lodge to be received through the womb centers of each woman here so that we may draw upon your wisdom and see the ways that are needed at this time. Come, be here now. So mote it be. Ho.

South: *I call upon the Grandmothers of the South.*

Bring forth your wisdom of spirit, of passion and creativity. Allow your fire to fill this Lodge to be received through the womb centers of each woman here so that we may draw upon your wisdom and gain the knowledge of how to create the women's ways from the place of inner child. Though we no longer dwell within the innocence of this child, we bring forth your passion and spirit. Come, be here now. So mote it be. Ho.

West: *I call upon the Grandmothers of the West.*

Bring forth your wisdom of relationship; of nurturing. Fill this lodge with the power of the mysteries great gift of life so that the women gathered here will receive this power into the womb center and draw upon your wisdom, gaining the understanding of what is required to establish the new ways in which love, life and peace are prevalent. Come, be here now. So mote it be. Ho.

North: *I call upon the Grandmothers of the North.*

Bring forth your wisdom of strength and endurance; providing the foundation upon which the women's ways may be laid. Fill this Lodge with nurturance so that the women gathered may receive this energy in their womb center and draw upon your rich wisdom. Come, be here now. So mote it be. Ho.

Above: *Father Sky, umbrella over us with your protective atmospheric arms. Shelter us from harm. Ho.*

Below: *Mother Earth, support us with your strength and abundant resources. Carry us through the changes. Ho.*

D. Evoke the Goddess Ishtar/Innana, or other Goddess to aide in the descent that will be taken inward to access the voices of the Grandmothers.

E. Activate the Lodge medicine using the deer medicine rattle. Gently lift the energy of the Lodge using the rattle in a spiral until you are rattling at the center of the ceiling.

F. Chants/Songs will be sung a total of thirteen times using the chanting beads. Whether one chant/song is used thirteen times, or several, the guider of this section should hold the chanting beads in her hand and move from one round to the next without pausing. Deciding the chants/songs to be used during the business time might be helpful. The reason for the thirteen rounds is to honor and remember the thirteen lunations of the current year we are working in. This part of the ceremony helps to altar the consciousness and place the participants into a trance state in preparation of seeking counsel with the Grandmothers.

G. Counsel with the Grandmothers. Upon ending the thirteenth round of chanting/singing, the women will call upon the voices of the Grandmothers and quietly begin individually recording the information flowing up from the womb center. Before the writing begins, one woman shall say:

Grandmothers, tell us what it is we should know now in order to serve myself, to serve my people, and to create the women's ways and a beautiful world?

Twenty to thirty minutes should be provided for the counsel. When each woman has finished writing, turns shall be taken reading the wisdom received and discussing it. Notes can be jotted down on the paper during the discussion. After all wisdoms have been read and discussed, make sure the paper is dated and the name of the woman who received the wisdom written at the bottom. Once this has been done, the pages are to be placed in the Voices of the Grandmothers' notebook kept in the Lodge. This notebook contains the women's ways which is the original intent of the Lodge work.

H. Personal time. If agreed upon before beginning the evening work, time can be provided for personal time. Meditation, Tarot spreads, creativity in the Vision Tapestry notebook (which is always kept in the Lodge), work with the belly rock, massaging each other, or just quiet time.

I. Moon Lodge Song. Before ending ceremony, hold hands and breath together. Feel the connectedness; the oneness. Sing the Lodge song, Sisters of the Moon, and while doing so really look at each other.

J. Thank Goddess Ishtar/Innana or Goddess evoked. Thank Mother Earth, Father Sky, and the Grandmothers of the directions.

K. Open circle by sharing the sacred kiss.

The woman who is now the Lodge keeper shall straighten the Lodge, close it up, pour the foot bath water on MaMa Earth, rinse out the container and return it to its place. She will return to clean the Lodge once a week during the next month. She will arrive at the Lodge thirty minutes before the next meeting to prepare it for that nights ceremony by opening up, dusting the walls and sweeping the rugs (this should get down twice that week), preparing the altar, candles, incense, and the foot bath water. If I am not attending that nights meeting, I will leave her the list of women who will be at the meeting.

Closing

The Sisters of the Moon Lodge is a communal place for women and will exist as long as I remain living at this location and/or there is a core of women. This is an equal participation. No one leads. No one follows. The up-keep of the Lodge is all our responsibility. Making sure there are adequate supplies in the Lodge is all our responsibility. When the Lodge no longer meets your needs it is your responsibility to share this, perhaps that is an indication that the original intent needs to be re-evaluated. If this is the case a meeting of the core will be scheduled and a new intention established. However, if this is not the case and you need to move on, go with blessings.

Blessed be, Sister.

Bibliography

Books

Allen, Paula Gun, *The Sacred Hoop*, Beacon Press, 1986.

Avalon, Arthur, *The Serpent*, Dover Publications, Inc. 1974.

Bell, Ruth, *Changing Bodies, Changing Lives*, Vintage Books, 1987.

Beyerl, Rev. Paul V., *The Holy Books of the Devas: an Herbal for the Aquarian Age*, Rowan Tree Publications, 1986.

Bierhorst, John (ed.), *The Sacred Path*, William Morrow & Co., Inc., 1983.

Billings, John, *The Ovulation Method*, The Liturgical Press, 1987.

Bolen, Jean Shinoda, *Goddesses In Every Woman*, Harper & Row, 1985.

Boston Women's Health Collective, *The New Our Bodies, Ourselves*, Touchstone Books, 1984.

Buckley, Thomas and Alma Gottlieb, *Blood Magic*, UCB Press, 1988.

Buchman, Dian Dincin, *Herbal Medicine*, Gramercy Publishing Co., 1979.

Budapest, Z., *The Holy Book of Women's Mysteries, Part II*, Susan B. Anthony Coven, #One, 1980.

Budapest, Zsuzsanna E., *The Grandmother of Time*, Harper & Row, 1989.

Cameron, Anne, *Daughters of Copper Woman*, Press Gang Publishers, 1981.

Carson, Anne, *Feminist Spirituality and the Feminine Divine*, The Crossing Press, 1986.

Chicago, Judy, *The Birth Project*, Doubleday, 1985.

Costlow, Judy, Maria Christina Lopez and Mara Taub, *Menopause: A Self–Care Manual*, Santa Fe, NM Health Education Project, 1989.

Cunningham, Scott, *Magical Herbalism*, Llewellyn Publications, 1983.

Culpeper's Color Herbal, Sterling Publishing Co., Inc., 1983.

d'Alviella, Count Goblet, *The Migration of Symbols*, University Books, 1956.

Daly, Mary, *Gyn/ecology*, Beacon Press, 1978.

———*Pure Lust*, Beacon Press, 1984.

Delaney, Janice, *The Curse*, Univ. of Ill Press, 1976.

Demetrakopoulos, Stephanie, *Listening to our Bodies*, Beacon Press, 1983.

Dillon, Mary and Shinan Barclay, *Flowering Woman: Moontime for Kory*, Sunlight Production, 1988.

Doress, Paula Brown, *Ourselves, Growing Older: Women Aging With Knowledge and Power*, Touchstone Books, 1987.

Flowers, Felicity Artemis, *The P.M.S. Conspiracy*, Circle of Aradia Publications, 1986.

Fitch, Ed, *Magical Rites from the Crystal Well*, Llewellyn Publications, 1984.

Francia, Luisa, *Dragontime: Magic & Mystery of Menstruation*, Ash Tree Publishing, 1990.

Friedman, Nancy, *Everything You Must Know About Tampons*, Berkley Books, 1981.

Gadon, Elinor W., *The Once and Future Goddess*, Harper & Row, 1989.

Gardner–Loulan, Jo Ann , *Period*, Volcano Press, 1981.

Gardner, Joy, *Healing Yourself During Pregnancy*, The Crossing Press, 1987.

Gaskin, Ina May, *Spiritual Midwifery*, The Book Publishing Co., 1978.

Gibson, Roberta, *Home Is The Heart*, Bear & Co., 1989.

Greenwood M.D., Sadja, *Menopause Naturally, Preparing for the Second Half of Life*, Volcano Press, 1989.

Grieve, M., *A Modern Herbal*, Vol. I & II, Dover Publication Inc., 1971.

Harding, M. Esther, *Woman's Mysteries*, Harper Colophon Books, 1971.

Hutchens, Alma R., *Indian Herbology of North America*, MERCO, 1973.

Kirk, Donald R., *Wild Edible Plants of Western and No. America*, Naturegraph Publishers, Inc., 1975.

Lander, Louise, *Images of Bleeding*, Orlando Press, 1988.

Lauersen, Niels H. & de Swaan, Constance, *The Endometriosis Answer Book*, Fawcett Columbine, 1988.

Madaras, Lynda, *The What's Happening to My Body Book for Girls*, 1988, Newmarket Press.

Millspaugh, Charles F., *American Medicinal Plants*, Dover Publications, Inc., 1974.

Nofziger, Margaret, *A Cooperative Method of Natural Birth Control*, Book Publishing Co., 1976.

——*The Fertility Question*, Book Publishing Co., 1982.

Pavarati, Jeannine, *Hygeia, A Woman's Herbal*, Freestone, 1978.

Parvati, Jeannine and Baker, Frederick, *Conscious Conception: Elemental Journey Through the Labyrinth of Sexuality*, Freestone Publishing, 1986.

Rosenblum, Art, *The Natural Birth Control Book*, Aquarian Research Foundation, 1984.

Royal, Penny C., *Herbally Yours*, Sound Nutrition, 1976.

Rudhyar, Dane, *The Lunation Cycle*, Aurora Press, 1967.

Rush, Anne Kent, *Moon, Moon*, Random House, 1976.

Scot, Reginald, *The Discoverie of Witchcraft* (1584), Centaur Press, Ltd., 1964.

Shuttle, Penelope, *The Wise Wound*, Richard Marek Publishers, 1978.

Slayton, Tamara, *Reclaiming The Menstrual Matrix*, Menstrual Health Foundation, 1990.

——*The Ecology of Being Female*, Menstrual Health Foundation. 1990.

Spretnak, Charlene, *The Politics of Women's Spirituality*, Anchor Books, 1982.

Starhawk, *Truth or Dare*, Harper & Row, 1987.

Stein, Diane, *The Kwan Yin Book of Changes*, Llewellyn Publications, 1985.

Stepanich, Kisma K., *An Act of Woman Power*, Whitford Press/A Division of Schiffer Publishing Ltd., 1989.

———*The Gaia Tradition: Celebrating Earth in Her Seasons*, Llewellyn Publications, 1991.

Stone, Merlin, *Ancient Mirrors of Womanhood*, Beacon Press, 1984.

Taylor, Dena, *Red Flower, Rethinking Menstruation*, Crossing Press, 1988.

Teish, Luisah, *Jambalaya, The Natural Woman's Book*, Harper & Row, 1985.

Walker, Barbara G., *The Woman's Encyclopedia of Myths and Secrets*, Harper & Row, 1983.

———*The Crone, Woman of Age, Wisdom, and Power*, Harper & Row, 1985.

———*The I Ching of the Goddess*, Harper & Row, 1986.

Weed, Susun, *Wise Woman Herbal: The Childbearing Year*, Ash Tree Publishing, 1987.

———*Wise Woman Herbal: Healing Wise*, Ash Tree Publishing, 1989.

Weideger, Paula, *Menstruation and Menopause*, Random House, 1976.

Wing, R. L., *The I Ching Workbook*, Doubleday, 1979.

Wosien, Maria–Gabriele, *Sacred Dance*, Thames & Hudson, 1974.

Wynne, Patrice, *The Womanspirit Source Book*, Harper & Row, 1988.

Journal Publications

Circle Network News, Spring 1990.

SageWoman, Spring 9990, Volume III, Issue #2.

Snake Power, Volume 1, Issue 2.

Woman of Power, Issue Eight, Winter 1988.

Articles

Berry, Carolyn, "Celebrating the Blood: Indian Women and Menstruation." *Bread and Roses,* Vol. 3, No. 2, 1984.

Campbell, Elizabeth Rose, "In Favor of Menstruation," *Mothering,* Summer 1984.

Goodman, Felicitas D. "Trance State & Spirit Journeys," *Shaman's Drum,* Spring 1990.

Grahn, Judy, "From Sacred Blood to the Curse and Beyond," in *The Politics of Women's Spirituality,* Anchor Press, 1982.

Keye, William R. "Premenstrual Syndrome," *The Western Journal of Medicine,* December 1988.

Kollmeyer, Alexandra, "The Joys of Menstruation," *Mothering,* Fall 1982.

Medicine Eagle, Brooke, "Women's Moontime: A Call to Power," *Shaman's Drum,* Spring 1986.

——"Sacred Time," Sacred Way, *Shaman's Drum,* Summer 1986.

——"Grandmother Lodge," *Shaman's Drum,* Summer 1986.

Mickelson, Jane, "Changing Woman," *Mothering,* Spring 1986.

Noble, Vicki, "Female Blood: Roots of Shamanism," *Shaman's Drum,* Spring 1986.

——"Shakti Woman," Vol. 1., Iss. I, *Snake Power Magazine,* October 31, 1989.

Robbins, Robin, "Rites of Passage," *Mothering,* Winter 1981.

Smith-Heavenrich, Sue, "Converting to Cloth," *Mothering,* Winter 1991.

Stepanich, Kisma, "The Ecology of Being Female." *Meditation Magazine,* 1991.

————— "Empowering the Feminine," *Sage Woman*, Lammas 1991, Iss. 16.

Sweeney, Kathleen, "Resources for the Menstrual Life Cycles," *Mothering*, Winter 1991.

Taylor, Dena, "The Power of Menstruation," *Mothering*, Winter 1991.

Washbourn, Penelope, "Becoming Woman: Menstruation as Spiritual Challenge" in *WomanSpirit Rising: A Feminist Reader in Religions*, ed. Carol P. Christ and Judith Plaskow, Harper and Row, 1979.

Cassette Tapes

Medicine Eagle, Brooke, *Moon Time*.

Medicine Eagle, Brooke, *Moon Lodge*.

STAY IN TOUCH

On the following pages you will find listed, with their current prices, some of the books now available on related subjects. Your book dealer stocks most of these, and will stock new titles in the Llewellyn series as they become available. We urge your patronage.

However, to obtain our full catalog, to keep informed of new titles as they are released and to benefit from informative articles and helpful news, you are invited to write for our bi-monthly news magazine/catalog. A sample copy is free, and it will continue coming to you at no cost as long as you are an active mail customer. Or you may keep it coming for a full year with a donation of just $5.00 in U.S.A. & Canada ($20.00 overseas, first class mail). Many bookstores also have *The Llewellyn New Times* available to their customers. Ask for it.

Stay in touch! In *The Llewellyn New Times'* pages you will find news and reviews of new books, tapes and services, announcements of meetings and seminars, articles helpful to our readers, news of authors, advertising of products and services, special money-making opportunities, and much more.

The Llewellyn New Times
P.O. Box 64383-Dept. 767, St. Paul, MN 55164-0383, U.S.A.

• • •

TO ORDER BOOKS AND TAPES

If your book dealer does not have the books described on the following pages readily available, you may order them direct from the publisher by sending full price in U.S. funds, plus $1.50 for postage and handling for orders *under* $10.00; $3.00 for orders *over* $10.00. There are no postage and handling charges for orders over $50. UPS Delivery: We ship UPS whenever possible. Delivery guaranteed. Provide your street address as UPS does not deliver to P.O. Boxes. UPS to Canada requires a $50 minimum order. Allow 4–6 weeks for delivery. Orders outside the U.S.A. and Canada: Airmail—add retail price of book; add $5 for each non-book item (tapes, etc.); add $1 per item for surface mail.

FOR GROUP STUDY AND PURCHASE

Because there is a great deal of interest in group discussion and study of the subject matter of this book, we feel that we should encourage the adoption and use of this particular book by such groups by offering a special "quantity" price to group leaders or "agents."

Our Special Quantity Price for a minimum order of five copies of *Sister Moon Lodge* is $44.85 cash-with-order. This price includes postage and handling within the United States. Minnesota residents must add 6.5% sales tax. For additional quantities, please order in multiples of five. For Canadian and foreign orders, add postage and handling charges as above. Credit card (VISA, Master Card, American Express) orders are accepted. Charge card orders only may be phoned free ($15.00 minimum order) within the U.S.A. or Canada by dialing 1-800-THE-MOON. Customer service calls dial 1-612-291-1970. Mail Orders to:

LLEWELLYN PUBLICATIONS
P.O. Box 64383-Dept. 767 / St. Paul, MN 55164-0383, U.S.A.

Prices subject to change without notice.

THE GAIA TRADITION
by Kisma K. Stepanich
The Gaia Tradition provides a spiritual foundation in which women, from all walks of life, can discover support and direction. It is an eclectic blend of Wicca, Native American Spirituality and Dianic Goddess worship.

Let author Kisma Stepanich guide you to spiritual attunement with Mother Earth through the evolution of the Goddess within and through the connection to the Goddess without.

The Gaia Tradition describes the Goddess philosophy and takes you month by month, season by season, through magical celebrations. Through a series of lessons, it helps women take a more dignified stance in their everyday lives and puts them on a path of a woman who is whole and self-assured. Let *The Gaia Tradition* build your spiritual foundations.
0-87542-766-9, 336 pp., 6 x 9, illus.   **$12.95**

IN THE SHADOW OF THE SHAMAN
by Amber Wolfe
Presented in what the author calls a "cookbook shamanism" style, this book shares recipes, ingredients, and methods of preparation for experiencing some very ancient wisdoms—wisdoms of Native American and Wiccan traditions, as well as contributions from other philosophies of Nature, as they are used in the shamanic way. Wolfe encourages us to feel confident and free to use her methods to cook up something new, completely on our own. This blending of ancient formulas and personal methods represents what Ms. Wolfe calls *Aquarian Shamanism*.

In the Shadow of the Shaman is designed to communicate in the most practical, direct ways possible, so that the wisdom and the energy may be shared for the benefits of all. Whatever your system or tradition, you will find this to be a valuable book, a resource, a friend, a gentle guide and support on your journey. Dancing in the shadow of the shaman, you will find new dimensions of Spirit.
0-87542-888-6, 384 pgs., 6 x 9, illus., softcover   **$12.95**

THE COMPLETE HANDBOOK OF NATURAL HEALING
by Marcia Starck

Got an itch that won't go away? Want a massage but don't know the difference between Rolfing, Reichian Therapy and Reflexology? Tired of going to the family doctor for minor illnesses that you know that you could treat at home—if you just knew how?

Now, all the information that has been uncovered during the holistic health movement is compiled in this one volume in concise and usable form. With this book you will acquaint yourself with the variety of natural therapies available as well as heal yourself and your family of most ailments.

Designed to function as a home reference guide (yet enjoyable and interesting enough to read straight through), this book addresses all natural healing modalities in use today: dietary regimes, nutritional supplements, cleansing and detoxification, vitamins and minerals, herbology, homeopathic medicine and cell salts, traditional Chinese medicine, Ayurvedic medicine, body work therapies, exercise, mental and spiritual therapies, subtle and vibrational healing, and diagnostic techniques. In addition, a section of 41 specific ailments outlines all natural treatments for everything from insect bites to varicose veins to AIDS.

0-87542-742-1, 384 pgs., 6 x 9, diagrams, softcover   **$12.95**

STROKING THE PYTHON
by Diane Stein

This book is a comprehensive course in psychic understanding, and ends women's psychic isolation forever. It contains the theory and explanation of psychic phenomena, women's shared and varied experiences, and how-to material for every woman's growth and psychic development. The reclamation of being psychic is women's reclamation of Goddess—and of their Goddess Be-ing.

That reclaiming of women's psychic abilities and psychic lives is a major issue in Goddess spirituality and in the wholeness of women. Learning that everyone is psychic, learning what the phenomena mean, sharing and understanding others' experiences, and learning how to develop women's own abilities is information women are ready and waiting for in this dawning Age of Aquarius and Age of Women.

In the Greek legends of Troy, Cassandra, daughter of Hecuba, was gifted with prophecy. She gained her gift as a child at Delphi when she Stroked the Pythons of Gaea's temple, becoming a psychic priestess. Gaea, the Python, was the Goddess of oracles and mother/creator of the Earth.

In this book are fascinating accounts of women's psychic experiences. Learn how to develop your own, natural psychic abilities through the extensive advice given in *Stroking the Python*.

0-87542-757-X, 381 pgs., 6 x 9, illus., softcover   **$12.95**

Prices subject to change without notice.